FLIGHTS OF **terror**

Aerial hijack and sabotage since 1930

As part of our ongoing market research, we are always pleased to receive comments about our books, suggestions for new titles, or requests for catalogues. Please write to: The Editorial Director, Patrick Stephens Ltd, Sparkford, Nr Yeovil, Somerset, BA22 7JJ.

FLIGHTS OF terror

Aerial hijack and sabotage since 1930

David Gero

PSL

Patrick Stephens Limited

First published in 1997

British Library Cataloguing-in-Publication Data:
A catalogue record for this book is
available from the British Library.

ISBN 1 85260 512 X

Library of Congress catalog card number: 97-70203

Patrick Stephens Limited is an imprint of
Haynes Publishing, Sparkford, Nr Yeovil,
Somerset, BA22 7JJ.

Haynes Publications Inc.
861 Lawrence Drive, Newbury Park,
California 91320 USA

Designed & typeset by
G&M, Raunds, Northamptonshire.
Printed and bound in Great Britain by
Butler & Tanner Ltd, London and Frome

Contents

Introduction

Aerial terrorism. Just the thought of a ticking bomb hidden in a suitcase, or a gun or knife-wielding assailant commandeering a commercial flight, is enough to send chills down the back of even the most seasoned air traveller.

Terrorism, like mid-air collisions, adverse weather conditions, and mechanical failure, is a real threat to aviation, and like other issues pertaining to air safety must be dealt with in a factual and responsible manner. This is what I have tried to do in *Flights of Terror*, which chronicles the various kinds of hostile actions committed against commercial aircraft from the earliest days of air travel.

I have employed a somewhat more casual format in this work than in *Aviation Disasters*, which used a straightforward chronological approach. Events have instead been broken down into several categories, such as all hijackings ending or intending to end in Cuba. All serious acts of terrorism are included, and one section deals with the closely related subject of aircraft attacked or downed in quasi-combat situations, but, generally speaking, bomb-scares have been omitted. To keep sticklers for detail happy, I have included registration numbers in cases where aircraft were destroyed.

As with my previous work, *Flights of Terror* is the result of considerable research throughout the world, by both myself and others, and, as with *Aviation Disasters*, I have included events occurring in all parts of the globe. Though I hope that everyone will find something of interest here, it is particularly exciting for me to share my interest, as well as my tremendous wealth of information, with other aviation enthusiasts, wherever they may be.

David Gero
San Gabriel,
California

Acknowledgements

The author would like to thank the following organizations and individuals for their help in the preparation of this book:

Airclaims Ltd; Air Incident Research; (UK) Civil Aviation Authority; Chris Kimura, author/ researcher; (US) Federal Aviation Administration; Graham K. Salt, researcher; Holly Jones, Wide World Photos; International Civil Aviation Organisation (ICAO); London Guildhall Library; London Newspaper Library; Poly-Languages Institute; Terry Denham, author; Victoria Aranda, translator; Marie Candice, translator; Rosana Volpert, translator.

Publications consulted:

Accident to Itavia DC-9 Paper by A. Frank Taylor, Cranfield University (ISASI Forum, March 1995).

Aircraft Hijackings and Other Criminal Acts Against Commercial Aviation, Statistical and Narrative Reports (US Department of Transportation, Washington, DC).

Airliner Production Lists by John Roach and Tony Eastwood (The Aviation Hobby Shop).

Air Piracy, Airport Security and International Terrorism: Winning the War Against Hijackers by Peter St John (Quorum Books).

Aviation Week magazine.

Aviation Terrorism, Historical Survey, Perspectives and Responses by Jin-Tai Choi (St Martin's Press).

Bloodletters and Badmen by Jay Robert Nash (M. Evans & Co.).

Flight International magazine.

Great Mysteries of the Air by Ralph Barker (Macmillan).

Hostile Actions Against Civil Aviation by Michael Morris (Air Incident Research).

La Opinion newspaper.

Lloyd's List newspaper.

Los Angeles Times newspaper.

Major Loss Record (Aviation Information Services Ltd).

New York Times newspaper.

The Times Atlas of the World.

Times of London newspaper.

Washington Post newspaper.

World Aircraft Accident Summary (Airclaims Ltd).

World Airline Accident Summary (UK Civil Aviation Authority).

World Commercial Aircraft Accidents by Chris Kimura.

World Directory of Airliner Crashes by Terry Denham (Patrick Stephens Ltd).

The Early Years

Before it had become an everyday tool in global trade and commerce, the aeroplane saw service as a weapon of war. Commercial aviation started in earnest after the First World War, with the introduction of both passenger and mail services, and it was not long before the peacetime aviation industry began experiencing hostilities of its own as the phenomenon of aerial terrorism was born.

First came the forced diversion of aircraft, or hijackings (sometimes referred to today as skyjackings, so as not to be confused with piracy at sea), followed by the even more frightening prospect of

An Imperial Airways Armstrong Whitworth Argosy, one of which was believed to have been the first commercial airliner destroyed in an act of aerial sabotage. (British Aerospace)

aerial sabotage. The number of aerial hijackings increased greatly after the Second World War, though the early post-war diversions were mostly of a 'benevolent' variety, often involving aircraft being pirated out of countries behind the 'Iron Curtain'. Ironically, after the fall of Cuba to Communism, hijackings again increased significantly, with aircraft going in the opposite direction (a subsequent chapter is devoted to this phenomenon). Para-military and guerrilla forces entered the hijacking scene in the late 1950s, while a decade later Middle Eastern politics became a motivating factor in many such actions.

With the exception of the North American sabotage-for-insurance schemes of the 1950s and 1960s, the following is a list of all acts of aerial terrorism prior to 1967.

21 February 1931

COMMERCIAL aviation got its first taste of terrorism with the hijacking of a Pan American Airways System trimotored Fokker F.7 in Peru. The US-registered mail aircraft was commandeered by a group of Peruvian revolutionaries with the intention of dropping propaganda leaflets. There were no casualties.

28 March 1933

THOUGH never proven with certainty, the first airline disaster believed to have been an act of sabotage was the destruction of the Imperial Airways 'City of Liverpool'. The trimotored Armstrong Whitworth Argosy (G-AACI) met a fiery demise in the Belgian countryside, near the town of Dixmude, located some 60 miles (100km) west-north-west of Brussels, where it had stopped during a scheduled service originating at Cologne, Germany, with an ultimate destination of London.

The airliner had been cruising at an altitude of about 4,000ft (1,200m) and a speed of around 100mph (150kph) when fire was observed near its tail assembly. Continuing to descend, the pilot apparently trying for an emergency landing in an open field, the Argosy finally suffered catastrophic structural failure at around 14:30 local time, its fuselage splitting in two at an approximate height of 250ft (75m) above the ground. It then plummeted to earth and burned. All 15 persons aboard, including three crew members, were killed. Investigation traced the origin of the fire to the rear of the passenger cabin, either in the lavatory or the luggage rack. Two explanations considered possible were the detonation of a timed incendiary device in a suitcase, or a fire being deliberately started in the lavatory. There was no evidence of a technical failure in the aircraft or its engines.

Found about a mile (1.5km) from the main wreckage was the body of a passenger named Albert Voss, who would become the centre of controversy in this case. Voss, a 69-year-old dentist, had been returning home from a business trip to Brussels. With burns apparent only on his hands and face, it would seem that he had jumped or fallen from the Argosy before the fire had intensified. Seated alone toward the rear of the cabin, he had the opportunity to start the blaze without being noticed. There also appeared to be ample motive for such behaviour: he was known to have been deeply in debt; in his work, he had access to anaesthetics, which can be highly inflammable; his background was tainted with rumours of drug trafficking and addiction; and he had reportedly spoken of suicide. Sufficient evidence did not exist to directly tie Albert Voss in with the loss of the 'City of Liverpool', but could he have been responsible? The question remains unanswered.

10 October 1933

ALL seven persons aboard, including a crew of three, were killed in the crash of a United Air Lines Boeing 247 (NC-13304), which occurred during a scheduled domestic US service. This was the first proven case of sabotage in the history of commercial aviation. The twin-engine transport was en route from Cleveland, Ohio, to Chicago, Illinois, one segment of a service originating at Newark, New Jersey, when it plummeted to earth and burned shortly after 21:00 local time near Chesterton, Indiana, located some 10 miles (15km) west of Gary.

Consolidation of the available evidence led to the conclusion by airline and federal officials that the aircraft had been destroyed by an explosive device that used nitro-glycerine and was probably attached to a timing device. The blast severed the empennage from the rest of the fuselage. The bomb was thought to have been put aboard at the Newark airport, possibly concealed in a brown package. However, no-one was ever prosecuted in connection with this case.

6 April 1948

THE first case of air piracy related to an escape from the Iron Curtain involved a Ceskoslovenske Aerolinie (CSA) DC-3 on a scheduled domestic service from Prague to Bratislava, Czechoslovakia. The transport was seized by about three-quarters of the 26 persons aboard, including the pilot and two other members of the crew. It landed safely in a US zone of Germany, near Munich.

4 May 1948

A Ceskoslovenske Aerolinie (CSA) DC-3 on a scheduled service from Brno, Moravia, to Ceske Budegovice, Czechoslovakia, was commandeered

The first proven case of aerial sabotage, occurring on 10 October 1933, involved a United Air Lines Boeing 247 such as this. (Boeing)

at gunpoint by five passengers, who forced it to land in Germany.

4 June 1948

A Yugoslav airliner carrying 28 persons, believed to have been a DC-3 operated by Jugoslovenski Aerotransport (JAT), was seized by the radio-operator and a passenger during a scheduled domestic flight from Belgrade to Sarajevo, landing safely in Italy, near Bari.

17 June 1948

A Transporturi Aeriene Romana Sovietica (TARS) Ju.52 trimotored airliner was commandeered during a scheduled domestic Romanian service with 23 persons aboard, landing at Salzburg, Austria.

30 June 1948

VIOLENCE marked this seizure, by half-a-dozen assailants, of a Bulgarske Vazdusne Sobsteine (BVS) trimotored Ju.52 that had been on a scheduled domestic flight from Varna to Sofia, Bulgaria, with 21 persons aboard. The pilot of the aircraft

was killed and two other crew members wounded before it made a safe landing at Istanbul, Turkey.

16 July 1948

THE first crash during an airline hijacking involved a Consolidated Catalina amphibian (VR-HDT) of the UK carrier Cathay Pacific Airways, which was on a scheduled flight from Macao to Hong Kong. Shortly after 18:00 local time, about 10 minutes after it had taken off, the twin-engine aircraft crashed in the Pearl River estuary, located in the Canton River delta approximately 10 miles (15km) north-east of Macao. All but one passenger among the 26 persons aboard were killed, including the crew of three. The bodies of nearly half of the victims were never recovered.

The sole survivor later admitted being part of a four-member robbery team that had commandeered the aircraft, which crashed out of control after the pilot and co-pilot were shot.

12 September 1948

WHILE on a scheduled domestic service from Athens to Salonika with 23 persons aboard, a DC-3 flown by the Greek carrier Technical Aeronautical

Exploitations (TAE) was commandeered by eight passengers, some of whom reportedly beat members of the crew. The transport landed safely at Tetovo, Yugoslavia.

4 January 1949

DURING a scheduled domestic service from Pecs to Budapest with 25 persons aboard, an Li-2 of the Hungarian airline Magyar-Szoviet Legiforgalmi Tarseaag was flown to Germany, landing at Munich. In a pre-arranged conspiracy, someone had taken over the controls from the pilot, who was also involved in the hijack.

30 January 1949

SIX persons hijacked a China National Aviation Corporation transport, believed to be either a DC-3 or a C-46, on a scheduled domestic flight from Shanghai to Tsingtso, forcing it to land at T'ainan, Taiwan. The other occupants were held for a month before being released; the aircraft was not returned.

29 April 1949

A young man armed with a revolver hijacked a Transporturi Aeriene Romana Sovietica (TARS) aircraft, possibly a Ju.52, which had been on a scheduled domestic Romanian service from Timisoara to Bucharest carrying 16 persons, forcing it to land at an airfield near Salonika, Greece.

29 April 1949

A Polskie Linje Lotnicze (LOT) aircraft, probably a twin-engine Li-2, was seized by four hijackers during a scheduled domestic flight with 16 persons aboard from Gdansk to Lodz, Poland, landing at a military airfield located near Stockholm, Sweden.

7 May 1949

A Philippine Air Lines Douglas DC-3 (PI-C-98) crashed in the Sibuyan Sea off the Philippine island of Elalat while en route to Manila from Daet, Camarines, one segment of a scheduled domestic service originating at Tacloban, on Leyte. All 13 persons aboard (10 passengers and a crew of three) were killed. The last radio communication with the flight was shortly after 16:00 local time. The following week, some wreckage and the body of the pilot were recovered, and examination of the former indicated a sudden explosion in the aircraft's tail assembly.

Two ex-convicts later confessed to planting a time bomb on the DC-3 in order to kill the husband of a woman who was involved with another man. Their payment for the mass murder: 185 pesos, or less than $100 US.

9 September 1949

THIS was the case of a love triangle degenerating into one of Canada's most horrific crimes, and ending with the offenders paying the ultimate price for their actions.

Operated by Quebec Airways, a subsidiary of Canadian Pacific Air Lines, the Douglas DC-3 (CF-CUA) had taken off from Quebec City at 10:25 local time, on a scheduled domestic service originating at Montreal, with an ultimate destination of Comeau Bay. Some 20 minutes later, the twin-engine transport was observed flying over the St Lawrence River, near the town of St Joachim, when suddenly an explosion occurred in the front fuselage section, and the aircraft turned to the right and started to descend. It ultimately slammed into a hill on the northern side of the river, near the village of Sault-Au-Cochon, Quebec, some 40 miles (65km) north-east of Quebec City. There was no fire, but all 23 persons aboard (19 passengers and four crew members) lost their lives. Investigation revealed that the violent blast had taken place in the forward luggage compartment, and probably either killed or incapacitated the two pilots, resulting in the uncontrolled descent.

A police investigation led to the subsequent arrest of two men and a woman in connection with the intentional destruction of the aircraft, under the guise of an accident. The mastermind of the plot was J. Albert Guay, a jeweller, whose wife had been a passenger on the flight and had been insured for $10,000, with her husband named as beneficiary. The woman with whom he was romantically involved was Marie Pitre, suspected of placing the bomb aboard the aircraft, her brother Genereux Ruest also being implicated in the crime. All three were later hanged.

9 December 1949

A Transporturi Aeriene Romana Sovietica (TARS) aircraft, possibly a trimotored Ju.52, was hijacked by four passengers during a scheduled internal Romanian service from Sibiu to Bucharest, with 24 persons aboard. A security guard was shot dead before the transport landed at Belgrade, Yugoslavia.

16 December 1949

A Polskie Linje Lotnicze (LOT) Li-2 airliner, on a scheduled domestic service from Warsaw to Gdynia, Poland, was flown to the West, landing near Roenne, on the Danish island of Bornholm. All but two of the 18 persons aboard were involved in the mass defection.

The grisly scene of the Canadian DC-3 crash in the woods of Quebec province in September 1949, which turned out to be an act of mass murder claiming 23 lives. (National Archives of Canada)

24 March 1950

THREE DC-3 transports flown by Ceskoslovenske Aerolinie (CSA) and carrying a total of 83 persons were flown to Erding Airfield, near Munich, West Germany, by their passengers and crews. All three of the aircraft involved in the mass defection were on scheduled domestic services, which had originated at Brno, Ostrava, and Bratislava respectively, and had an ultimate destination of Prague, Czechoslovakia.

13 April 1950

OPERATING on a scheduled service to Paris from Northolt Airport, serving London, a British European Airways (BEA) Vickers Viking 1B was approximately half-way across the English Channel and flying at 3,500ft (c1,050m) when it was extensively damaged by the detonation of an 'infernal' device in the lavatory, which probably had been placed in the used towel receptacle. Of the 32 persons aboard, a stewardess was seriously injured, but the airliner returned safely to its point of origin.

17 April 1950

THIS case of attempted sabotage was motivated by a combination of greed and passion. The saboteur, John Grant, had placed a bomb in a valise that was to be loaded aboard a United Air Lines flight bound from Los Angeles to San Diego, California. Among the passengers were his wife and children, whom he had insured for $25,000. Reportedly, he was heavily in debt and infatuated with an airline stewardess. However, the device detonated as it was being loaded on to the aircraft; there were no injuries. John Grant was convicted and sentenced to 20 years imprisonment.

17 October 1951

A Jugoslovenski Aerotransport (JAT) DC-3, on a scheduled Yugoslav domestic flight, was seized by

A British European Airways Viking of the type which survived a sabotage attempt over the English Channel on 13 April 1950. (British Airways)

the pilot and co-pilot, who were accompanied by their wives and two children, and flown to Zurich, Switzerland, where they asked for political asylum. The three other crew members and 22 passengers returned to Yugoslavia.

26 June 1952

THREE hijackers commandeered a Jugoslovenski Aerotransport (JAT) DC-3 that was on a scheduled domestic service from Zagreb to Pola, Yugoslavia, with 32 persons aboard. Two of them held the passengers at gunpoint as the third broke into the cockpit with an axe and took over the controls, landing the aircraft at an airstrip near Foligno, Italy, where they requested political asylum.

24 September 1952

TWO passengers suffered serious injuries aboard a Compania Mexicana de Aviacion SA DC-3 when a bomb placed in a suitcase exploded in its luggage compartment during a scheduled domestic flight from Mexico City to Oaxaca de Juarez. The airliner

managed a safe emergency landing despite sustaining substantial damage in the blast.

30 December 1952

THE pilot and purser of a Philippine Air Lines DC-3 were shot and killed in the attempted hijacking of the transport aircraft during a scheduled domestic service from Laoag to Aparri. Although the gunman demanded to be flown to China, the aircraft was damaged by machine-gun fire from a Nationalist Chinese fighter and landed on the Taiwanese island of Quemoy, where he was captured. He was later sentenced to a life prison term in the Philippines.

23 March 1953

A Ceskoslovenske Aerolinie (CSA) DC-3 with 29 persons aboard was hijacked by four assailants while on a scheduled domestic flight from Prague to Brno, Czechoslovakia. Pilot Miroslav Slovak 'hedgehopped' the aircraft across the border into Germany, where it had to circle for about half-an-

Pilot Miroslav Slovak (centre) and four others celebrate their successful flight from Communist Czechoslovakia in a commandeered airliner, March 1953. (UPI/Corbis Bettmann)

hour as the defectors sought permission to land from US authorities before setting down at Rhein-Main Airport, serving Frankfurt. Two other passengers joined the defectors seeking asylum.

6 July 1954

AN armed 15-year-old boy who stormed aboard and tried to commandeer an American Airlines DC-6 was shot dead by its captain at Hopkins Municipal Airport, serving Cleveland, Ohio, where the aircraft had stopped during a scheduled international service from New York City to Mexico City.

11 April 1955

POLITICAL terrorism was the apparent motive behind the sabotage of an Air-India International Lockheed 749A Constellation (VT-DEP). The airliner was on a non-scheduled service originating at Hong Kong, its passengers consisting of Chinese delegates and journalists on their way to a conference at Bandung, Indonesia. Whilst cruising at 18,000ft (c5,500m) over the South China Sea, a muffled

explosion was heard, and almost immediately smoke started entering the cabin; soon thereafter, a localised fire was detected on the starboard wing.

The flight crew, who had already initiated an emergency descent, then put into effect fire-fighting procedures, during which time the No 3 power plant was feathered, but the aircraft experienced both hydraulic and electrical systems failure due to the effects of the blaze. Dense smoke in the cockpit reduced visibility to almost nil, and the Constellation ultimately crashed in the sea about 100 miles (150km) north of Kuching, Sarawak, at about 17:30 local time. Of the 19 persons aboard, only three members of the crew survived.

A Chinese aircraft cleaner had reportedly been bribed to place an incendiary device in the starboard wheel well of VT-DEP, with its subsequent detonation puncturing the No 3 fuel tank and leading to the uncontrollable fire.

4 March 1956

AN explosive device detonated in the forward cargo compartment of a Skyways Ltd Handley

Page Hermes 4 as the British-built and registered airliner was parked at the airport serving Nicosia, Cyprus, resulting in considerable damage. There were, however, no injuries.

13 July 1956

SEVEN hijackers commandeered a Magyar-Szoviet Legiforgalmi Tarseaag Li-2 carrying 20 persons on a scheduled domestic service from Gyor to Szombathely, Hungary. After a struggle with crew members and passengers, in which several were injured, one of the hijackers took over the controls and landed the airliner at an unused airbase near Ingolstadt, West Germany. The hijackers asked for political asylum; their hostages and the transport returned to Hungary.

19 December 1957

AN Air France Armagnac was on a scheduled flight to Paris from Oran, Algeria, when a bomb detonated in a lavatory, tearing a large hole in the fuselage. There were no injuries among the 95 persons aboard, and the airliner landed safely at Lyon, France, about half-an-hour after the explosion.

16 February 1958

A Korean National Airlines DC-3, operating as Flight 302 on a domestic service from Pusan to Seoul, South Korea, with 34 persons aboard, was hijacked by what were reported as North Korean agents. The aircraft landed at Pyongyang, North Korea, and was not returned to the South, though most of the passengers and crew were released some three weeks after the hijacking. South Korea subsequently enacted tighter security measures throughout its air carrier operations.

9 April 1958

IN the first of a series of hijackings involving pre-Castro Cuba, a Compania Cubana de Aviacion SA DC-3, on a domestic service from Havana to Santa Clara, was flown by its crew to Merida, Mexico. The aircraft and passengers were returned to Cuba.

13 April 1958

A Compania Cubana de Aviacion SA DC-3 airliner carrying 15 persons on a scheduled domestic run from Havana to Santa Clara was flown to Miami, Florida, by its crew, who complained that the Cuban Government was requiring them to fly over areas in Cuba where guerrilla fighting was taking place.

22 October 1958

A Compania Cubana de Aviacion SA DC-3 airliner was commandeered by anti-government rebels during a scheduled domestic flight from Cayo Mambi to Moa Bay, with 14 persons aboard. Although its pilot was shot and wounded, the hostages were subsequently released.

1 November 1958

COMPANIA Cubana de Aviacion SA Flight 495, a four-engine turboprop Vickers Viscount 755D (CU-T603), had departed from Miami, Florida, the previous evening, bound for Veradero, Cuba, a trip of about 200 miles (320km). But it never reached its destination. Hijacked by five Cuban rebels, the airliner was observed circling in the vicinity of Antilla, Oriente province, before finally making a wide turn, and, after passing over the town, crashing in Nipe Bay. All but three passengers among the 20 persons aboard were killed, including the crew of four.

The crash occurred in darkness shortly after 02:00 local time, as the Viscount attempted to land at Preston Airport. During the final approach its fuel supply was effectively exhausted, with only eight gallons left in the tanks. Following a loss of control, it plunged into water about 10ft (3m) deep some 1,300ft (400m) offshore and approximately 1.2 miles (2km) from the airport, its tail initially striking the surface of the bay and separating from the rest of the fuselage.

Most of its wreckage and nearly all of the victims' bodies were later recovered.

6 November 1958

HIJACKED during a scheduled Cuban domestic service from Manzanillo to Holguin, a Compania Cubana de Aviacion SA DC-3 with 25 persons aboard was held at a rebel airstrip before the hostages were released. As a result of this latest incident, the airline cancelled most domestic flights.

9 April 1959

Half-a-dozen revolutionaries commandeered a DC-3 of the Haitian airline COHATA on a scheduled domestic service from Auxcayes to Port-au-Prince, carrying 34 persons. Killing its pilot, they forced the co-pilot to land at Santiago de Cuba.

16 April 1959

Three hijackers took over an Aerovias 'Q' SA C-46 as the Cuban airliner was on a scheduled domestic service from Havana to the Island of Pines with 22 persons aboard. It subsequently landed at Miami, Florida.

25 April 1959

A Compania Cubana de Aviacion SA Viscount

turboprop airliner with 16 persons aboard was commandeered shortly after it had taken off from Varadero, Cuba, on a scheduled domestic service to Havana. The four hijackers, who included a military general who had served under former Cuban President Fulgencio Batista and two women who had reportedly hidden pistols under their skirts, asked to be taken to Miami, but as the aircraft was low on fuel they settled for Key West, Florida.

8 July 1959

While on a scheduled domestic flight from Cattaro to Belgrade, Yugoslavia, a Jugoslovenski Aerotransport (JAT) airliner, believed to have been a DC-3, was hijacked by a lone gunman who fired a warning shot and then ordered the pilot to land at the nearest Italian airport, which happened to be Bari.

8 September 1959

A passenger aboard a Compania Mexicana de Aviacion SA Douglas DC-3, who was suspected of carrying a bomb hidden in his suitcase, was blasted out of an access door and killed when the device detonated as the airliner was flying at 11,000ft (c3,400m) over the Bay of Campeche, on a scheduled domestic service originating at Mexico City, with an ultimate destination of Merida de Yucatan. Among the other 15 persons aboard, including three crew members, six passengers and the co-pilot suffered injuries.

Following the explosion, which occurred around 12:30 local time, the transport successfully force-landed at Poza Rica, Vera Cruz, despite a fire that was successfully extinguished by the crew.

2 October 1959

THREE passengers armed with pistols and a hand-grenade commandeered a Compania Cubana de Aviacion SA Viscount turboprop that was on a scheduled domestic flight from Havana to Santiago de Cuba, carrying 37 persons. The airliner landed safely at Miami, Florida.

2 December 1959

A Panair do Brasil SA Constellation on a scheduled Brazilian domestic service from Rio de Janeiro to Belem was commandeered by a group of hijackers engaged in a revolt against the Brazilian Government. The airliner was flown to Buenos Aires, Argentina.

12 April 1960

THE pilot, two other crew members, and one passenger seized Cubana Flight 800 as the Viscount turboprop was on a scheduled domestic service from Havana to Santiago de Cuba. After landing at Miami, Florida, the hijackers disabled the airliner by setting fire to its four engines.

28 April 1960

A Douglas DC-3 (YV-C-AFE), flown by the airline Linea Aeropostal Venezolana on a scheduled domestic Venezuelan service originating at Caracas, with an ultimate destination of Puerto Ayacuceho, crashed in flames following a mid-air explosion about 10 miles (15km) from Calabozo, in Guarico, an en-route stop. All 13 persons aboard were killed, including the crew of four. Two victims were found alive in the wreckage, and before succumbing to their injuries these confirmed that the aircraft's destruction had been caused by the detonation in the cabin of a hand-grenade brought aboard by another passenger, identified as a Russian immigrant. The blast had occurred around 08:20 local time when the captain tried to disarm the man, after what may have been an attempt to commandeer the flight.

5 July 1960

A Cubana airliner, which may have been a four-engine turboprop Britannia, was hijacked by two members of its flight-crew and diverted to Miami, Florida, while on a scheduled transatlantic service to Havana from Madrid, Spain.

17 July 1960

THE pilot of a Cubana Viscount commandeered the turboprop airliner during a scheduled service to Miami, Florida, from Havana, landing it in Jamaica.

19 July 1960

AN attempt to hijack a Trans-Australia Airlines four-engine turboprop Electra to Singapore during a scheduled domestic service from Sydney to Brisbane failed when the air pirate was overpowered by the first officer and an off-duty pilot near its destination.

28 July 1960

A Cubana airliner on a scheduled domestic service to Havana from Cuba's Oriente province was commandeered by the pilot, with the help of two passengers. The trio were then joined by two women and two children when the aircraft landed at Miami.

21 August 1960

THE attempted take-over of an Aeroflot aircraft by

a couple, which occurred during a scheduled domestic service in the USSR, was thwarted when members of the crew, though wounded, overpowered the hijackers.

29 October 1960

NINE men commandeered a Cuban C-46, believed operated by the airline Aerovias 'Q' SA, which was on a scheduled domestic flight from Havana to the Island of Pines with 38 persons aboard. A security guard was shot dead during the hijacking, and the pilot, co-pilot, and one passenger, a 13-year-old boy, were wounded, though the aeroplane landed safely at Key West, Florida.

8 December 1960

THE attempted hijacking by five passengers of a Cuban C-46 that was on a scheduled domestic service erupted into a gun battle that left one person dead and four wounded. Subsequently the transport, believed operated by the carrier Aerovias 'Q' SA, crash-landed at the airport serving Cienfuegos, Cuba, the act of air piracy ending in failure.

1 January 1961

TWO male hijackers took a pilot hostage while in the Havana airport terminal and forced him to fly them out of Cuba in a Cubana airliner, which subsequently landed in New York City.

1 May 1961

THE first successful US domestic hijacking involved National Airlines Flight 337, as the twin-engine Convair 440 was on a service from Miami to Key West, Florida, with 10 persons aboard. Armed with a revolver and a knife, the lone assailant forced the aircraft to Cuba. He was arrested in Miami 14 years later, and subsequently sentenced to 20 years' imprisonment for kidnapping (there was no federal law for aerial piracy in the US at the time of the hijacking).

10 May 1961

AN Air France Lockheed 1649A Starliner (F-BHBM) crashed and burned in the Sahara Desert, eastern Algeria, about 30 miles (50km) south-west of Ghadamis, Libya. All 78 persons aboard (69 passengers and nine crew members) perished.

Operating as Flight 406, the airliner had been en route from Fort Lamy (Ndjamena), Chad, to Marseille, France, one segment of a service originating at Brazzaville, Congo, with an ultimate destination of Paris. It broke up in darkness and

The first successful hijacking on a US domestic service occurred in May 1961, involving a Convair 440 identical to this, but flown by National Airlines. (General Dynamics)

clear meteorological conditions while cruising at an approximate height of 20,000ft (6,000m). The airline concluded that the most probable cause of the catastrophe was sabotage with a nitro-cellulose explosive.

3 July 1961

A group of 11 men and three women commandeered a Cubana DC-3 that was on a scheduled domestic service from Havana to Veradero. A security guard assigned to the aircraft was shot and wounded during the hijacking, which ended in Miami.

24 July 1961

OPERATING as Flight 202, an Eastern Air Lines Electra turboprop was hijacked to Cuba by a single gunman during a domestic intrastate service from Miami to Tampa, Florida, with 38 persons aboard.

31 July 1961

WHILE a Pacific Air Lines DC-3, designated as Flight 327, was at the airport in Chico, California, preparing for an intrastate service to San Francisco, its pilot and a ticket agent were shot and wounded, the former being blinded. The assailant was later convicted of three counts of assault with intent to commit murder and sentenced to three terms of up to 14 years in prison each, to run consecutively.

3 August 1961

A Continental Air Lines Boeing 707 jetliner, operating as Flight 54 and carrying 73 persons on a domestic service from Phoenix, Arizona, to El Paso, Texas, was commandeered by a man and his 16-year-old son, who were armed with pistols. The attempted hijacking to Cuba ended on the ground at El Paso airport when law enforcement personnel shot out the aircraft's tyres and captured both suspects.

As there was no US air piracy law in effect at the time, the father was convicted of 'obstruction of commerce by extortion' and 'intrastate transportation of a stolen aircraft', and sentenced to 20 years in prison. Facing juvenile charges on the same two counts, his son spent three years in a correctional facility.

9 August 1961

PAN American World Airways Flight 501, a DC-8 jetliner carrying 79 persons on a service between Mexico City and Guatemala, got hijacked to Cuba by a single man armed with a pistol. He was subse-

August 1961: law enforcement officers in four vehicles shoot out the tyres of Continental Air Lines Boeing 707 using sub-machine-guns, bringing to an end the hijacking of the jetliner. (UPI/Corbis-Bettmann)

quently deported to Mexico and convicted there of robbery and illegal possession of firearms, receiving a prison sentence of eight years and nine months. He reportedly later returned to the US by ship from France.

9 August 1961

IN the hijacking of an Aerovias 'Q' SA C-46 airliner, which occurred during a domestic Cuban service from Havana to the Island of Pines, the pilot and two other persons were killed and six more wounded. The co-pilot crash-landed the aircraft near the capital.

10 November 1961

WITH the intention of dropping leaflets over the Portuguese capital, six men commandeered a Transportes Aereos Portugueses (TAP) Super Constellation that was on a scheduled service to Lisbon from Casablanca, Morocco. The aircraft landed at Tangier, Morocco, and the hijackers were then expelled to Senegal, and subsequently granted political asylum in Brazil.

27 November 1961

AN AVENSA DC-6B got hijacked during a scheduled domestic Venezuelan service from Caracas to Maracaibo with 43 persons aboard. The airliner landed at Curacao, Netherlands Antilles, from where the five assailants were extradited back to Venezuela, and there served prison sentences of more than four years each.

28 November 1963

SIX hijackers commandeered an AVENSA twin-engine Convair 440 as it was on a scheduled domestic service from Ciudad Bolivar to Caracas, Venezuela, with 11 persons aboard. The aircraft landed in Trinidad, from where the assailants were extradited back to Venezuela for prosecution.

Fall 1964

BOTH pilots were wounded in the attempted hijacking of an Aeroflot An-2 biplane by two men during a scheduled domestic service in the USSR, from Shadur-Lungu to Izmail, Ukraine. The two assailants were captured after the aircraft landed at Kishinev.

8 December 1964

ALL 17 persons aboard (13 passengers and a crew of four) were killed in the crash of an Aerolineas Abaroa DC-3 (CP-639) near Tripuani, La Paz, Bolivia. The airliner was on a non-scheduled domestic service from Caranavi to the city of La Paz when it exploded in flight shortly after 10:00 local time, falling in the Andes Mountains, where the terrain was about 14,000ft (4,300m) above sea level. The cause of the tragedy was determined to be a violent explosion of a 'criminal origin' in the rear of the transport, which tore off its empennage. A suicide-for-insurance swindle was suspected.

Spring 1965

IN the attempted hijacking by a man and a woman of an Aeroflot airliner on a scheduled domestic service in the USSR, the flight engineer was shot and killed by the assailants before they were overpowered by other members of the crew.

31 August 1965

A Hawaiian Airlines DC-3, operating as Flight 358 on an inter-island service from Honolulu, Oahu, to Kauai, was commandeered by a 16-year-old boy armed with a knife and a broken bottle, who wanted the aircraft to return to its point of origin. He was captured after the transport landed at the Honolulu international airport. Convicted of interference with an aircraft crew, he was sentenced to a juvenile correctional facility, and paroled in November 1967.

11 October 1965

AN attempt to hijack Aloha Airlines Flight 755, a twin-engine turboprop F-27, occurred as it was boarding passengers on the Hawaiian island of Molokai in preparation for an inter-island service to Honolulu, Oahu. The assailants were two US Navy sailors armed with knives, who were overpowered by the crew. Court-martialled by the Navy, both were sentenced to four years' imprisonment and dishonourably discharged from the service.

26 October 1965

A lone assailant armed with an air pistol tried to commandeer a National Airlines Electra turboprop, designated as Flight 209, which was on an intrastate service from Miami to Key West, Florida. Overpowered by the crew, he was captured but subsequently acquitted of aircraft piracy and assault charges on grounds of mental incompetence.

17 November 1965

GUNSHOTS were fired during an attempt to commandeer a National Airlines DC-8 jet, operating as Flight 30, on a domestic US service from Houston, Texas, to Melbourne, Florida. Subdued by another passenger, the 16-year-old hijacker was convicted of assault and incarcerated for 18 months in a juvenile facility.

An Ilyushin Il-18, shown in the old livery of the Soviet airline Aeroflot, which was the type flown by Cubana involved in an unsuccessful hijacking in March 1966. (Aviation Photo News)

27 March 1966

TWO crew members were shot to death in the unsuccessful attempt to commandeer an Empresa Consolidada Cubana de Aviacion four-engine turboprop Ilyushin Il-18V during a scheduled domestic service from Santiago de Cuba to Havana with 91 persons aboard. The hijacker was the flight engineer, who first killed a guard and then the pilot, who had duped him into believing he had landed at Miami, Florida, but had actually set down at Havana's Jose Marti Airport under cover of darkness. He also wounded the co-pilot when he learned of the trick, causing the aircraft to swerve off the runway and strike a fence. The assailant escaped, only to be captured about two weeks later.

7 July 1966

THIS successful hijacking of an Empresa Consolidada Cubana de Aviacion Il-18 turboprop was carried out by nine persons, including the pilot, during a scheduled domestic service from Santiago de Cuba to Havana. The co-pilot was wounded, but the aircraft landed safely in Jamaica.

August 1966

ONE passenger was wounded and the three hijackers were captured during an attempt to comman-deer an Aeroflot aircraft that was on a domestic Soviet service, and which landed at Batumi, Georgian SSR.

28 September 1966

AN Aerolineas Argentinas DC-4 was hijacked by a group of 20 persons while on a scheduled domestic flight from Buenos Aires to Rio Gallegos, landing in the Falkland Islands. After being extradited back to Argentina, the five leaders of the group were sentenced to five years' imprisonment and the others three years.

22 November 1966

AN Aden Airways Douglas DC-3 (VR-AAN) was destroyed in an act of sabotage during a scheduled domestic service from Meifah to Aden. Flying at 6,000ft (c1,800m), about 20 minutes after an after-noon take-off, the airliner plunged into the desert some 130 miles (210km) east of its destination following an in-flight blast, all 30 persons aboard (27 passengers and a crew of three) losing their lives.

The crash was linked to the detonation of an explosive charge in hand luggage being carried in the cabin, which occurred on the port side just above the wing.

Destination Cuba

Cuba's fall to Fidel Castro in 1959 was a blow to the Western World, especially to the United States, which, for the first time in a century, found itself facing a hostile nation on its very doorstep.

As had been the case with Eastern Europe, the first few years of Communism in Cuba saw a number of defections by air. Subsequently, however, the island would become a haven for drop-outs, misfits, and political dissidents at odds with Western culture. Following several incidents in the early 1960s – few of which were successful – the hijacking-to-Cuba craze got into full swing late

What was to become a common sight in the late 1960s: US air travellers returning home after an unplanned diversion to Cuba. (Wide World Photos)

in the decade, reaching its peak in the period 1968–70. They continue to occur periodically, despite the implementation of preventative policies and procedures.

While most of the aircraft taken to Cuba were American, such diversions could begin at almost any point in the world. The following is a list of every hijacking to Cuba that took place after 1966, with the exception of those resulting in fatalities.

6 August 1967

CARRYING 78 persons, a DC-4 flown by the Colombian carrier Aerovias Condor de Colombia Ltda (Aerocondor) was commandeered by five men during a scheduled domestic service from Barranquilla to the island of San Andres, and forced to fly to Havana.

9 September 1967

FLYING on a scheduled Colombian domestic service from Barranquilla to Magangue, an AVIANCA DC-3 airliner was hijacked to Cuba by three men.

21 February 1968

THE modern hijack craze began in earnest with the case of Delta Air Lines Flight 843, a DC-8 jetliner commandeered shortly after take-off from West Palm Beach, Florida, bound for Miami, the final, intrastate segment of a service that had originated at Chicago, Illinois. The aircraft landed safely around 17:00 at Jose Marti Airport, serving Havana, Cuba, which would be seeing a lot of American commercial transports over the next few years. The aircraft and the 108 persons aboard, including a crew of seven, were returned safely with the single exception of the pistol-wielding hijacker.

The air pirate surrendered in Spain two years later, and after his extradition to the United States he was committed to a psychiatric facility.

5 March 1968

A four-engine DC-4 operated by the Colombian airline AVIANCA was hijacked during a scheduled domestic flight from Riohacha to Barranquilla with 32 persons aboard. The air pirates were identified as three young men, two of whom were reportedly taking their guerrilla leader to Cuba for medical attention. The transport landed safely at Santiago de Cuba, its fuel supply nearly exhausted due to the strong head winds it had encountered.

12 March 1968

OPERATING as Flight 28, a National Airlines DC-8 jetliner was hijacked over Florida while on the Tampa to Miami intrastate segment of a service originating at San Francisco, California. The aircraft, with 58 persons aboard, had been commandeered by three armed men, one of whom disembarked weeping at Havana, apparently having 'lost his nerve' about committing the hijacking shortly before the landing. Unconfirmed reports indicated that two members of the trio later died in Cuba.

21 March 1968

AN AVENSA twin-engine turboprop Convair 580 became the first Venezuelan airliner hijacked to Cuba. The aircraft, carrying 50 persons on a domestic service from Caracas to Maracaibo, landed safely, but precariously low on fuel, at Santiago de Cuba.

19 June 1968

VENEZOLANA Internacional de Aviacion SA (VIASA) Flight 797 was commandeered while en route from Santo Domingo, Dominican Republic, to Curacao, Netherlands Antilles, one segment of a service originating at Miami, Florida, with an ultimate destination of Caracas. The twin-jet DC-9 Series 10, with 78 persons aboard, landed safely at Santiago de Cuba.

After leaving Cuba, the hijacker was sentenced to 20 years' imprisonment by a Dominican court in August 1970.

29 June 1968

SOUTHEAST Airlines Flight 101, a twin-engine DC-3, was bound for Miami from Key West, Florida, when forced to Havana by a passenger, one of its 17 occupants. Staying behind after the release of the aircraft was both the hijacker and the pilot, Captain George Prellezo, who had flown from Cuba aboard an airliner he had commandeered eight years earlier and was now jailed as a defector. He was released by the Cuban authorities and returned to the US after being held for more than three weeks.

1 July 1968

ORIGINATING at Minneapolis, Minnesota, Northwest Airlines Flight 714 was commandeered while en route from Chicago, Illinois, to Miami, Florida, with 92 persons aboard. The Boeing 727 jet returned to the US mainland sans passengers, who were flown back on a piston-engine Douglas DC-7B. This marked the beginning of a policy by Cuban officials of not allowing fully-loaded Western jets to take off from an airfield not suited to them.

12 July 1968

THIS unsuccessful hijacking, which ended with the air pirate surrendering to the first officer, involved Delta Air Lines Flight 977, a Convair 880 jetliner on a domestic US service from Baltimore, Maryland, to Houston, Texas, with 55 persons aboard. Charges against the pistol-wielding hijacker, who wanted to be taken to Cuba, were dismissed, and he was committed to a mental hospital.

17 July 1968

NATIONAL Airlines Flight 1064, a DC-8 jet carrying 64 persons on a transcontinental domestic US service from Los Angeles, California, to Miami, Florida, was hijacked shortly after taking off from Houston, Texas, an en-route stop. The pilot managed to talk the armed hijacker – a Cuban who was heard to say 'Fidel ordered me back' – into landing at New Orleans, Louisiana, for refuelling before proceeding on to Havana.

The passengers were driven to Veradero and then flown back to the US aboard a chartered aircraft, the Cuban authorities again unwilling to risk a take-off from Jose Marti Airport by a heavily-loaded jet transport.

11 September 1968

A US citizen commandeered an Air Canada Viscount 700 turboprop airliner that was on a scheduled domestic service from Moncton, New Brunswick, to Toronto, Ontario. He surrendered in Montreal, Quebec, and asked for asylum in Canada. Instead, he was sentenced to prison there, and after being deported to the US in 1971 was jailed again, this time for a bank robbery and a related offence committed in Texas a month before the hijacking.

20 September 1968

WHILE en route from San Juan, Puerto Rico, to Miami, Florida, carrying 53 persons, Eastern Airlines Flight 950 was hijacked over the Bahamas by an armed passenger who identified himself as a Cuban. The Boeing 720 jetliner returned from Cuba without its passengers, these coming back on a Lockheed Electra turboprop.

22 September 1968

TWO aircraft flown by the Colombian carrier AVIANCA were hijacked to Cuba after their departure from Barranquilla, Colombia. The first was a Boeing 727-59 jetliner carrying 78 persons, which landed at Camaguey. Some three hours later, the second, a piston-engine DC-4 with 61 aboard, touched down safely at Santiago de Cuba.

6 October 1968

AN Aeromaya SA twin-engine turboprop Hawker Siddeley 748 was hijacked while flying from the Island of Cozumel to Merida, Mexico. Commandeered by an armed woman accompanied by two children, the Mexican airliner, with a total of 17 persons aboard, landed safely at Havana, where a fourth passenger also defected.

4 November 1968

DESIGNATED as Flight 186 and carrying 65 persons, a National Airlines Boeing 727-235 jetliner was hijacked by a self-styled 'black nationalist freedom fighter' shortly after take-off from New Orleans, Louisiana, an intermediate stop during a domestic service originating at Houston, Texas, with an ultimate destination of Miami, Florida. Before landing at Havana, the gunman robbed the passengers, ordering a stewardess to collect the loot in a sack. The money was subsequently returned to the victims by the Cuban authorities; the hijacker was not.

18 November 1968

A Compania Mexicana de Aviacion SA DC-6 airliner, on a scheduled domestic flight from Merida to Mexico City with 23 persons aboard, was hijacked to Cuba by two armed men, landing safely at Havana.

23 November 1968

A band of five men, a woman, and three children, who complained of 'juvenile delinquency and corruption existing in the United States', commandeered Eastern Airlines Flight 73, which was on a service to Miami from Chicago, Illinois. A total of 90 persons were aboard the Boeing 727-25 jet, which landed at Jose Marti Airport, serving Havana.

A man who reportedly purchased the tickets for the passengers but did not directly participate in the hijacking was later arrested.

24 November 1968

ONLY hours after the Eastern Airlines hijacking, Pan American World Airways Flight 281, a Boeing 707 jetliner with 103 persons aboard en route from New York City to San Juan, Puerto Rico, was commandeered by three armed men who told a stewardess that this was the 'easiest way' to get to Cuba. Two of them were apprehended separately in Puerto Rico in the mid-1970s and sentenced to 15 and 12 years' imprisonment respectively, for endangering the lives of an aircraft crew with a gun and knife; the third member of the hijack trio remained in Cuba.

Eastern Airlines would experience more of its aircraft being hijacked to Cuba than any other carrier, including a Boeing 727-25 like this one in November 1968. (Eastern Airlines)

30 November 1968

EASTERN Airlines Flight 532 was commandeered during a domestic US service from Miami, Florida, to Dallas, Texas. The Boeing 720 jet, with 45 persons aboard, reached Cuba safely.

3 December 1968

A National Airlines Boeing 727 jetliner, operating as Flight 1439 and carrying 35 persons, was commandeered by a hijacker armed with a pistol and a hand-grenade after taking off from Tampa, Florida, an en-route stop during a domestic US service from New York City to Miami, Florida.

11 December 1968

TRANS World Airlines Flight 496, a Boeing 727-31 jet with 39 persons aboard, inaugurating a new domestic route to Miami from St Louis, Missouri, was hijacked by a married couple after it had taken off from Nashville, Tennessee, an intermediate stop. The aircraft reached Havana without further incident.

19 December 1968

EASTERN Airlines Flight 47, a McDonnell Douglas DC-8 Super 61 jetliner carrying 151 persons, bound for Miami from Philadelphia, Pennsylvania, was commandeered to Havana by a man accompanied by his four-year-old daughter.

Cuban radio later described the 'weapons' he had used as a toy pistol and a fake container of nitro-glycerine. The hijacker returned to the US via Canada about a year later and would serve 16 months in prison for interfering with an aircraft crew member.

2 January 1969

THE new year was but two days old when an Eastern Airlines McDonnell Douglas DC-8 Super 61 jetliner, designated as Flight 401, on a New York City to Miami domestic service with 146 persons aboard, was commandeered by a couple accompanied by their infant daughter. The man was killed in a bank hold-up in New York two years later.

7 January 1969

A piston-engine DC-4, flown by Colombian airline AVIANCA on a scheduled domestic service from Riohacha to Maicao, was forced to Cuba by a lone hijacker.

9 January 1969

EASTERN Airlines Flight 831, a Boeing 727 jet operating on an international service to the Bahamas from Miami, Florida, with 79 persons aboard, was commandeered to Cuba by a knife-wielding assailant, who returned to the US via Canada later in the year and received a 20-year prison sentence for air piracy in 1972.

11 January 1969

AEROLINEAS Peruanas SA (APSA) Flight 60, a Convair 990A Coronado jet airliner en route from Buenos Aires, Argentina, carrying 118 persons, was hijacked while preparing to land at Miami, Florida, landing instead at Havana. The air pirate was sent to Mexico four years later, where he received a 25-year prison sentence. He was later returned to Cuba with 29 other prisoners released by Mexico.

11 January 1969

UNITED Air Lines joined the ranks of carriers experiencing hijackings when its Flight 459 was commandeered over Florida while on an intrastate service from Jacksonville to Miami with 20 persons aboard. The tri-jet Boeing 727 reached Havana without further incident. The hijacker returned to the US via Canada four months later, and was subsequently acquitted of all charges on grounds of temporary insanity.

13 January 1969

AN unsuccessful attempt to hijack Delta Air Lines Flight 297 ended with the capture of the shotgun-armed assailant, who subsequently received a 15-year sentence for interference with a flight crew member. The Convair 880 jet, carrying 77 persons, had been on a domestic US service to Miami from Detroit, Michigan.

19 January 1969

AN Eastern Airlines McDonnell Douglas DC-8 Super 61 jetliner, designated as Flight 9, was en route from New York City to Miami with 171 persons aboard when it was commandeered by a man holding an apparently live hand-grenade. The suspect was later captured and sentenced to 5 years' imprisonment in the Dominican Republic.

19 January 1969

TEN persons were captured after the attempted hijacking of a Compania Ecuatoriana de Aviacion SA Lockheed Electra turboprop, which had been on a scheduled domestic Ecuadorean service from Guayaquil to Quito, with 88 persons aboard. All 10 were later successfully prosecuted.

24 January 1969

NATIONAL Airlines Flight 424, a Boeing 727 jet with 47 persons aboard, was hijacked by a 19-year-old deserter from the US Navy who said he didn't want to go to Vietnam. Holding a knife at the throat of a stewardess, he commandeered the aircraft to Havana during an intrastate service to Miami from Key West, Florida.

28 January 1969

NATIONAL Airlines Flight 64, a McDonnell Douglas DC-8 Super 61 jet on a transcontinental service from Los Angeles to Miami with 32 persons aboard, was commandeered by two men armed with a revolver and dynamite. They were escapees from the California Institute for Men, where they had been serving time for robbery. The aircraft landed safely at Havana.

28 January 1969

ONLY hours after the National Airlines hijacking, Eastern Airlines Flight 121 was diverted to Cuba by three armed men during a domestic service to Miami that had originated at Philadelphia, Pennsylvania. There were 113 persons aboard the DC-8 Super 61 jetliner. One hijacker was caught in Cleveland, Ohio, in 1975, and received a 5-year suspended sentence; his cohorts returned to the US in 1978, both later being sentenced to 7 years' imprisonment for interference with a flight crew.

31 January 1969

A National Airlines DC-8 jetliner, designated as Flight 44, got diverted to Cuba during a domestic US service from San Francisco, California, to Tampa, Florida, with 63 persons aboard. The lone hijacker, who had used a pistol to commandeer the aircraft, was extradited to the US from Yugoslavia in 1976, and the following year received a 15-year prison sentence for interfering with a flight crew.

3 February 1969

A couple armed with a knife and an aerosol can filled with insecticide attempted to hijack a National Airlines Boeing 727 jet, operating as Flight 11, on a domestic service from New York City to Miami, but were convinced by the pilot that they should land at the intended destination and were then captured. Both served 19 months in prison for the lesser charge of interfering with an aircraft crew.

3 February 1969

EASTERN Airlines Flight 7, a Boeing 727-25 jetliner with 94 persons aboard, on a domestic US service to Miami from Newark, New Jersey, was commandeered by a trio of hijackers armed with a knife and an alleged bomb, reaching Havana without further incident.

5 February 1969

A DC-4 flown by the Colombian carrier Socieded Aeronautica de Medellin Consolidada SA (SAM), on a scheduled domestic service from Barranquilla to Medellin, was taken to Cuba by a lone hijacker. He later fled to Czechoslovakia, and then to Sweden, where he was arrested and sentenced to 20 months' imprisonment in 1972.

8 February 1969

THE attempted hijacking of a Compania Mexicana de Aviacion SA DC-6, which was on a scheduled domestic service from Mexico City to Villahermosa, Tabasco, ended when the air pirate was overpowered by other passengers and captured.

10 February 1969

EASTERN Airlines Flight 950, a DC-8 Super 61 jetliner carrying 119 persons on an international service from San Juan, Puerto Rico, to Miami, Florida, was commandeered by a lone gunman and diverted to Havana.

11 February 1969

A twin-jet DC-9 of Linea Aeropostal Venezolana was hijacked to Cuba by three men during a scheduled domestic Venezuelan service from Maracaibo to Caracas, with 73 persons aboard.

25 February 1969

AN Eastern Airlines DC-8 jetliner, operating as Flight 955 and carrying 67 persons, was commandeered during a domestic US service to Miami from Atlanta, Georgia. In September 1969 the

hijacker, who had used a revolver, surrendered to US authorities in Prague, Czechoslovakia, and the following July he was sentenced to life imprisonment for air piracy and kidnapping.

5 March 1969

A National Airlines Boeing 727 jet on a New York City to Miami run with 26 persons aboard, designated as Flight 97, was hijacked by what witnesses described as a 'grubby-looking character' armed with a revolver, who also robbed some of the passengers in the process of forcing the aircraft to Havana. The air pirate returned to the US more than a decade later, and in 1981 was sentenced to five years' probation for air piracy.

15 March 1969

A piston-engine DC-6 of the carrier Aerovias Condor de Colombia Ltda (Aerocondor) was commandeered by a lone hijacker during a domestic service from Barranquilla to San Andres Island, with 47 persons aboard.

17 March 1969

DURING a domestic US service originating at Dallas, Texas, with an ultimate destination of Charleston, South Carolina, a Delta Air Lines twin-jet DC-9 Series 30, designated as Flight 518, was commandeered between Atlanta and Augusta, Georgia, by a man who claimed to be carrying a shoebox filled with dynamite. The bomb proved to be a fake, but it got him a trip to

A Delta Air Lines DC-9 identical to this found itself winging its way to Cuba on 17 March 1969, one of two aircraft hijacked in a single day. (McDonnell Douglas)

Havana, along with the other 62 persons aboard the aircraft.

Later that year, the hijacker returned to the US via Canada, and was subsequently confined to a mental health facility for three years.

17 March 1969

LESS than two hours after the hijacked Delta DC-9 had landed at Havana, a Boeing 727 jetliner of Peru's Compania de Aviacion Faucett SA touched down at Jose Marti Airport, having been seized while on a scheduled domestic service from Lima to Arequipa. During a refuelling stop at Guayaquil, Ecuador, the four hijackers, who were carrying explosives, allowed the other 69 passengers to disembark before the aircraft proceeded on to Cuba.

19 March 1969

DELTA Air Lines Flight 918, a Convair 880 jet with 97 persons aboard, was the target of an attempted hijacking between Dallas, Texas, and New Orleans, Louisiana, by a man armed with a revolver. Charges against him would later be dismissed on the basis of insanity, and he was then transferred to a mental health facility in Arizona.

25 March 1969

DELTA Air Lines Flight 821, a Douglas DC-8 jetliner on a transcontinental service to Los Angeles from Newark, New Jersey, was commandeered shortly after taking off from Dallas, Texas, one of two en-route stops. Among the 114 persons aboard the aircraft were some two dozen Marine recruits on their way to San Diego, California. The hijacker was reported to have died in Cuba in 1975.

11 April 1969

A group of hijackers composed of about 10 men accompanied by three women and four children commandeered a Compania Ecuatoriana de Aviacion SA DC-6 flying on a scheduled domestic route between Guayaquil and Quito, Ecuador, and carrying 60 persons, ordering it to Cuba.

13 April 1969

FOUR men took over Pan American World Airways Flight 460, with more than 90 persons aboard, between San Juan, Puerto Rico, and Miami, forcing the Boeing 727 jetliner to fly to Havana.

14 April 1969

A Sociedad Aeronautica de Medellin Consolidada SA (SAM) DC-4 got hijacked to Cuba during a scheduled domestic service from Medellin to Barranquilla, Colombia, with 29 persons aboard.

5 May 1969

TWO hijackers commandeered a National Airlines Boeing 727 jet, operating as Flight 91 and carrying 75 persons, during a domestic service from New York City to Miami. Both men returned to Canada a decade later, where one received a six-month prison term for bombings in that country; extradition to the US was later denied for both of them.

20 May 1969

AN AVIANCA Boeing 737 jet airliner was hijacked to Cuba during a scheduled domestic Colombian service from Bogota to Pereira, with 59 persons aboard.

26 May 1969

NORTHEAST Airlines Flight 6 was commandeered by three armed men while en route from Miami to New York City. The Boeing 727 jet and its 20 passengers and crew members reached Havana without further incident.

30 May 1969

A man who claimed to be carrying a hand-grenade but was in fact unarmed unsuccessfully tried to commandeer Texas International Airlines Flight 669, a twin-engine turboprop Convair 600 on an intrastate service to New Orleans from Alexandria, Louisiana. Criminal charges against him were later dropped on grounds of insanity and he was committed to a psychiatric facility for two years.

17 June 1969

A Trans World Airlines Boeing 707 jetliner, operating as Flight 154, was hijacked to Cuba by a lone gunman after it had taken off from Oakland, California, on a domestic US transcontinental service to New York City carrying 89 persons.

20 June 1969

A vintage DC-3 flown by the Colombian airline Lineas Aereas La Urraca, on a scheduled domestic service from Villavicencio to Monterrey, was hijacked to Cuba by three men and a woman.

22 June 1969

WHILE on a domestic service to Miami from Newark, New Jersey, Eastern Airlines Flight 7, a DC-8 Super 61 jet with 89 persons aboard, was forced to Cuba by a lone hijacker armed with a knife and a jar marked 'poison'.

25 June 1969

ABOUT a quarter of an hour after its take-off from Los Angeles, on a transcontinental service to New York City, United Air Lines Flight 14, a DC-8 Super 61 jetliner with 58 persons aboard, was commandeered by a single gunman while still over California, landing early the following morning at Havana.

28 June 1969

EASTERN Airlines Flight 173, a Boeing 727 jetliner with 104 persons aboard, was hijacked off the east coast of Florida while on a service to Miami from Baltimore, Maryland, and diverted to Cuba. The knife-wielding air pirate returned to the US via Canada five months later, and was sentenced to 15 years' imprisonment in 1970 for interference with an aircraft crew.

3 July 1969

A group of 13 persons commandeered a Sociedad Anonima Ecuatoriana de Transportes Aereos (SAETA) DC-3 airliner with 21 aboard on a domestic Ecuadorian service from Tulcan to Quito.

10 July 1969

AN attempt to commandeer an AVIANCA DC-4 after it had left Barranquilla, Colombia, on a scheduled domestic flight to Santa Maria, ended when the hijacker was overpowered. The aircraft returned safely to its point of departure.

10 July 1969

FOR the second time in a single day, a Colombian DC-4 airliner was targeted for a hijacking during a scheduled domestic service, this one flown by the carrier Sociedad Aeronautica de Medellin Consolidada SA (SAM) and en route from Cali to Bogota. And as with the first attempt, this one ended with the lone air pirate being overpowered and the transport landing safely in Colombia.

26 July 1969

IN one of Mexico's comparatively rare hijackings to Cuba, a Compania Mexicana de Aviacion SA DC-6 was commandeered while on a scheduled domestic service from Minatitlan, Veracruz, to Villahermosa, Tabasco, with 32 persons aboard.

26 July 1969

CONTINENTAL Air Lines Flight 156, a DC-9 jet, was commandeered by a knife-wielding man after it had taken off from El Paso, Texas. The aircraft stopped for refuelling at Midland, Texas, where it was scheduled to land, and proceeded on to Havana

after its passengers had been allowed to disembark. The hijacker returned to the US later the same year, and in 1970 he was sentenced to 50 years' imprisonment for air piracy.

29 July 1969

DURING a scheduled domestic service, a male hijacker dressed as a female tried to take over a Nicaraguan airliner, possibly a C-46 flown by Lineas Aereas de Nicaragua SA (LANICA), but was subdued and captured.

31 July 1969

THIS daring hijack was committed by a man who had been arrested in connection with a bank robbery which had occurred four years earlier. The prisoner was being accompanied by two guards on Trans World Airlines Flight 79, a Boeing 727-231 jetliner on a domestic US service from Pittsburgh, Pennsylvania, to Los Angeles, California, when he asked to go to the lavatory. Here he apparently found a razor blade, which, after hiding it until the right moment, he suddenly put to the throat of a stewardess and ordered the aircraft to Cuba.

The hijacker was arrested in the state of Indiana 12 years later, and was sentenced that year to 25 years in prison for air piracy and kidnapping.

4 August 1969

AN AVIANCA DC-4 on a scheduled domestic Colombian service from Santa Marta to Riohacha was hijacked to Cuba by a trio of men.

5 August 1969

THE unsuccessful hijacking of an Eastern Airlines DC-9 jet on a domestic US service from Philadelphia, Pennsylvania, to Tampa, Florida, designated as Flight 379, resulted in the capture of the 73-year-old suspect, who had been armed with a knife and a straight razor. Criminal charges against him were dropped the following year, and he was later committed to a mental health facility.

14 August 1969

A Northeast Airlines Boeing 727 jetliner, operating as Flight 43 on a domestic US service to Miami from Boston, Massachusetts, with 52 persons aboard, was hijacked in the vicinity of Jacksonville, Florida, by two men armed with a revolver and a knife, proceeding on to Cuba.

23 August 1969

TWO men commandeered an AVIANCA Avro 748 twin-engine turboprop airliner to Cuba. It had been on a scheduled Colombian domestic service from Bucaramanga to Bogota with 30 persons aboard.

29 August 1969

NATIONAL Airlines Flight 183, a Boeing 727 jet carrying 55 persons on a domestic US service from Miami to New Orleans, Louisiana, was diverted to Cuba by a lone armed assailant.

7 September 1969

AN Eastern Airlines DC-8 Super 61 jetliner, designated as Flight 925 and carrying 96 persons, was hijacked to Cuba by a single gunman during an international service from New York City to San Juan, Puerto Rico.

10 September 1969

THE unsuccessful attempt to commandeer Eastern Airlines Flight 929 as the DC-8 Super 61 jet was en route from New York City to San Juan, Puerto Rico, with 202 persons aboard, ended with the unarmed assailant being subdued by other passengers and members of the crew. He was committed to a mental health facility in January 1970.

24 September 1969

A National Airlines Boeing 727 jetliner got hijacked to Cuba while operating as Flight 411 on a domestic service to Miami from Charleston, South Carolina. The air pirate, who had used a pistol and an alleged bomb in the take-over, returned to the US with Cuban refugees in 1980, and the following year was sentenced to five years' imprisonment for interfering with an aircraft flight crew.

8 October 1969

A Brazilian Servicos Aereos Cruzeiro do Sul SA Caravelle jet airliner with 67 persons aboard was hijacked to Cuba by four men during a scheduled domestic service from Belem to Manaus.

8 October 1969

AN Aerolineas Argentinas Boeing 707 jetliner, carrying 50 persons, was commandeered to Cuba by a single hijacker during a scheduled international service to Miami from Buenos Aires, Argentina.

9 October 1969

DESIGNATED as Flight 42, a National Airlines DC-8 jetliner was hijacked during a transcontinental domestic US service from Los Angeles to Miami with 70 persons aboard. The aircraft landed safely at Havana's Jose Marti Airport. The lone gunman had reportedly told the pilot that he was 'homesick'.

21 October 1969

A Pan American World Airways Boeing 720B jetliner, operating as Flight 551 on an internal Mexican service from Mexico City to Merida, was hijacked by a 17-year-old armed with a revolver, landing safely in Havana.

28 October 1969

A Colombian twin-engine Beechcraft, on a domestic air taxi service from Buenaventura to Bogota with eight persons aboard, was hijacked to Cuba by two men.

4 November 1969

THE first hijacking of the day involved a Brazilian SA Empresa de Viacao Aerea Rio Grandense (VARIG) Boeing 707 jet airliner, designated as Flight 863, which was commandeered to Cuba during a service from Buenos Aires, Argentina, to Santiago, Chile, with 101 persons aboard.

4 November 1969

THE second hijacking of the day almost failed when the commandeered Lineas Aereas de Nicaragua SA (LANICA) BAC One-Eleven jetliner, which had been on a scheduled service from Managua, Nicaragua, to San Salvador, El Salvador, carrying 32 persons, landed on Grand Cayman Island, in an attempt to trick the two air pirates into believing that it was Cuba. One of the hijackers was in fact captured after getting off, but was released when the other one, still aboard, threatened a stewardess with a gun. The aircraft then proceeded to Cuba with both assailants aboard.

8 November 1969

THIS potentially tragic hijacking of an Argentine jet airliner had a peaceful conclusion. The Austral Lineas Aereas SA BAC One-Eleven was seized on a scheduled domestic flight from Cordoba to Buenos Aires by a man who threatened to shoot a child unless the pilot headed for Cuba. However, after the aircraft had landed for refuelling at Montevideo, Uruguay, the gunman was persuaded to release all the passengers, and some 80 minutes later he gave himself up to the authorities.

12 November 1969

TWO juveniles who attempted to hijack a LAN-

Chile Caravelle jet airliner, which had been on a scheduled domestic service from Santiago to Puerto Montt, were overpowered by the two members of the flight crew after taking off from Antofagasta, Chile.

12 November 1969

ON a scheduled domestic service from Manaus to Belem with 12 persons aboard, a twin-engine turboprop NAMC YS-11, operated by the Brazilian carrier Servicos Aereos Cruzeiro do Sul SA, was hijacked to Cuba by a single assailant.

13 November 1969

AN AVIANCA DC-4, carrying 61 persons on a scheduled domestic Colombian service between Cucuta and Bogota, was hijacked to Cuba by six men. During a refuelling stop at Barranquilla, a pregnant woman and one other passenger were allowed to disembark.

29 November 1969

THIS was the first case of a hijacking to Cuba from Europe. A Brazilian SA Empresa de Viacao Aerea Rio Grandense (VARIG) Boeing 707 jet, carrying 95 persons on a transatlantic service originating at London and destined for Rio de Janeiro, was commandeered over Portugal by an assailant armed with a revolver and a knife.

2 December 1969

TRANS World Airlines Flight 54, a Boeing 707 jet on a domestic US service from San Francisco, California, to Philadelphia, Pennsylvania, with 28 persons aboard, was forced to Cuba by a passenger who held a knife to the throat of a stewardess and forced his way into the cockpit. Though the 707 reached Havana safely, a US Air National Guard F-102 jet fighter that was to have provided an escort for the airliner crashed near Jacksonville, Florida, the pilot parachuting to safety.

The air pirate returned to the US a decade later and was then sentenced to 10 years in prison for interfering with an aircraft crew.

19 December 1969

A Linea Aerea Nacional de Chile (LAN-Chile) Boeing 727 jetliner, on a scheduled domestic service from Santiago to Arica with 99 persons aboard, was hijacked to Cuba by a single assailant.

23 December 1969

A vintage twin-engine C-46 flown by Lineas Aereas Costaricenses SA (LASCA) got comman- deered by a single hijacker while on a scheduled domestic flight from Puerto Limon to San Jose, Costa Rica. During a stop, 30 passengers were allowed to disembark before the airliner proceeded on to Cuba.

26 December 1969

OPERATING as Flight 929 en route from New York City to Chicago, Illinois, a United Air Lines Boeing 727 jet with 32 persons aboard was commandeered by a lone gunman shortly after its departure from La Guardia Airport, landing at Havana. In 1983 the hijacker turned himself in to the authorities in San Juan, Puerto Rico, and the following year was sentenced to life imprisonment for air piracy.

1–3 January 1970

THIS prolonged hijacking involved a Servicos Aereos Cruzeiro do Sul SA Sud-Aviation Caravelle, the Brazilian twin-jet airliner having been commandeered while en route to Rio de Janeiro, Brazil, from Montevideo, Uruguay. Due to a technical problem, the aircraft had to land at Lima, Peru, where police helplessly looked on as a new generator was flown in from Santiago, Chile, and then installed. The trouble didn't end at that point, as the Caravelle had to land in Panama because of more generator troubles. After electricians had wired up 22 automobile batteries in order to start the engines, the aircraft finally took off for Havana, landing 46 hours after the start of the hijacking.

24 January 1970

TWO men and two women hijacked an ALM Dutch Antillean Airlines Fokker F.27 Friendship, the twin-engine turboprop being forced to Cuba during a scheduled service from Santo Domingo, Dominican Republic, to Curacao, Netherlands Antilles.

16 February 1970

WHILE on a service to Miami from Newark, New Jersey, an Eastern Airlines Boeing 727-225 jetliner, designated as Flight 1, was hijacked by a Spanish-speaking man accompanied by his wife and two children. At one point the man held a flaming Molotov cocktail and exclaimed 'Viva Cuba!' However, the aircraft, carrying a total of 104 persons, landed safely at Havana despite the fiery threat.

11 March 1970

OPERATING as Flight 361, a United Air Lines

An Eastern Airlines Boeing 727-225 was diverted to Cuba in February 1970, as US hijackings continued into the new decade. (Eastern Airlines)

Boeing 727-222 jetliner carrying 106 persons on a domestic US service from Cleveland, Ohio, to Atlanta, Georgia, was hijacked by an armed assailant who was accompanied by his wife and four children. Imprisoned in Cuba, he was shot and killed during an escape attempt in 1973, his family returning to the US the following year.

11 March 1970

A Boeing 727 jet, operated by the Colombian airline AVIANCA on a scheduled domestic service from Bogota to Barranquilla with 78 persons aboard, was hijacked to Cuba by four men.

12 March 1970

A Brazilian VARIG Boeing 707 jet airliner, operating as Flight 866 on a transatlantic service to London from Santiago, Chile, was hijacked to Cuba with 41 persons aboard.

24–25 March 1970

AN Aerolineas Argentinas Comet 4 jet airliner, carrying 68 persons on a scheduled domestic flight from Cordoba to Tucuman, was commandeered by a couple. Stopping at Lima, Peru, for repairs, it reached Cuba the following day.

25 April 1970

A single hijacker commandeered a Brazilian Viacao

Aerea Sao Paulo SA (VASP) Boeing 737 jet flying on a scheduled domestic service from Brasilia to Manaus. All but one of the other passengers, who stayed aboard voluntarily, were released when the aircraft landed for refuelling in Guyana before proceeding on to Cuba.

1 May 1970

TWO hijackers took over a British West Indian Airways Boeing 727 jetliner on a scheduled service from Kingston, Jamaica, to Grand Cayman Island in the Bahamas, with 68 persons aboard. After it had landed in Cuba, the authorities there managed to convince the assailants that a proposed flight on to Algeria would be beyond the aircraft's range.

12 May 1970

A group of eight Dutch revolutionaries armed with automatic weapons and hand-grenades pirated an ALM Dutch Antillean Airlines Fokker F.27 Friendship twin-engine turboprop, which was carrying 33 persons on a scheduled flight from Santo Domingo, Dominican Republic, to Curacao, Netherlands Antilles, and forced it to fly to Cuba.

14 May 1970

A Boeing 737 jet of the Brazilian carrier Viacao Aerea Sao Paulo SA (VASP), carrying 48 persons, was commandeered by a single assailant armed with a pistol and explosives during a scheduled domestic service from Brasilia to Manaus. The aircraft made two refuelling stops before proceeding on to Cuba.

21 May 1970

AN AVIANCA DC-3 on a scheduled Colombian domestic service from Yopal to Sogomoso en Boyaca with 26 persons aboard was commandeered by four hijackers, landing at Barrancabermeja and Barranquilla, Colombia, before proceeding on to Cuba.

24 May 1970

THE Mexican airline industry, which had established routes to and from Cuba, had been understandably victimized far less by hijackers than its US counterpart. But on this occasion, revenge for the killing by Mexican authorities of a Guatemalan guerrilla leader two years earlier was the apparent motive behind the piracy by four men of a Compania Mexicana de Aviacion SA Boeing 727 jetliner, which was on a service to Mexico City from Merida with 79 persons aboard.

25 May 1970

THE first of two US airline hijackings in a single day involved American Airlines Flight 206, a Boeing 727 jet on a domestic service from Chicago to New York City with 74 persons aboard. It was taken over by a single assailant armed with a pistol.

25 May 1970

DELTA Air Lines Flight 199, a Convair 880 jetliner, was commandeered after it had taken off from Atlanta, Georgia, while carrying 102 persons on a domestic service from Chicago to Miami. The armed hijacker was a Spanish-speaking woman, whose 12-year-old son served as translator. She returned to the US a decade later with Cuban refugees, and was subsequently sentenced to 20 years in prison for air piracy.

31 May 1970

A couple accompanied by five children took over an Avro 748 twin-engine turboprop airliner being flown by the Colombian carrier AVIANCA on a scheduled domestic service from Bogota to Bucaramanga, forcing it to Cuba.

26 June 1970

AN AVIANCA Boeing 727 jet airliner with 99 persons aboard was hijacked to Cuba by two assailants during a scheduled Colombian domestic service from Cucuta to Bogota.

1 July 1970

NATIONAL Airlines Flight 28, a DC-8 jet with 39 persons aboard, was diverted to Cuba while en route from New Orleans, Louisiana, to Tampa, Florida, one segment of a domestic transcontinental service originating at San Francisco, with an ulti-

Delta Air Lines, with an extensive route structure in the American South-east, was the victim of numerous hijackings, one in May 1970 involving a Convair 880 jet. (Delta Air Lines)

mate destination of Miami. Four passengers, all US service personnel, were reportedly 'roughed up' by Cuban authorities on the ground at Havana.

1 July 1970

WHILE attempting to hold its passengers as hostages in exchange for jailed terrorists, this attempted hijacking to Cuba of a Brazilian Servicos Aereos Cruzeiro do Sul SA Caravelle jetliner ended with the capture of the four assailants on the ground at Rio de Janeiro, where the flight – a scheduled domestic service to Sao Paulo – had originated. The pilot of the aircraft and a police officer were wounded in the hijacking.

4 July 1970

A YS-11 twin-engine turboprop, operated by Servicos Aereos Cruzeiro do Sul SA on a scheduled Brazilian internal flight from Belem to Macapa with 63 persons aboard, was commandeered by a single hijacker carrying a bottle of what he said was nitro-glycerine. All the passengers were allowed to disembark during two of the five stops made along the way to Cuba.

25 July 1970

AFTER being hijacked, Aeronaves de Mexico SA Flight 600, a DC-9 jet airliner carrying 31 persons on a scheduled domestic service from Acapulco to Mexico City, landed at the capital for refuelling before proceeding on to Cuba. Three of the four assailants were Dominican prisoners, who had been released and sent to Mexico in exchange for a US diplomat kidnapped earlier in the year.

28 July 1970

AN Aerolineas Argentinas Boeing 737 jetliner carrying 32 persons was taken over during a scheduled domestic service from Salta to Buenos Aires. About half of the passengers disembarked at Cordoba, but while on the way to Cuba the aircraft encountered a snowstorm over the Andes and had to turn back. The hijacker, who was armed with two pistols, surrendered to police after the aircraft had returned to Cordoba.

2 August 1970

CUBA got its first glimpse of a wide-bodied jetliner with the hijacking of Pan American World Airways Flight 299, a Boeing 747-121 on a service from New York City to San Juan, Puerto Rico, with 377 persons aboard. The lone air pirate, who had carried out the hijack by means of a pistol and an alleged nitro-glycerine explosive, returned to the US in 1978, and was convicted of kidnapping. He was sentenced to life imprisonment later that year.

19 August 1970

A Trans-Caribbean Airways DC-8 jetliner, operating as Flight 401, got hijacked to Cuba during a service from Newark, New Jersey, to San Juan, Puerto Rico, with 154 persons aboard.

Cuba would see its first wide-bodied Boeing 747 when a Pan American aircraft was hijacked there in August 1970. (Pan American World Airways)

20 August 1970

A Delta Air Lines twin-jet DC-9, designated as Flight 435 and carrying 82 persons on an intrastate service from Atlanta to Savannah, Georgia, was hijacked to Cuba by a single assailant allegedly carrying a bomb. He was arrested five years later in San Juan, Puerto Rico, and after being returned to the US received a 20-year prison term for air piracy.

24 August 1970

A man who said he had a bomb (which turned out to be a fake) commandeered Trans World Airlines Flight 134, a Boeing 727 jet on a service from Las Vegas, Nevada, to Philadelphia, Pennsylvania, with 86 persons aboard. The hijacker was deported back to the US from Cuba the following month, but found mentally incompetent to stand trial, and was committed to a psychiatric facility for three years.

19 September 1970

ALLEGHENY Airlines Flight 730, a Boeing 727 jetliner on an intrastate service from Pittsburgh to Philadelphia, Pennsylvania, carrying 98 persons, got hijacked to Cuba by a lone assailant armed with a pistol and, according to him, explosives. He returned to the US in 1978 and was sentenced to 15 years' imprisonment for air piracy the same year.

22 September 1970

A single assailant threatened to start a fire during the attempted hijacking of Eastern Airlines Flight 945, a DC-8 jetliner on a service from Boston, Massachusetts, to San Juan, Puerto Rico, but the aircraft nevertheless landed at its intended destination. The suspect surrendered there. Rather than air piracy, he was convicted on outstanding state charges of murder and robbery and was sentenced to life imprisonment.

21 October 1970

A twin-engine C-46 operated by Lineas Aereas Costaricenses SA (LASCA), on a scheduled domestic service from Limon to San Jose with 44 persons aboard, was commandeered by a group of five men and two women. The flight landed on San Andres Island for refuelling, whereupon the hijackers boarded a second aircraft for the trip to Cuba.

30 October 1970

OPERATING as Flight 43, a National Airlines DC-8 jetliner with 58 persons aboard was hijacked to Cuba by an armed man accompanied by his wife and five children during an intrastate service from Miami to Tampa, Florida.

1 November 1970

UNITED Air Lines Flight 598, a Boeing 727 jet on an intrastate service from San Diego to Los Angeles, California, was hijacked by a gunman accompanied by his two children. The aircraft landed for refuelling at Tijuana, Mexico, before proceeding on to Cuba.

13 November 1970

DESIGNATED as Flight 257, an Eastern Airlines twin-jet DC-9 was hijacked to Cuba by an armed man during a domestic service from Raleigh, North Carolina, to Atlanta, Georgia, with 78 persons aboard.

19 December 1970

AN unsuccessful attempt to detour a Continental Air Lines DC-9 jet, which was operating as Flight 144 on a domestic US service from Albuquerque, New Mexico, to Tulsa, Oklahoma, with 30 persons aboard, ended with the capture of the unarmed hijacker. He was later sentenced to five years in prison for 'conveying false information to commit air piracy'.

3 January 1971

TWO pistol-wielding couples, one of them accompanied by their four children, commandeered a National Airlines DC-8 jetliner, operating as Flight 36 on a domestic service from Los Angeles, California, to Miami, Florida, with 96 persons aboard. The married couple and their family were apprehended in San Juan, Puerto Rico, in 1975, the husband receiving a sentence of 20 years for air piracy, while charges against the wife were dropped. The other couple were arrested in Chicago the same year, the man likewise receiving a 20-year sentence and the woman getting five years on a lesser charge.

22 January 1971

ARMED with a hatchet and an alleged bomb, a single assailant hijacked Northwest Airlines Flight 433, a Boeing 727 jet on an interstate domestic service from Milwaukee, Wisconsin, to Detroit, Michigan, with 60 persons aboard. He first asked to go to Algeria but settled for Cuba instead. Returning to the US in 1978, he received a 15-year prison sentence for air piracy and kidnapping.

26 January 1971

THE attempted hijacking of a Dominican Republic-registered Constellation, flown by Aerovias Quisqueyanas C por A on a scheduled service from

Santo Domingo, Dominican Republic, to San Juan, Puerto Rico, with 74 persons aboard, ended with the transport landing in the nation of registry and the crew overpowering the single assailant.

4 February 1971

DESIGNATED as Flight 379, a Delta Air Lines DC-9 jet was commandeered to Cuba during a service from Chicago to Nashville, Tennessee, with 27 persons aboard. The hijacker, who had allegedly been carrying nitro-glycerine, was captured four years later and subsequently sentenced to 20 years' imprisonment for air piracy.

25 February 1971

WESTERN Air Lines Flight 328, a Boeing 737 jetliner carrying 98 persons on a domestic service originating at San Francisco, California, with an ultimate destination of Seattle, Washington, was diverted to Vancouver, British Columbia, by a 19-year-old military draftee who had first asked to be taken to Cuba. He was deported to the US the following month and later sentenced to 10 years' imprisonment for interfering with an aircraft crew.

31 March 1971

A 14-year-old boy tried to hijack a Delta Air Lines twin-jet DC-9, designated as Flight 400 and carrying 22 persons, while it was on the ground at Birmingham, Alabama. He was later sentenced to three years' probation on the lesser charge of carrying a weapon aboard an aircraft.

31 March 1971

EASTERN Airlines Flight 939, a stretched DC-8 jetliner with 82 persons aboard, on a service from New York City to San Juan, Puerto Rico, was commandeered to Cuba by a single assailant allegedly carrying a pistol and a bomb. He returned to the US via Bermuda in 1974, and was released on probation the following year.

25 April 1971

THE attempted hijacking of an AVIANCA DC-4, which took place during a scheduled Colombian domestic service from Barranquilla to Medellin, ended with other passengers and the crew overpowering the lone assailant.

29 April 1971

A Boeing 707 jet airliner operated by the Colombian carrier AVIANCA was commandeered while on a scheduled service from Los Angeles, California, to Bogota, Colombia, but the lone hijacker was captured when it landed in Panama.

29 May 1971

A hijacker armed with two knives took over Pan American World Airways Flight 442, a Boeing 707 jetliner en route from Caracas, Venezuela, to Miami, Florida, with 69 persons aboard.

18 June 1971

THE attempted hijacking of Piedmont Airlines Flight 25, a Boeing 737 jet that was on the ground at the airport serving Winston-Salem, North Carolina, ended with the capture of the lone assailant, who said he had a bomb and a container of acid but was, in fact, unarmed. He was sentenced to five years in prison for the lesser crime of conveying false information in an attempt to commit air piracy.

21 June 1971

THE lone hijacker who attempted to commandeer a DC-4 of Colombia's airline AVIANCA during a scheduled domestic service from Monteria to Medellin was overpowered and disarmed by the crew.

24 July 1971

DESIGNATED as Flight 183, a National Airlines DC-8 jet, carrying 83 persons on an intrastate service from Miami to Jacksonville, Florida, was hijacked to Cuba by a man armed with a pistol and a stick of dynamite. One passenger and a stewardess were shot and slightly wounded.

3 September 1971

OFF-DUTY crew members and other passengers overpowered a hijacker who, armed with an ice-pick, tried to take over an Eastern Airlines twin-jet DC-9, operating as Flight 993 on a domestic service from Chicago to Miami with 86 persons aboard. In 1972 he was sentenced to 20 years in prison for interfering with the crew of an aircraft.

9 October 1971

EASTERN Airlines Flight 953, a Boeing 727 jet en route from Detroit, Michigan, to Miami, Florida, carrying 46 persons, was commandeered by an armed assailant. He was apprehended in Michigan in 1976 and subsequently sentenced to 40 years' imprisonment.

12 October 1971

AN AVENSA twin-engine turboprop Convair 580, operating as Flight 564, got hijacked to Cuba during a scheduled domestic Venezuelan service from Barcelona to Caracas with 41 persons aboard.

18 October 1971

AN attempt to hijack to Cuba a Wien Consolidated Airlines Boeing 737 jet, designated as Flight 15 and carrying 35 persons on an intrastate Alaskan service from Anchorage to Bethel, ended with the lone gunman surrendering to Canadian authorities at Vancouver, British Columbia. He was deported to the US and subsequently sentenced to 20 years in prison for air piracy.

20 October 1971

SIX hijackers, two of them women, took over a Sociedad Anonima Ecuatoriana de Transportes Aereos (SAETA) Viscount 700 as the turboprop airliner was on a domestic Ecuadorean service from Quito to Cuenca, and ordered it to Cuba.

25 October 1971

WHILE on a service from New York City to San Juan, Puerto Rico, with 236 persons aboard, an American Airlines Boeing 747 wide-bodied jetliner, designated as Flight 98, was commandeered by a single assailant armed with a pistol that was actually a fake. The hijacker returned to the US in 1978 and was later sentenced to three years in prison for interference with the crew of an aircraft.

17 November 1971

AN Arawak Airlines aircraft, possibly a twin-engine Convair 440, was taken over by a single assailant during a domestic intra-island service in Trinidad and Tobago. He surrendered after the aircraft had returned to its departure point.

27 November 1971

OPERATING as Flight 106 and carrying 49 persons, a Trans World Airlines Boeing 727 jet was hijacked by three men armed with pistols and a knife while on the ground at Albuquerque, New Mexico, preparing to depart for Chicago, Illinois. One of the three assailants reportedly died of accidental drowning in Cuba 16 months later.

26 December 1971

IN one of the few Canadian airline hijackings, an Air Canada twin-jet DC-9, designated as Flight 932 and carrying 89 persons, was commandeered to Cuba during a domestic service from Thunder Bay to Toronto. The hijacker was armed with a gun and a hand-grenade, the airport at Thunder Bay having no weapon detection system at the time.

7 January 1972

PACIFIC Southwest Airlines (PSA) Flight 902, a Boeing 727-214 jetliner on an intrastate service from San Francisco to Los Angeles, California, with 151 persons aboard, got hijacked by a couple armed with a pistol and a shotgun and accompanied by a child. They initially asked to be taken to Africa, but subsequently settled for Cuba. The male assailant returned to the US in 1978 and was later sentenced to 50 years' imprisonment for air piracy.

26 January 1972

AN S-61N turbine-engine rotorcraft operated by San Francisco & Oakland Helicopter Airlines was

An Air Canada DC-9 similar to this was involved in one of Canada's few hijackings, the day after Christmas 1971. (Air Canada)

the target of this attempted hijacking on the ground at Berkeley, California. The pistol-wielding suspect surrendered, and was later committed to a psychiatric facility.

7 March 1972

TWO armed men commandeered a Grumman 73 Mallard amphibian, operated by the US air-taxi company Chalk's International Airline, during a flight from Miami, Florida, to the Bahamas, with nine persons aboard. One of the assailants was shot and killed three years later in Jamaica; the second was sentenced to 10 years' imprisonment in 1985.

8 April 1972

TWO hijackers who attempted to take over a Peruvian Compania de Aviacion Faucett SA Boeing 727 jetliner during a scheduled domestic service from Piura to Chiclayo were overpowered and disarmed by the crew.

5 May 1972

WESTERN Air Lines Flight 407, a Boeing 737 jet en route from Salt Lake City, Utah, to Los Angeles, California, with 81 persons aboard, was hijacked by a lone gunman who first wanted to be taken to North Vietnam but settled for Cuba, owing to the limited range of the aircraft. He returned to the US in 1975 and was later sentenced to 10 years in prison.

15 August 1972

AN Austral Lineas Aereas SA BAC One-Eleven twin-jet airliner, operating as Flight 811 on a domestic service from Trelew to Buenos Aires, Argentina, with 96 persons aboard, was commandeered by a group of 10 terrorists and convicts who had broken out of a prison in southern Argentina. The aircraft subsequently landed at Santiago, Chile, where the hijackers were granted political asylum before eventually going on to Cuba via a regular flight.

25 August 1972

FOUR men commandeered to Cuba an Aerolineas TAO Viscount 785D turboprop airliner that was on a scheduled domestic Colombian service from Neiva to Bogota with 30 persons aboard.

6 November 1972

A hijacker who took over a Japan Air Lines Boeing 727 jetliner on a scheduled domestic service from Tokyo to Fukuoka demanded $2 million and a flight to Cuba, but while boarding a longer-range

DC-8 at Tokyo he was captured by police. He was later sentenced to 20 years' imprisonment.

8 November 1972

A Compania Mexicana de Aviacion SA Boeing 727 jet airliner, operating as Flight 705 on a domestic service from Monterey to Mexico City with 110 persons aboard, was hijacked by four terrorists. These demanded the release of six colleagues being held in prison, as well as four million pesos, automatic weapons, and a doctor to accompany a wounded prisoner. All their demands were met, and the 10 flew on to Cuba, which returned the ransom money and automatic weapons to Mexico.

10–12 November 1972

THE longest and perhaps most gruelling of the Cuban hijackings involved Southern Airways Flight 49. Commandeered by three fugitives shortly after its departure from Birmingham, Alabama, on an intrastate service to Montgomery, the 30-hour odyssey would see the DC-9 jet hopping about all over the American South-east and Midwest, landing at Jackson, Mississippi; Lexington, Kentucky; Key West, Florida; Cleveland, Ohio; and even Toronto, Canada; before eventually arriving at Havana, Cuba.

At one point, it circled the country retreat of the American President, Richard Nixon, and at another the hijackers threatened to crash the aircraft into the atomic power plant located at Oak Ridge, Tennessee. In its last stop in the US, the DC-9 landed at McCoy Air Force Base, near Orlando, Florida, where the FBI decided to take action, shooting out the aircraft's left two tyres. This enraged the hijackers, who shot and wounded the first officer while the aircraft was still on the ground. Miraculously, the captain nevertheless managed to get the aircraft off the ground despite the flat tyres.

The aircraft and its 31 occupants finally returned to Havana, where it had already landed once, skidding to a stop. Cuban authorities would later return the $2 million dollars received by the hijackers – a portion of the $10 million they had demanded – and imprisoned all three men. They were returned to the US in 1980, and sentenced to further prison terms there, one receiving a 25-year sentence and the others 20 years each.

18 May 1973

THREE men and a woman commandeered an AVENSA twin-engine turboprop Convair 580, which was on a scheduled domestic Venezuelan service from Velera to Barquisime with 37 persons aboard, with the intention of freeing 79 prisoners

Law enforcement personnel using a fuel truck to deliver ransom and food to a hijacked Southern Airways DC-9 in November 1972. (UPI/Corbis-Bettmann)

held in Venezuela. When their demand was refused, the aircraft instead proceeded to Cuba.

4 July 1973

AN Aerolineas Argentinas Boeing 737 jetliner, on a scheduled domestic service from Buenos Aires to Tucuman, was hijacked by a single assailant with a strange demand. He asked the government of Argentina to provide $200,000 to medical agencies in the country. Passengers were released at stops in Argentina, Chile, Peru, and Panama, before the aircraft proceeded on to Cuba.

20 October 1973

FOUR hijackers commandeered an Aerolineas Argentinas twin-jet Boeing 737, carrying 49 persons on a scheduled domestic flight from Buenos Aires to Salta. They released most of the other occupants after landing at Yacuiba, Bolivia, and two days later freed the rest and surrendered when promised safe passage to Cuba.

31 October 1973

THE hijacker of an AVENSA DC-9 jetliner, who threatened a stewardess with a pistol during a scheduled domestic Venezuelan service from Barquisimeto to Caracas, shot and seriously wounded himself when told by the pilot that the aircraft was low on fuel and had to land.

21 January 1974

AN Aeropesca Colombia Viscount 700 turboprop airliner on a scheduled domestic service from Pasto to Popayan was hijacked to Cuba, landing for refuelling at Cali, where the 22 other passengers were allowed to disembark.

25 April 1975

AN unarmed passenger who said he was carrying a pistol and a bomb attempted to hijack a United Airlines Boeing 727 jetliner, designated as Flight 344, on a domestic service from Raleigh, North Carolina, to Newark, New Jersey, but later surrendered. He was convicted of the lesser charge of conveying false information regarding destruction of an aircraft, and sentenced to five years' imprisonment.

9 September 1975

THREE hijackers tried to commandeer a Haiti Air Inter Twin Otter turboprop to Cuba during a scheduled domestic service from Port-au-Prince to Cap-Haitien, but when the aircraft landed at Gonaives for refuelling they were overpowered by two passengers.

25 December 1977

DURING the attempted hijacking of Eastern

Airlines Flight 668, a twin-jet DC-9 en route from Jacksonville, Florida, to Atlanta, Georgia, the lone assailant – who was carrying a toy pistol and a fake explosive device – was overpowered by police and FBI agents. He was later sentenced to 25 years in prison for air piracy.

18 January 1978

DURING a domestic flight from Quito to Guayaquil with 60 persons aboard, a man and a woman commandeered a Sociedad Anonima Ecuatoriana de Transportes Aereos (SAETA) Viscount turboprop airliner, forcing it to fly to Cuba.

28 January 1978

AN unarmed man who claimed to have a gun commandeered Piedmont Airlines Flight 964 as the twin-engine turboprop YS-11 was on the ground at Kinston, North Carolina, an en-route stop during a domestic service from Washington, DC, to Wilmington, North Carolina. He was overpowered by other passengers and the crew, and later sentenced to 35 years in prison for air piracy.

13 March 1978

A lone assailant who claimed to have a bomb hijacked United Airlines Flight 696, a Boeing 727 jet on a domestic service from San Francisco, California, to Seattle, Washington, demanding to be taken to Cuba. After the aircraft had landed at Denver, Colorado, he surrendered to the authorities. No explosives were found. The hijacker was declared legally insane and committed to a psychiatric hospital.

14 December 1978

REPORTEDLY intoxicated, a man who motioned as though he had a gun in his pocket tried to hijack National Airlines Flight 97, a Boeing 727 jetliner on a domestic service from New York City to Miami with 54 persons aboard. He was persuaded to return to his seat and later taken into custody. His punishment was five years' probation for interference with an aircraft crew.

16 March 1979

A man who said he had a 'cutter' in his pocket, but was in reality unarmed, took over Continental Air Lines Flight 62 shortly after the Los Angeles-bound Boeing 727 jet had taken off from Phoenix, Arizona, with 94 persons aboard. He demanded $200,000 and a trip to Cuba, but after the aircraft had landed at Tucson, Arizona, the passengers and all but one of the cabin attendants were released.

Subsequently, the three-member flight crew escaped through a cockpit window and the remaining stewardess locked herself in a restroom, allowing FBI agents to move in and arrest the suspect. He was found mentally incompetent and committed to a psychiatric facility.

11 June 1979

THE first successful hijacking of a US airliner to Cuba in six years involved Delta Air Lines Flight 1061, an L-1011 TriStar wide-bodied jet on a service from New York City to Fort Lauderdale, Florida, with 204 persons aboard. Armed with a pocket-knife, the lone assailant also claimed to have a gun and a bomb planted in the aircraft, but neither were found after the L-1011 had landed at Havana.

30 June 1979

SHOUTING pro-Castro remarks and wielding a bottle of rum, a single assailant tried to commandeer an Eastern Airlines L-1011 TriStar to Cuba as the wide-bodied jetliner, operating as Flight 932, was en route from San Juan, Puerto Rico, to Miami, Florida, carrying 306 persons. He was overpowered by other passengers and members of the crew, but criminal charges against him were later dropped on grounds of mental incompetence.

20 July 1979

DESIGNATED as Flight 320, a United Airlines Boeing 727 jetliner with 126 persons aboard, on a domestic service from Denver, Colorado, to Omaha, Nebraska, was commandeered by a lone assailant who knocked on the cockpit door and asked to be taken to Cuba, saying that he had plastic explosives in his pocket. After landing at Omaha, he released the other passengers and the cabin attendants. While the aircraft was on the ground, the hijacker allowed the cockpit door to remain open, and once he had taken both his hands out of his pockets, FBI agents, on receiving a signal from the flight engineer, rushed aboard and overpowered him. No explosives were found, and the suspect would later be found not guilty by reason of insanity.

16 August 1979

A passenger who said he was carrying a bomb, and who threatened a flight attendant with a pen-knife, tried to hijack to Cuba an Eastern Airlines Boeing 727 jet, operating as Flight 980, during a service to Miami from Guatemala City, Guatemala, with 91 persons aboard. As the aircraft was approaching to land at Varadero, Cuba, the hijacker was convinced to go to Key West, Florida, where he was subsequently overpowered. He was found mentally incompetent and was later admitted to a psychiatric hospital.

25 January 1980

DELTA Air Lines Flight 1116, an L-1011 TriStar wide-bodied jetliner carrying 63 persons, was diverted to Cuba during a domestic service to New York City from Atlanta, Georgia. While on the ground at Havana, the armed hijacker, who was accompanied by his wife and two young daughters, refused either to let anyone get off or any Cuban authorities to board the aircraft, and at one point he demanded to be flown to Iran.

After several hours, with the assailant remaining in the cockpit, the cabin attendants and most of the passengers escaped through a floor hatch. Upon discovering this, the hijacker demanded that the aircraft take off, but this was prevented by a truck blocking its path. A short while later he disembarked and surrendered. He was arrested in New York later in the year and subsequently sentenced to 40 years' imprisonment.

9 April 1980

A lone assailant armed with a pistol scaled a fence at the airport in Ontario, California, then boarded an American Airlines Boeing 727 jetliner which, as Flight 348, was being readied for a domestic service to Chicago, Illinois; no passengers were aboard. The gunman forced the crew to take off and proceed to Cuba, stopping for refuelling at Dallas, Texas. Late the next year he was arrested after returning to Southern California, and was subsequently sentenced to 50 years' imprisonment for air piracy.

22 July 1980

A Delta Air Lines L-1011 TriStar wide-bodied jet, operating as Flight 1135 and carrying 158 persons, was commandeered to Cuba during a service from Miami, Florida, to San Juan, Puerto Rico. Bad weather prevented the aircraft from landing at Havana, and it proceeded on to Camaguey, where the hijacker surrendered. He reportedly received a three-year prison term in Cuba.

10 August 1980

DESIGNATED as Flight 4, an Air Florida Boeing 737 jet airliner with 35 persons aboard, on an intrastate service from Miami to Key West, Florida, was hijacked by a Spanish-speaking passenger holding what resembled a bomb and shouting several times 'Cuba!' The aircraft reached Havana safely, where the assailant surrendered; his package was found to contain only soap.

13 August 1980

SHORTLY after it had taken off, an Air Florida twin-jet Boeing 737 on a service to Miami from Key West, Florida, designated as Flight 707, was commandeered by seven hijackers who poured gasoline in the aisle and in other parts of the aircraft, then raised lit matches and cigarette-lighters while shouting 'Cuba!' The aircraft, with 74 persons aboard, reached Havana safely, where the assailants surrendered. They reportedly all wound up serving prison sentences in Cuba.

14 August 1980

EN route from Miami to San Juan, Puerto Rico, National Airlines Flight 872, a wide-bodied DC-10 carrying 224 persons, was commandeered by two men, one of whom held up a quart-sized bottle of liquid and the other a cigarette-lighter. After the jet landed in Havana, the hijackers were taken into custody, the Cuban authorities subsequently sentencing both to prison, for four and five years respectively.

16 August 1980

THIS day saw three American jetliners hijacked to Cuba, and in every case the weapon used was a flammable liquid. Eastern Airlines Flight 90, a Boeing 727 with 53 persons aboard, was commandeered by a half-dozen assailants during an intrastate service from Miami to Orlando, Florida; Republic Airlines Flight 228, a DC-9 carrying 116 persons on the same route, was taken over by five hijackers; and a Delta Air Lines wide-bodied L-1011, designated as Flight 1065, on a service from Miami to San Juan, Puerto Rico, with 193 persons aboard, was hijacked by a lone assailant. All of the air pirates involved reportedly ended up in Cuban jails, serving sentences of from two to four years.

18 August 1980

JUST before Eastern Airlines Flight 348 was about to land at Atlanta, Georgia, on a service from Melbourne, Florida, a cabin attendant received a two-page note written by a hijacker, claiming that he had a bomb in the baggage compartment and a means of detonating it by remote control. He was demanding $3.4 million, the release of two prisoners, and a trip to Cuba. As the aircraft was already on final approach, the crew elected to land at Atlanta airport, where the assailant was taken into custody by the local police. His baggage contained a handgun, but no bomb. Charges against him were later dropped due to his mental incompetence.

26 August 1980

EASTERN Airlines Flight 401, an L-1011 wide-bodied jet carrying 242 persons on a service from New York City to Miami, was hijacked by three assailants who, speaking through a translator, threatened to start a fire unless taken to Cuba, having already poured a liquid throughout the interior of the aircraft. All three ended up in prison in Cuba, sentenced to terms of from two to three years.

8 September 1980

A man holding what appeared to be an unlit Molotov cocktail commandeered Eastern Airlines Flight 161, a Boeing 727 jet on a service from New York City to Tampa, Florida, with 90 persons aboard. Landing for refuelling at Tampa, the aircraft proceeded on to Cuba, where the hijacker was reportedly sentenced to two years in prison.

12 September 1980

A lone assailant, holding a cigarette-lighter and two red sticks that had 'TNT' marked on them, tried to hijack to Cuba an Eastern Airlines Boeing 727 jet, designated as Flight 5, which was carrying 85 persons on a service to Miami from Newark, New Jersey. Correctly judging that the red sticks were not explosives, a flight attendant hit him on the wrist, and he was then overpowered by two passengers. Convicted of air piracy, he was sentenced to 20 years' imprisonment.

13 September 1980

USING what was by now a proven hijacking technique, two men commandeered a Delta Air Lines Boeing 727 jet, which was operating as Flight 334 on a domestic service from New Orleans, Louisiana, to Atlanta, Georgia, with 88 persons aboard. The pair, who threatened to set fire to what was believed to have been rubbing alcohol that had been splashed about in the interior of the aircraft, were taken to Cuba as demanded, but there were sentenced to three and four years' imprisonment respectively.

14 September 1980

BY threatening to set off a bomb somewhere in the city of Tampa, Florida, where Flight 115 had originated, a lone assailant tried to hijack the Eastern Airlines Boeing 727 jet to Cuba. The aircraft, with 102 persons aboard, instead landed at Miami, its intended destination, where the man was arrested. His bomb threat proved to be a hoax; the 15-year prison sentence he received for interfering with an airline crew member was not.

17 September 1980

WHEN nearing the end of a domestic service from Atlanta, Georgia, to Columbia, South Carolina, Delta Air Lines Flight 470, a Boeing 727 jet with 111 persons aboard, was commandeered to Cuba by two assailants holding cigarette-lighters and bottles of what was apparently gasoline. In a surprise change of policy, the Cuban authorities turned the two hijackers over to US Marshals in Havana. Both were later sentenced to 40 years' imprisonment in the US for air piracy.

25 October 1980

A passenger on Continental Air Lines Flight 67, a Boeing 727 jet en route to Houston, Texas, with 132 persons aboard, threatened a cabin attendant in Spanish that he would start a fire unless taken to Cuba. The captain, second officer, and a flight attendant then attacked and overpowered him, and the aircraft returned safely to Miami, Florida, its point of origin. The would-be hijacker was later sentenced to 30 years in prison for air piracy.

6 November 1980

AN AVENSA DC-9 jet airliner was seized during a scheduled domestic Venezuelan service from Caracas to Puerto Ordaz with 60 persons aboard. The two hijackers, who claimed to have a bomb wrapped in a gasoline-soaked cloth, were taken into custody after landing in Havana.

12 November 1980

A twin-engine turboprop Convair 600 operated by the Uruguayan airline Argo was hijacked during a scheduled service from Colonia, Uruguay, to Buenos Aires, Argentina, with 37 persons aboard. The assailant, armed with a pistol and a small can that he said contained explosives, first demanded to be taken to Cuba, but was told this was not possible. The aircraft then landed in Buenos Aires, where he released most of his hostages. One of three women who tried to disarm him was shot and wounded. The assailant was subsequently talked into surrendering by his uncle, who had been allowed on board, and he later received an 11-year prison sentence.

15 December 1980

SEVEN armed men, members of the Colombian guerrilla group M-19, commandeered an AVIANCA Boeing 727 jet airliner during a scheduled domestic Colombian service from Bogota to Pereira with 137 persons aboard. Before proceeding on to Havana, the aircraft landed twice in Colombia, once in Panama, and at Mexico City, with a number of passengers being released at every stop.

5 February 1981

A passenger on Eastern Airlines Flight 929 told a cabin attendant that he had a bomb, and demanded to be taken to Cuba. The L-1011 TriStar jet, on a service from New York City with 242 persons aboard, proceeded on to San Juan, Puerto Rico, its intended destination, the crew having convinced the hijacker that it was going to Cuba. In an altercation after the aircraft landed, the assailant was knocked out of a door and tumbled down a stairway. He was later found not competent to stand trial and was committed to a psychiatric facility.

10 July 1981

TWO men, who were accompanied by two women and four children, hijacked Eastern Airlines Flight 71, an L-1011 TriStar wide-bodied jetliner, during a domestic service to Miami from Chicago, Illinois. Bursting into the cockpit holding three small bottles with burning wicks, they demanded to be taken to Havana. The Cuban authorities were not as affable as the hijackers might have believed, reportedly sentencing both of them to 10 years in prison.

7 December 1981

ON this day, three Venezuelan jetliners carrying a total of 262 persons were hijacked while on scheduled domestic operations, all having taken off earlier from Caracas. Two DC-9s flown by Linea Aeropostal Venezolana were commandeered by three and four men respectively, one aircraft en route to Puerto Ordaz and the other to Barcelona; and seven men took over an AVENSA Boeing 727 during a service to San Antonio Detachira. The hijackers were asking for $10 million in ransom, the release of a number of prisoners, and the publication of a manifesto citing their political complaints and demands.

The three aircraft hopped about over South and Central America, landing at various locations where a number of passengers were released in exchange for fuel and supplies. At one point, both DC-9s landed at Tegucigalpa, Honduras, and the 727 at Guatemala City, where the hijackers demanded to speak to the respective Venezuelan ambassadors. All were then flown to Panama, where the same demands were made. Eventually, all three aircraft reached Havana, where the 14 air pirates surrendered to the Cuban authorities.

27–29 January 1982

NINE members of the M-19 guerrilla organisation commandeered an Aerotal Colombia Boeing 727 jetliner that was on a scheduled domestic flight from Bogota to Pereira with 128 persons aboard.

Returning first to the capital city, the aircraft then proceeded on to Cali, where about a third of the passengers were released. Here the 727 was damaged when it collided with military vehicles blocking the runway, followed by an exchange of gunfire between the hijackers and military personnel. After the terrorists agreed to free the rest of their hostages, a corporate jet was made available with a crew, which flew them on to Cuba.

2 February 1982

A lone assailant, carrying a cigarette-lighter and a plastic bottle allegedly filled with a flammable liquid, commandeered an Air Florida Boeing 737 jet, designated as Flight 710, which was on an intrastate service from Miami to Key West, Florida, with 77 persons aboard. The aircraft proceeded on to Havana, where the Cuban authorities reportedly sentenced the hijacker to 12 years' imprisonment.

1 March 1982

A passenger carrying a bottle of liquid and a cigarette-lighter, and who claimed that he had a bomb, tried to hijack United Airlines Flight 674, a Boeing 727 jetliner carrying 97 persons, during a domestic service from Chicago to Miami. When he found that the crew had tricked him and landed in Miami instead of Cuba he became very agitated, but was subsequently overpowered by the pilot and other passengers. Charges against him were dismissed on grounds of mental incompetence.

5 April 1982

THREE men commandeered Delta Air Lines Flight 591, a Boeing 727 jet carrying 103 persons en route from Chicago to Miami. Pouring gasoline throughout the cabin, they demanded to be taken to Cuba; one of them splashed some on a stewardess when she asked him to stop, resulting in injury to both her eyes. Arriving in Cuba, they received stiff penalties, all three reportedly being sentenced to 20 years' imprisonment.

28 April–1 May 1982

FOUR men armed with pistols and explosives commandeered an Aerovias Nacionales de Honduras SA (ANHSA) Dash-7 turboprop airliner that was on a scheduled domestic service from La Ceiba to San Pedro Sula with 48 persons aboard. Claiming to be a group opposed to the Honduran Government, the terrorists demanded the release of 86 prisoners, a ransom of one million lempiras, publication of a political statement, and fuel for the aircraft. The other passengers were eventually released or escaped from the aircraft, with two of them suffering injuries. Three days after the start of

A de Havilland Dash-7 flown by the Honduran airline ANHSA was successfully diverted to Cuba in April 1982. (de Havilland Canada)

the siege the hijackers were transferred to another aircraft and flown to Cuba.

22 July 1982

TWO hijackers who poured gasoline on the floor and seats and shouted that they wanted to be taken to Cuba, successfully commandeered a US-registered Marco Island Airways Martin 404, operating as Flight 39 on an intrastate service from Miami to Key West, Florida, with 12 persons aboard. Both men were reportedly sentenced to 15 years' imprisonment in Cuba.

16 August 1982

A passenger aboard a Dolphin Airways EMBRAER Bandeirante, which was designated as Flight 296, told the pilot that he had a bomb in the bag he was carrying and demanded to be flown to Cuba after the twin-engine turboprop had landed during an intrastate service from Tampa to West Palm Beach, Florida. The bomb threat proved to be a hoax. Later captured by law enforcement officers, he was sentenced to five years' imprisonment for air piracy, with the stipulation that he would be released upon completion of an alcohol rehabilitation programme.

15 February 1983

A Rio Airways de Havilland Dash-7, operating as

Flight 252 on an intrastate service from Killeen to Dallas/Ft Worth, Texas, was commandeered by a lone assailant armed with a sub-machine-gun and a bag in which he claimed to have explosives. He demanded to be taken first to Mexico, and then to Cuba. The four-engine turboprop, with 20 persons aboard, landed in Nuevo Laredo, Nuevo Leon, Mexico, where negotiations went on for several hours.

In exchange for the release of his hostages, the gunman was taken to Mexico City, and during this flight he surrendered. He was subsequently sentenced to eight years' imprisonment for air piracy.

1 May 1983

DURING a service to Miami from San Juan, Puerto Rico, a passenger aboard a Capitol Air stretched DC-8 jet airliner, designated as Flight 236 and carrying 212 persons, scattered notes in the cabin citing his unemployment, misery, and grief, and threatened to blow the US-registered aircraft up with a bomb if not taken to Cuba. On landing at Havana, the hijacker was found not to be carrying any weapons or explosives. Reportedly, he was hospitalized in a psychiatric facility in Cuba.

12 May 1983

A woman armed with a flare pistol hijacked Capital Air Flight 236, a stretched DC-8 jet, shortly before

Three stretched DC-8 jets flown by the US carrier Capitol Air were involved in hijackings to Cuba during a four-month period in 1983. (McDonnell Douglas)

it was to have landed at Miami while on a service from San Juan, Puerto Rico, with 231 persons aboard. She was taken into custody by Cuban authorities after landing at Havana.

19 May 1983

EASTERN Airlines Flight 24, a Boeing 727 jet with 132 persons aboard, was hijacked to Cuba during a domestic service to New York City from Miami. The lone assailant shouted 'Cuba' several times and held up what appeared to be a stick of dynamite. He was taken into custody after the aircraft landed at Havana.

14 June 1983

AN Eastern Airlines Airbus A300 wide-bodied twin-jet transport, designated as Flight 414, en route from Miami to New York City with 95 persons aboard, was hijacked to Cuba by a lone assailant allegedly carrying a bottle of flammable liquid.

24 June 1983

A lone assailant who held a razor to the neck of a cabin attendant tried to commandeer an Aeromexico DC-9 jetliner to Cuba shortly before it was to have landed at Merida, Mexico, an en-route stop during a scheduled flight from Mexico City to Miami, Florida. As it was low on fuel, the aircraft

still landed at Merida, where a police officer disguised as a mechanic went aboard and captured the hijacker.

2 July 1983

PAN American World Airways Flight 378, a Boeing 727 jet on an intrastate service from Miami to Orlando, Florida, carrying 61 persons, was hijacked to Cuba by two men, one carrying a plastic bottle containing what smelled like gasoline and the other displaying a pear-shaped object wrapped in cloth that had a protruding wick.

7 July 1983

AN Air Florida Boeing 737 jet, carrying 47 persons on an intrastate service from Ft Lauderdale to Tampa, Florida, got hijacked to Cuba by a passenger who said he had an explosive device, taking the alleged bomb out of an athletic bag.

17 July 1983

STANDING up and shouting 'Cuba' several times, three men armed with knives and an aerosol can seized a Delta Air Lines Boeing 727 jet, operating as Flight 722, on an intrastate service from Miami to Tampa, Florida, with 107 persons aboard. The pilot got the message and diverted to Havana, where Cuban authorities boarded the aircraft and took the hijackers into custody.

19 July 1983

HAVING nearly completed a service from New York City to Miami, Eastern Airlines Flight 1, an L-1011 wide-bodied jetliner carrying 232 persons, was commandeered by a passenger who distributed several copies of type-written notes in broken English claiming to have a bomb and demanding to be taken to Cuba; he also held a briefcase as if it contained such a device. The aircraft proceeded to Havana without further incident.

21 July 1983

THIS bungled hijacking involved Northwest Airlines Flight 714, a Boeing 727 jet on an intrastate service to Miami from Tampa, Florida, with 97 persons aboard. The lone assailant threatened a cabin attendant with a knife and instructed the pilot to take him to Cuba. When he set the weapon down to accept a drink, two others passengers attacked and subdued him. He was later sentenced to 10 years in prison for air piracy.

2 August 1983

SHORTLY after it had taken off from Miami, bound for Houston, Texas, an attempt was made to hijack a Pan American World Airways Boeing 727 jet, operating as Flight 925 and carrying 130 persons. Speaking in Spanish, the assailant made a statement to the effect that he intended to take command of the aircraft and force it to fly to Cuba. Three other passengers then grabbed him and tied him to a seat. He would later receive a 12-year prison sentence for interference with an air crew.

4 August 1983

FOR the third time in approximately three months, a Capitol Air stretched DC-8 jet, designated as Flight 236, was hijacked to Cuba during a service to Miami from San Juan, Puerto Rico. This time a lone assailant carrying a very real-looking toy pistol, a bottle of a clear liquid, and what resembled sticks of explosives, took over an aircraft with 264 persons aboard. He was taken into custody by the Cuban authorities after the aircraft had landed at Havana.

18 August 1983

DELTA Air Lines Flight 784, a Boeing 727 jet with 79 persons aboard on an intrastate service from Miami to Tampa, Florida, was successfully commandeered by a passenger who, after take-off, stood up and shouted 'Take this national to Cuba!' He had also displayed a plastic bottle containing a fluid that smelled like kerosene or gasoline, pouring it on himself and the seat he occupied and then lighting a candle to validate his order.

22 September 1983

EN route from New York City to St Thomas, Virgin Islands, with 112 persons aboard, an American Airlines Boeing 727 jet, operating as Flight 625, was hijacked to Cuba by a passenger who, in a note, threatened to blow up the aircraft. His purported bomb appeared to be a small box with a battery taped to its side and several wires extending out.

3 February 1984

AN A300 wide-bodied jetliner operated by the Brazilian airline VARIG, on a scheduled domestic service from Rio de Janeiro to Manaus, was hijacked by a man and a woman, who had a small child with them. The aircraft landed in Surinam, where the passengers were released, before proceeding on to Camaguey, Cuba.

27 March 1984

A lone assailant, claiming to have explosives and two accomplices, commandeered Piedmont Airlines Flight 451, a twin-jet Boeing 737 on a domestic service to Miami, Florida, from Charleston, South Carolina, with 59 persons aboard. Among his demands were a $5 million ransom and the release of his brother from prison in South Africa. Even though the captain advised him that the aircraft was low on fuel, the hijacker threatened that passengers would be killed if not taken to Cuba. The aircraft managed to reach Havana, with the assailant, who was found to have not been carrying any explosives, reportedly being sentenced to 15 years in a Cuban prison.

28 March 1984

DELTA Air Lines Flight 357, a Boeing 727 jet carrying 26 persons on a domestic service from New Orleans, Louisiana, to Dallas, Texas, got hijacked to Cuba by a passenger holding a bottle of liquid, threatening to set fire to a cabin attendant if his demand was not met.

2 October 1984

A Colombian Lineas Aereas del Caribe DC-8 cargo jet was commandeered by a gunman, accompanied by family members, while on the ground at Cartagena, Colombia, an en-route stop during a domestic service from Barranquilla to Bogota. The aircraft proceeded on to Havana.

On 27 March 1984 a Piedmont Airlines Boeing 737 identical to this was diverted to Cuba by a lone assailant who turned out to be unarmed. (Boeing)

31 December 1984

AN American Airlines DC-10 wide-bodied jet, designated as Flight 626 and bound for New York City from St Croix in the Virgin Islands with 198 persons aboard, was diverted to Cuba by a convicted mass-murderer who had been under escort by three armed law enforcement officers but suddenly emerged from a lavatory carrying a pistol. The weapon he used had apparently been planted aboard by someone else as part of a well-executed escape plan.

18 January 1985

THE attempted hijacking of an Eastern Airlines A300 was foiled by trickery on the part of the crew. Operating as Flight 403 and carrying 132 persons, the wide-bodied jet was en route to Miami from Newark, New Jersey, when the assailant emerged from a lavatory shouting in Spanish that he wanted to go to Cuba. He was holding a cigarette-lighter in one hand and what appeared to be explosives in the other, and also stated that he had poured gasoline on himself.

The hijacker was informed that the aircraft had arrived in Cuba when in fact it landed at Orlando, Florida, and after dropping the bag and lighter he was overpowered by crew members. His 'bomb'

turned out to be a fake, but he was nevertheless charged with air piracy.

7 March 1987

A man whose only words that English-speaking passengers could understand were 'Cuba! Cuba!' tried to commandeer Alaska Airlines Flight 93, a Boeing 727 jet carrying 109 persons on a domestic US service from Seattle, Washington, to Anchorage, Alaska, but he was subdued by members of the crew and other passengers.

23 May 1988

AN AVIANCA Boeing 727 jetliner, carrying 136 persons on a scheduled domestic Colombian service from Medellin to Bogota, got hijacked by a lone assailant who said he was terminally ill and wanted to die in another country. He ordered the aircraft to Cuba, but due to insufficient fuel it had to land in Panama. It then stopped at Aruba before flying to Cartagena, Colombia, where the hijacker escaped. He was captured the following day.

11 December 1988

TRANS World Airlines Flight 469, a Boeing 727

jet en route to Miami from San Juan, Puerto Rico, with 128 persons aboard, was hijacked by a lone assailant who claimed to have a bomb and wanted to go to Cuba. He was tricked and captured when the aircraft landed instead on Grand Turk Island.

27 May 1989

A man who had escaped from a psychiatric facility and wanted to return to his native Cuba tried to take over American Airlines Flight 1098, a Boeing 727 jetliner that was on a domestic US service to Miami from Dallas, Texas, but after it had landed at its intended destination, he surrendered.

16 January 1990

A lone assailant who claimed to have an explosive device tried to hijack to Cuba an America West Airlines twin-jet Boeing 737, designated as Flight 727, on a domestic service from Houston, Texas, to Las Vegas, Nevada. When it landed for refuelling at Austin, Texas, he was overpowered by a police officer who had entered the aircraft through an escape hatch.

10 February 1991

SMOKING is prohibited on US domestic flights, but that didn't deter one passenger from wanting to light up aboard a Southwest Airlines Boeing 737 jetliner, operating as Flight 335 and on an intrastate service from Oakland to San Diego, California. He first began arguing with the crew over the issue and was so perturbed by the rule that, in anger, he shortly afterward passed them a note saying he was carrying explosives and demanding $13 million and a flight to Cuba. He later said the threat was just a joke!

FBI agents weren't amused however, and arrested him on charges of air piracy after the aircraft landed at its intended destination. A federal judge did not get the joke either when he sentenced him in 1992 to 30 years in prison.

Hijacks Turn Deadly

With a few exceptions that occurred in Third World countries during the 1940s and 1950s, hijackings remained relatively peaceful: actual violence was rare during hijackings in the Western World, and killings were non-existent. This was somewhat miraculous, considering the potential for death and disaster when the volatile mixture of a perpetrator armed with a knife, firearm, or explosive was blended with an aircraft loaded with passengers.

However, perhaps in consequence of a combination of more resolute policies being adopted by governments and operators, and the greater desperation of air pirates, the use of deadly force reappeared in 1969, and became frighteningly commonplace during the 1970s. The prospect of a few fatalities resulting from such incidents grew to scores when the first modern aircraft crashed during acts of air terrorism. Swift action, or sometimes just plain luck, prevented numerous other potential disasters.

With the exception of those cases related to Middle Eastern affairs, the following is a list of all hijackings that resulted in loss of life after 1966.

11 March 1969

THE first hijacking in the 'modern' era to result in a fatality involved a Colombian Sociedad Aeronautica de Medellin Consolidada SA (SAM) DC-4 carrying 40 persons on a scheduled domestic

11 March 1969: The flight engineer of a Colombian DC-4 runs from the aircraft moments before he was mistakenly killed; the real hijacker lies wounded beside the aircraft. (UPI/Corbis-Bettmann)

service from Medellin to Cartagena. In a case of badly-timed aerial piracy, a 17-year-old boy holding a stick of dynamite demanded to be taken to Cuba shortly before the aircraft's planned arrival at Cartagena's Crespo Airport, only to learn that it had to land due to its low fuel supply. He gave the pilot 10 minutes to refuel, but the police and military authorities had other plans, moving in closer when the engines were shut down. Before they could take any action, however, some occupants of the DC-4 took the situation into their own hands.

A passenger first struck the hijacker, causing him to drop the dynamite. During a struggle, the assailant, the other passenger, and a mechanic all tumbled out of a door and on to the tarmac, whereupon airport guards, believing all three to be hijackers, opened fire. The mechanic was killed and the air pirate seriously wounded. The drama ended around 12:40 local time, some 105 minutes after it had begun.

3 June 1969

TWO men and a woman armed with a machine-gun, a rifle, and a hunting knife, tried to hijack to Finland an Aeroflot Il-14, operating as Flight 3794 on a domestic Soviet service from Leningrad to Tallin. Although shots were fired at the cockpit, the crew managed to land the aircraft. One of the men was killed and the other two hijackers were captured, the second man later being sentenced to 11 years' imprisonment and three years in exile, while the woman, who was married to the dead assailant and sister of the other man, was sentenced to 13 years' imprisonment and five years in exile.

6 September 1969

TWO DC-3 airliners operated by the carrier Transportes Aereos Militares Ecuatorianos (TAME) were commandeered in an apparently co-ordinated effort by a band of about a dozen terrorists shortly after they had taken off from Quito, Ecuador, at around dawn, on scheduled domestic flights to Esmeraldas. A total of more than 50 persons were aboard the two aircraft, whose hijackers demanded to be flown to Cuba because they wanted 'freedom'.

Both aircraft landed for refuelling at Tumaco, Colombia, where the co-pilot of one was killed when he resisted and another flight crewman was wounded. The transport on which the shooting had taken place was left behind, the hijackers herding some of their hostages on to the second DC-3, which reached its intended destination late that evening.

12 December 1969

ETHIOPIA'S hard-line policy of dealing with air piracy was illustrated in this attempted hijacking of an Ethiopian Airlines Boeing 707. The jetliner was bound for the capital, Addis Ababa, from the northern city of Asmara, one segment of a service originating at Madrid, Spain, when two members of the Eritrean Liberation Front guerrilla organisation, reportedly carrying explosives, ordered the crew to fly to Aden.

The aircraft diverted instead to Athens, Greece, with both young male assailants dead. Security guards, placed aboard Ethiopian aircraft after two earlier hijackings, had overpowered and tied them up, and then slit their throats. There were no other casualties.

9 January 1970

A twin-engine C-47 operated by the carrier Rutas Aereas Panamenas SA (RAPSA) was commandeered by a lone assailant during a scheduled domestic Panamanian flight from David to Bocas del Toro, but after returning to its point of origin for refuelling National Guard personnel refused to let it take off. One guardsman then entered the aircraft through a cockpit window and shot dead the hijacker. Another passenger, whom he had been holding hostage, was wounded.

6 February 1970

ONE air pirate was killed and four other persons were wounded, a stewardess seriously, in an unsuccessful attempt to hijack a Linea Aerea de Chile (LAN-Chile) Caravelle VI-R to Cuba. Two students commandeered the twin-jet airliner, which was on a scheduled domestic service from Puerto Montt to Santiago, and it then landed at the capital for refuelling. The hijackers released 29 of the 71 passengers, all women and children, before a police detective went aboard, disguised as a catering employee. Shooting then broke out in the aircraft's cabin, apparently after another passenger had tried to disarm one of the hijackers. The second air pirate, who was amongst the wounded, was captured.

10 March 1970

TWO armed 'bandits', later identified as a married couple, reportedly committed suicide after failing in their attempt to hijack a twin-engine turboprop Antonov An-24 operated by the East German airline Interflug, which was on a scheduled domestic flight from East Berlin to Leipzig.

17 March 1970

THE first fatality in a US airline hijacking since the dawn of the jet age occurred aboard an Eastern Airlines DC-9 Series 31, designated as Flight 1320,

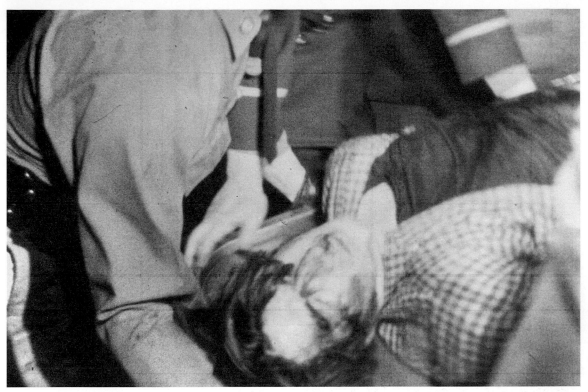

The wounded gunman who shot two Eastern Airlines pilots on 17 March 1970 is taken to hospital after the safe landing of the DC-9. (UPI/Corbis-Bettmann)

on a domestic service from Newark, New Jersey, to Boston, Massachusetts, with 73 persons aboard. During the landing approach to Logan International Airport, a male passenger, identified as 27-year-old John DiVivo, showed the stewardess a .38 calibre revolver as she was collecting fares, then asked to see the captain.

Shortly after the gunman entered the flight deck, at around 20:30 local time, shots were heard. It was later revealed that the assailant had ordered the crew to fly east until the aircraft 'runs out of gas', then suddenly opened fire. The hero proved to be First Officer James Hartley, who, though mortally wounded, managed to disarm the gunman and shoot him with the same weapon. The hijacker was wounded, as was Captain Robert Wilbur, who nevertheless managed to land the twin-engine jet safely. Convicted of the crime, John DiVivo committed suicide in prison in October 1970.

15 October 1970

THOUGH several attempts had been reported, no successful hijacking of a Soviet airliner ever occurred until this incident, which involved an Aeroflot Antonov An-24V on a scheduled domestic service from Batumi to Sochi, carrying 51 persons.

According to the hijacker, Proinas Brazinskas,

who was accompanied by his 14-year-old son, the pilot ignored his orders and instead put the twin-engine turboprop into an 'acrobatic' manoeuvre, causing him to lose his balance and fire the shotgun he was carrying. A stewardess was hit and killed. A subsequently declassified Russian report indicated that the stewardess was shot when she tried to stop one assailant from entering the cockpit. The captain later said that the hijackers burst into the cockpit when the flight crew tried to radio the ground, shooting and wounding three of its members.

The aircraft managed a safe landing at Trabzon, Turkey, located on the Black Sea. Turkish authorities refused the two hijackers political asylum due to the nature of their crime, and they spent two years in prison there before moving to the United States.

23 January 1971

A Korean Air Lines Fokker F.27 Friendship Mark 500 (HL-5212), carrying 60 persons on a scheduled domestic South Korean service from Kangnung to Seoul, was seized and ordered to fly to North Korea. However, South Korean military aircraft forced the twin-engine turboprop to crash-land on a beach near Sokcho, South Korea, approximately 20 miles (30km) from the border. The assailant then

The commandeered Aeroflot An-24 on which a stewardess was killed sits on the apron at Trabzon after being seized by a father-and-son hijacking team in October 1970. (Wide World Photos)

set off a hand-grenade, killing himself and the first officer. Another 22 persons aboard were wounded in the blast and the aircraft was destroyed.

11 June 1971

THE first instance of a US airline passenger being killed in a hijacking involved Trans World Airlines Flight 358, a Boeing 727-231 on a domestic service to New York City from Albuquerque, New Mexico.

Armed with a .38 calibre pistol, the 23-year-old assailant forced his away aboard the jetliner after it had landed at Chicago's O'Hare International Airport, an en-route stop. Seizing one of the stewardesses as a hostage, he released the passengers, though a 65-year-old man was shot and killed when he went back into the cabin, apparently to retrieve his coat. The aircraft then took off and headed east, the air pirate not only demanding to be flown to North Vietnam but also $75,000 in ransom money.

Unbeknown to the gunman, a deputy US marshal had been 'smuggled' in through a cockpit window at O'Hare, and about 30 minutes after the 727 had left Chicago, when the stewardess stepped away from her captor, he shot and wounded the hijacker. The aircraft later landed in New York City.

The hijacker committed suicide by hanging himself in a psychiatric hospital in 1978.

11 July 1971

AFTER an unsuccessful attempt by two assailants

to hijack an Empresa Consolidada Cubana de Aviacion aircraft, possibly a twin-engine Ilyushin Il-14, which had been operating as Flight 740 on a domestic service from Havana to Cienfuegos, a hand-grenade was detonated. One passenger was killed and three persons were wounded, although the transport landed safely.

23 July 1971

IN this incident, a pistol-wielding suspect would lose his life after commandeering Trans World Airlines Flight 335, which had taken off from New York City on a US domestic service to Chicago, Illinois. He asked to be taken to Milan, Italy, but was convinced by the pilot that the tri-jet Boeing 727 could not make the transatlantic trip.

After the aircraft had returned to La Guardia Airport, the gunman and the stewardess he was holding hostage were driven to nearby John F. Kennedy International Airport, where a longer-range Boeing 707 stood by for the flight to Italy. But it was never needed, the hijacker being felled by an FBI sharpshooter at around 14:40 local time as he walked about 20ft (6m) behind his hostage; he died approximately half-an-hour later. There were no other casualties.

12 December 1971

COSTA Rican President Jose Figueres Ferrer personally oversaw an attack on a Lineas Aereas de

Gunman holding stewardess Maria Concepcion hostage while transferring from the TWA Boeing 727 to another aircraft on 23 July 1971, moments before being shot. (Wide World Photos)

Nicaragua (LANICA) BAC One-Eleven Series 400 at El Coco Airport, San Jose, Costa Rica. The twin-jet airliner, operating as Flight 419 and carrying 54 persons, had been commandeered by three men during a service from Miami, Florida, to Managua, Nicaragua, demanding to be taken to Cuba.

After it had landed for refuelling, Costa Rican authorities refused to allow the One-Eleven to depart. During a siege lasting more than two hours, the aircraft's tyres were shot out and one power plant erupted into flames after being hit, though the fire was extinguished. In a subsequent assault by members of the civil guard, one hijacker was killed. The other two were captured and sent back to Managua, but both escaped from custody in the Nicaraguan earthquake of 23 December 1972.

16 December 1971

THE hijacker of a Lloyd Aereo Bolivano SA Fairchild F-27 was shot and killed by police and military troops at Cochabamba, Bolivia, where the twin-engine turboprop airliner had landed for re-fuelling. He had already killed the pilot of the aircraft after commandeering it while on a scheduled domestic service from Sucre to La Paz, ordering the co-pilot to fly to Arica, Chile.

26–27 January 1972

IT was 10 hours of terror for Eileen McAllister, the stewardess of Mohawk Airlines Flight 452, which was commandeered during an intrastate service from Albany, New York, to La Guardia Airport, serving New York City. The 45-year-old hijacker held a gun against the cabin attendant and also said he had a bomb.

The 42 other passengers disembarked safely when the twin-engine turboprop FH-227 landed at Westchester Airport, White Plains, New York. In line with the air piracy craze begun the previous year, ie hijacking for ransom instead of transport, the assailant demanded $200,000 and two para-chutes, for himself and, to her surprise, the stew-ardess. As such aircraft have no rear ramp, the jump would have had to be made from a side door, adding to its difficulty and danger. The airline in fact offered to exchange a company vice-president for her. The money was finally delivered around 01:30 local time on the second day, three hours past the hijacker's deadline. The aircraft then took off and proceeded to circle the White Plains area.

In an act of defiance that probably saved her life, Stewardess McAllister refused to jump; her deter-mination was enough for her captor to change his mind. He now ordered that the aircraft should land at Poughkeepsie airport and that a car be made available for his getaway. An unmarked vehicle was waiting upon his arrival there, but so were FBI agents. After placing his hostage in the front passenger seat, he got behind the steering wheel, whereupon he was immediately killed by a single shotgun blast. Stewardess McAllister was unharmed.

The body of the hijacker lies beside his getaway car at Poughkeepsie, where he was killed following a 10-hour ordeal aboard Mohawk Airlines FH-227 on 26–27 January 1972. (Wide World Photos)

5 April 1972

THE hijacker of a Merpati Nusantara Airlines Viscount was shot dead by the pilot at Maguwo Airport, Jogjakarta, Indonesia. Armed with two hand-grenades, the assailant had commandeered the four-engine turboprop aircraft during a scheduled domestic flight from Surabaja to Djakarta, demanding a Rp.20 million ransom and a parachute. He later lowered his ransom demand to Rp.5 million and released the other passengers.

During the siege, an army officer had slipped a pistol to the pilot, who then killed the hijacker.

23 May 1972

A Compania Ecuatoriana de Aviacion SA Electra turboprop was commandeered and forced to return to Quito, Ecuador, from where it had taken off earlier, on a scheduled domestic service to Guayaquil. The hijacker demanded $40,000 in ransom and a parachute. On the pretext of showing him how to use the parachute, a military officer boarded the aircraft and immediately opened fire, killing the assailant. The captain and a female passenger were slightly wounded.

30 May 1972

AN Empresa de Viacao Aerea Rio Grandense (VARIG) Lockheed Electra was hijacked while on a scheduled Brazilian domestic flight from Sao Paulo to Curitiba. The gunman released all the passengers and the cabin attendants at the Sao Paulo airport after receiving a ransom of $254,000 dollars from the airline. Subsequently, the flight crew escaped through the cockpit of the four-engine turboprop and federal troops rushed the aircraft, the hijacker shooting and killing himself before he could be captured.

8 June 1972

A group of 10 Czechs – seven men and three women, accompanied by a child – hijacked a Slov-Air Let 410 twin-engine turboprop commuter airliner that was carrying them, along with seven other persons, on a scheduled domestic service from Marianske Lazne to Prague. The pilot was shot and killed when he resisted and two others aboard also suffered injuries. The aircraft landed safely at a small airfield in West Germany, where the hijackers asked for asylum. One of them later committed suicide in prison, while the other nine adults were sentenced to prison terms varying between three and seven years.

2 July 1972

PAN American World Airways Flight 841, a Boeing 747-121 wide-bodied jet with 153 persons aboard, was hijacked by a knife-wielding Vietnamese man about 45 minutes after it had taken off from Manila in the Philippines, an en-route stop during a service originating at San Francisco, California, with an ultimate destination of Saigon, South Vietnam. The assailant sent the captain a note stating that he was carrying explosives and would blow up the aircraft unless flown to Hanoi, North Vietnam. A second note written in blood reiterated his demand. Nevertheless, the captain landed at Tan Son Nhut Airport, Saigon.

As they were negotiating in the aircraft once it was on the ground, the captain jumped the hijacker, who had been holding a stewardess at knifepoint. Grasping the assailant by the throat, the captain ordered another passenger, who was armed, to shoot him; the dead hijacker was then tossed out of a cabin door. During the hasty disembarkation of the aircraft that ensued, numerous other passengers suffered minor injuries.

The armed passenger who shot the hijacker was a civilian security officer who, at the beginning of

the flight, had checked in his weapon with the crew. They were able to smuggle it back to him after the hijack attempt commenced.

5 July 1972

THIS daring act of aerial piracy with a violent conclusion began about 10:00 local time, shortly after Pacific Southwest Airlines (PSA) Flight 710 had taken off from Sacramento, California. There were 86 persons aboard the twin-jet Boeing 737-214, which was on an intrastate service to Los Angeles, with an en-route stop at San Francisco.

The two young men who commandeered the aircraft, both armed with automatic pistols, were demanding $800,000, two parachutes, and a trip to the Soviet Union. Landing briefly at San Francisco International Airport, the 737 took off and proceeded to circle as the airline tried to meet these demands. It returned to the same airport around noon, which would mark the beginning off a four-hour stand-off with FBI agents, who surrounded the jetliner. One agent, posing as a pilot ostensibly bringing the ransom, parachutes, and charts needed for the transcontinental flight, was asked to strip down to his underclothes to prove that he was unarmed before being allowed to re-dress and board the aircraft. The assailants did not know about the small pistol that had been stashed in a coat pocket.

A dead hijacker is taken away at Saigon after being shot during an attempt to commandeer a Pan Am 747. (UPI/Corbis-Bettmann)

Soon after the first agent had entered, a second one rushed aboard and almost immediately confronted one hijacker in the cockpit, killing him with two shotgun blasts. The second suspect in the rear of the cabin then opened fire, wounding three passengers, a 66-year-old man fatally. Emptying his weapon, the assailant was himself shot to death after threatening the agent with a knife. The gun battle was over moments after it began at around 16:00 local time.

The family of the innocent man killed in the incident received a modest compensation for their loss: $100,000 in air travel insurance.

6 October 1972

OPERATING on a scheduled domestic Italian service with an ultimate destination of Bari, an Aero Trasporti Italiani SpA (ATI) Fokker F.27 Friendship Mark 200 was hijacked by a young man and forced to return to Ronchi dei Legionari Airport, serving Trieste, from where it had taken off earlier. The assailant demanded L.200 million and a flight to Cairo, Egypt.

After the six passengers had been released, the three crew members of the twin-engine turboprop managed to escape; shortly thereafter, the hijacker hurled an explosive device from a cockpit window, and police opened fire. Early the next morning, they stormed the airliner and found him shot to death.

29 October 1972

FOUR gunmen, including a father and his two adult sons wanted for murdering a bank manager and a policeman during an attempted robbery the previous week, shot their way aboard an Eastern Airlines Boeing 727 jetliner at the Houston, Texas, Intercontinental Airport. A ticket agent was killed and a second employee wounded before the assailants forcefully boarded the aircraft, which, designated as Flight 496, was preparing for departure on a domestic service to Atlanta, Georgia, with 47 persons aboard. They then ordered the aircraft to fly to Cuba. Subsequently returning to the US, the father and his sons were apprehended in July 1975 and later sentenced to 50 years' imprisonment each for kidnapping and air piracy. The fourth suspect remained a fugitive.

15 November 1972

ONE of Australia's rare cases of aerial hijacking involved a Fokker F.27 Friendship twin-engine turboprop of Ansett Airlines of Australia, on a scheduled domestic service from Adelaide to Darwin. It was commandeered by a single assailant armed with a .22 calibre rifle, who, after landing at Alice Springs, Northern Territory, demanded a light aircraft and a parachute. He allowed one cabin attendant and all female passengers to disembark.

Subsequently, while walking to the general aviation aeroplane provided, with the second stewardess as hostage, he was jumped by a plain-clothes detective. Running into nearby bushes, he shot himself, and later succumbed in hospital.

24 November 1972

A previous fatal hijacking was an important element in this attempted act of air piracy, which led to the death of the assailant. The gunman kidnapped a stewardess and boarded an Air Canada DC-8 Super 63 jetliner that was parked at Rhein-Main Airport, serving Frankfurt, West Germany. Operating as Flight 807, the aircraft had been preparing for a transatlantic service with an ultimate destination of Montreal, Canada.

The hijacker had threatened to set off dynamite unless German authorities released several Czech prisoners, including one of those who, on 8 June, had participated in the take-over of a Czech airliner, the pilot of which had been killed. However, he was himself killed by a police marksman.

8 December 1972

IN a blazing gun-battle with security guards, seven members of the Eritrean Liberation Front, two of them women, were killed after the attempted hijacking of an Ethiopian Airlines Boeing 720B. Operating as Flight 708 and carrying 94 persons, the jetliner was en route from Addis Ababa to Asmara, the domestic segment of a service with an ultimate destination of Paris, when the seven terrorists, armed with pistols and hand-grenades and intent on holding the passengers and crew members for ransom, put their ill-fated plan into effect.

During the assault, a courageous American passenger picked up a grenade that had been dropped by a wounded hijacker and tossed it into an unoccupied section of the cabin. The blast damaged the aircraft substantially, knocking out one engine and briefly causing a loss of control. Nine persons were wounded, most in the explosion, but the 720B returned safely to Addis Ababa.

23 April 1973

UNLESS he was taken to Sweden, a lone assailant threatened to set off an explosive device aboard an Aeroflot Tu-104 jetliner, which had been on a scheduled domestic Soviet service from Leningrad to Moscow with an estimated 80 persons aboard. He did just that when the crew instead elected to land at another Leningrad airport, the explosion killing himself and the flight engineer. The aircraft was approximately 500ft (150m) above the ground at the time, but nevertheless landed safely.

18 May 1973

THE first catastrophic disaster occurring during a hijacking was the crash of an Aeroflot Tupolev Tu-104A. All 81 persons aboard perished when the Soviet twin-jet airliner crashed east of Lake Baikal in Siberia. Reportedly, an explosive device carried by the assailant had detonated aboard the aircraft at an altitude of about 30,000ft (10,000m) after he had demanded to be taken to China during a scheduled domestic service from Moscow to Chita, RSFSR.

8 October 1973

AN Air France Boeing 727-228 jet airliner on a scheduled domestic service from Paris to Nice was hijacked by a woman who wanted to go to Cairo; she also demanded that all air traffic in France be halted for 24 hours. The aircraft landed at the airport serving Marseille, ostensibly for refuelling, where she allowed the 110 passengers and most of the crew to disembark. Following a subsequent attempt to overpower her she opened fire with a rifle and was then killed by police.

2 November 1973

FOUR young men commandeered an Aeroflot Yak-40 as the Soviet-built and registered three-engine jet airliner, designated as Flight 19, was on a domestic service from Moscow to Bryansk, demanding half-a-million dollars' ransom. The flight engineer and one passenger were wounded in the take-over, although the aircraft managed to land at Vnukovo Airport, serving the capital. One assailant who was also wounded later died, while a second shot himself before he could be arrested.

20 February 1974

TRICKERY by the pilot foiled this attempt to hijack an Air Vietnam DC-4 to North Vietnam. The airliner was taken over minutes after its departure from Dalat, South Vietnam, on a scheduled domestic service to Qui Nhon with 52 persons aboard. Shortly before noon, local time, it landed at Hue, also in the South, but the hijacker was fooled into believing that it was in the Communist North.

During a scuffle with the co-pilot which ensued when the hijacker learned of the truth, he dropped the live hand-grenade he had been carrying, and it detonated in the cabin, killing him and two other passengers. Another 15 persons were injured and the aircraft was extensively damaged in the blast.

22 February 1974

A gunman who was also carrying an incendiary bomb shot dead a security guard at Baltimore-Washington International Airport, near Baltimore, Maryland, then stormed aboard a Delta Air Lines twin-jet DC-9, designated as Flight 523, which was boarding passengers in preparation for a domestic service to Atlanta, Georgia. The assailant then shot

An Aeroflot Tu-104 similar to the one that crashed in a hijacking attempt while on a Soviet domestic service in May 1973. (Aircraft Photographic)

both pilots, the first officer fatally, when they refused his demand to take off. He was then wounded by police, and subsequently committed suicide with his revolver. The incident was over minutes after it began, at approximately 07:00 local time.

American newspaper columnist Jack Anderson would later reveal that the man who committed the crime had, more than a month earlier, sent him a tape-recording detailing plans to hijack an airliner and crash it into the Presidential White House in Washington, DC.

10–11 May 1974

AN Aerovias Nacionales de Colombia SA (AVIANCA) Boeing 727-59 jet airliner, with 92 persons aboard, was commandeered shortly before it was to have landed at El Dorado Airport, serving Bogota, during a scheduled domestic service from Pereira. The three assailants, armed with pistols and what they said was a bomb, originally wanted to be taken to Cuba, but then changed their demand to 8 million pesos in return for the rest of the passengers after releasing 25 women and children on the ground at Bogota.

The aircraft then took off, landing at Perua and Cali before returning to the capital, where, on the second day of the hijacking, the 727 was stormed by police. One of the assailants was killed, and the other two, one of whom had been wounded, were captured. In the emergency evacuation of the aircraft, 14 passengers and a stewardess suffered injuries.

24 July 1974

A man who had hijacked a flight to Cuba in 1969 had considerably less success in this attempted take-over of an Aerovias Nacionales de Colombia SA (AVIANCA) Boeing 727-24C jetliner. Operating on a scheduled domestic service from Bogota to Barranquilla carrying 129 persons, the aircraft had last stopped at Pereira, where the assailant got aboard, armed with a revolver. After it had landed in Cali, two passengers suffered injuries evacuating the 727. Only the flight crew and a young woman with an infant, who had accompanied the assailant, remained aboard. Subsequently the hijacker was shot by police, and later died in hospital.

15 September 1974

AN Air Vietnam Boeing 727-121C jet airliner (XV-NJC), operating as Flight 706, was hijacked during a domestic service from Da Nang to Saigon (now Ho Chi Minh City). The aircraft subsequently crashed as it was attempting to land at the Phan Rang airport, located about 150 miles (250km)

Passengers escape from an AVIANCA Boeing 727 at Bogota, 11 May 1974, where one gunman was killed by police and two others captured. (UPI/Corbis-Bettmann)

north-east of the South Vietnamese capital, and all 75 persons aboard (67 passengers and a crew of eight) perished.

It was believed that the assailant had detonated two hand-grenades when the pilot refused his order to fly to Hanoi, North Vietnam. The aircraft flew past the centreline of Runway 22 while on the base leg of the airport circuit in what may have been a missed approach manoeuvre, then plunged into the ground from an approximate height of 1,000ft (300m) and exploded.

22 February 1975

A Viacao Aerea Sao Paulo SA (VASP) Boeing 737 jetliner carrying 80 persons on a scheduled domestic service from Goiania to Brasilia was commandeered by a gunman who set down an infant in the cockpit and grabbed a stewardess. During eight hours of negotiations at Brasilia, he demanded 10 million cruzeiros, guns, parachutes, and the release by the Brazilian government of at least two prisoners.

After he had released the women and children aboard, the assailant was killed by police who had slipped aboard as the other passengers were leaving the aircraft. One of the pilots was wounded in the hand.

14–15 September 1975

WHAT began as a hold-up led to kidnapping, the attempted hijacking of a commercial jet and, ultimately, to the death of the assailant. After trying to rob a grocery store, where a woman was stabbed, the gunman commandeered an automobile and its driver, then took a doctor hostage at a hospital. He next kidnapped a security guard at Reid-Hillview Airport in San Jose, California, switching vehicles and driving with his three captives to San Jose Municipal Airport, where he took hostage two maintenance personnel before herding all five of them on to a Continental Air Lines Boeing 727.

The gunman had the maintenance workers start the jetliner and taxi it into position for take-off, but police shot out its tyres. Subsequently, the doctor was shot and tumbled down the rear stairway, critically wounded. After it had stopped, the assailant emerged from the aircraft and was himself shot dead after pointing his gun at one of the more than two dozen police officers who had surrounded the 727. The drama ended around 01:30 local time, some two hours after it began.

29 February 1976

Police shot and killed the hijacker of an Aerolineas Centrales de Colombia (ACES) twin-engine turbo-prop Saunders ST-27 after it landed at the airport serving Medellin, Colombia. He had commandeered the aircraft during a scheduled domestic Colombian service, demanding $300,000 but releasing the 15 passengers.

18–19 April 1976

A lone assailant already facing charges of vehicular homicide and larceny commandeered a twin-engine Piper Navajo, with its pilot and a mechanic aboard, at Grand Island, Nebraska. Forced to fly to Denver, Colorado, the Navajo set down at that city's Stapleton International Airport, then took off and circled for about half-an-hour before landing again.

To satisfy the gunman's demand for a flight to Mexico, the authorities offered the use of a larger general aviation aircraft, a Convair 990A Coronado four-engine jet operated by Denver Ports of Call. Waiting aboard it were FBI agents, who shot and killed him in the passenger cabin shortly after midnight. His two hostages escaped harm.

21–23 May 1976

THIS hijacking and subsequent stand-off between a group of terrorists and military forces, lasting some 45 hours, ended in death and the destruction of a jet transport. The Philippine Airlines twin-jet BAC One-Eleven Series 527FK (RP-C-1161), designated as Flight 116, was commandeered about 15 minutes after its departure from Davao, on a domestic service to Manila. Including a crew of six, there were 103 persons aboard the aircraft, which diverted to the airport at Zamboanga, located on Mindanao.

The hijackers were demanding $375,000 in ransom, semi-automatic rifles, and a longer-range DC-8 to take them to Libya. Through negotiation, 14 women and children were initially released, followed by two more passengers and a cabin attendant.

To help persuade them to give up peacefully, relatives of the hijackers, bringing food with them, were allowed aboard. But when they began to leave and some of the other occupants tried to slip out with them, shots were fired and one of the assailants loosed a hand-grenade. Troops then rushed the aircraft, shortly after 12:30 local time on 23 May. In the blast, ensuing fire, and indiscriminate shooting, 13 persons lost their lives, including three hijackers. Another 22 persons were injured and the jetliner was gutted by flames.

The three surviving terrorists, one of whom was seriously wounded, were captured and subsequently sentenced to death.

28 August 1976

AN Air France Caravelle III jet airliner on a scheduled service to Bangkok, Thailand, was commandeered by a lone assailant and held on the ground at

An Air France Caravelle of the type on which a hijacker set off hand-grenades in August 1976, killing himself. (Aircraft Photographic)

Tan Son Nhut Airport, serving Ho Chi Minh City, Vietnam. The hijacker released the other 20 persons aboard, but when security forces rushed the aircraft he set off two hand-grenades, killing himself. The Caravelle sustained some damage in the blast.

17 March 1977

THE attempted hijacking of an All Nippon Airways Boeing 727-281 jetliner, which was operating as Flight 817 on a domestic Japanese service from Tokyo to Sendai with 180 persons aboard, ended in the suicide of the lone assailant. Shortly before the aircraft returned to its point of origin, he entered a lavatory and then swallowed poison. Two other passengers had been slightly injured by the would-be hijacker.

25 April 1977

TWO members of the Eritrean Liberation Front were shot and killed by the crew after their attempted hijacking of an Ethiopian Airlines DC-3, which had been on a scheduled domestic service from Makele to Gondar. Several passengers were reportedly wounded, although the transport landed safely.

30 September 1977

AN Air Inter Caravelle 12 jetliner, carrying 107 persons on a scheduled French domestic service to Lyon, was commandeered and forced to return to Paris, from where it had taken off earlier, landing at Orly Airport. A stewardess was shot and wounded trying to stop the lone air pirate from entering the flight deck.

When police stormed the aircraft at around 14:00 local time, the assailant tossed a hand-grenade, the resulting explosion killing one passenger and injuring four other persons, as well as causing considerable damage to the aircraft. He was nevertheless captured and was later sentenced to 18 years' imprisonment.

20 October 1977

FRONTIER Airlines Flight 101, a twin-jet Boeing 737 carrying 34 persons, was commandeered by a shotgun-armed assailant during a domestic intrastate service from Grand Island to Lincoln, Nebraska, landing at Atlanta, Georgia. There, following lengthy negotiations, the gunman shot and killed himself.

29 October 1977

TWO crew members were killed and a third wounded in the hijacking of an Air Vietnam DC-3, which occurred as the airliner, carrying 40 persons, was on a scheduled service from Ho Chi Minh City, Vietnam, to Phu Quoc Island, Thailand. The DC-3 was diverted to Singapore, where the four assailants were sentenced to 14 years' imprisonment each.

4 December 1977

A hijacking with a disastrous conclusion involved a Malaysian Airline System Boeing Advanced 737-2H6 jetliner (9M-MBD), designated as Flight 653, which was commandeered during a domestic service from Penang to Kuala Lumpur. As it was proceeding on to Singapore, the aircraft entered a descent from a height of 21,000ft (6,400m). Subsequently, it was observed to pitch up from level flight, and then plunged into a swamp about 30 miles (50km) south-west of Johor Baharu, exploding and disintegrating on impact. All 100 persons aboard (93 passengers and seven crew members) perished.

It was later concluded that the two pilots must have been shot. Following this disaster, security measures were implemented in Malaysian airline operations.

9 March 1978

THE flight engineer of a China Airlines Boeing 737 jet tried to hijack the aircraft as it was on a scheduled service from Taiwan to Hong Kong with 101 persons aboard, attacking the pilot and co-pilot with a hammer and scissors. However, he was shot dead by a security guard, and the 737 landed safely at its intended destination.

1 May 1978

AN attempt to hijack an Aeroflot Il-18 turboprop airliner to Iran during a scheduled Soviet domestic service from Ashkhabad to Mineral'nyye Vody ended with the assailant, who was carrying a training grenade, being shot dead by the co-pilot.

9 November 1978

AN armed passenger rushed into the cockpit of an Aeroflot An-24 turboprop, which had been on a scheduled Soviet domestic service originating at Krasnodar and ultimately destined for Baku, firing off a few shots and wounding the flight engineer before being locked in the baggage compartment, where he subsequently killed himself.

4 April 1979

A lone assailant commandeered Pan American World Airways Flight 816, a Boeing 747 wide-bodied jet on a service to Auckland, New Zealand, while it was on the ground at the international airport serving Sydney, Australia, a woman and a police officer suffering stab wounds. The hijacker was shot dead by police before the aircraft could take off.

13 October 1980

A Turkish Airlines Boeing 727-200 jet, operating as Flight 890 and carrying 148 persons, was commandeered during a domestic service from Istanbul to Ankara. Landing at Diyarbakir, Turkey, the aircraft was stormed by troops. One passenger was killed and about a dozen persons wounded in the assault, including the four hijackers, who were all captured.

2–14 March 1981

A Pakistan International Airlines Boeing 707 jetliner designated as Flight 326, a domestic service from Karachi to Peshawar with 159 persons aboard, was hijacked to Kabul, Afghanistan. The air pirates demanded the release by Pakistan of 'political prisoners' and mortally wounded one passenger, who was still alive when tossed out of the aircraft. Pakistan gave in to their demands, and on the twelfth day of the siege, after flying to Damascus, Syria, the hijackers surrendered.

28–30 March 1981

GARUDA Indonesian Airways Flight 206, a twin-jet DC-9 carrying 57 persons on a domestic service from Palembang to Medan, was hijacked by five assailants and ultimately flown to Bangkok, Thailand. Shortly after 02:30 on the third day of the ensuing siege, Indonesian commandos rushed the aircraft at Don Muang Airport. All five hijackers were killed, as well as one soldier and the pilot; two other persons had earlier been shot and wounded.

10 April 1981

IN an attempted hijacking to Cuba, a passenger armed with a flammable liquid grabbed a stewardess aboard an Eastern Airlines A300B wide-bodied jet, which was operating as Flight 17 on a service from New York City to Miami with 148 persons aboard. He died of asphyxiation while being overpowered and captured by a passenger and a member of the crew.

20 August 1982

INDIAN Airlines Flight 492, a Boeing 737 jet with 71 persons aboard, was hijacked during a domestic service from Jodhpur to New Delhi and forced to Pakistan, which denied it clearance to land. Subsequently it set down at Amritsar, India, where the lone assailant was shot dead by police when he stuck his head out of the cabin door.

20 January 1983

A convicted hijacker, on 20 years' probation for a crime committed three years earlier, commandeered a Northwest Airlines Boeing 727 jetliner, operating as Flight 608 on a domestic service from Seattle, Washington, to Portland, Oregon, with 41 persons aboard. He wanted to be taken to Afghanistan. This time, however, he was shot and killed by FBI agents after the aircraft had landed at its scheduled destination.

18 February 1983

SECURITY guards shot and killed the would-be

hijacker of a Ceskoslovenske Aerolinie (CSA) Tu-134 jet after he attacked a stewardess and tried to enter the flight deck as the aircraft was on a scheduled domestic service from Poprad to Prague, Czechoslovakia.

7 March 1983

FOUR assailants who demanded to be taken to Turkey hijacked a Balkan Bulgarian Airlines twin-engine turboprop An-24 that had been on a scheduled domestic service from Sofia to Varna. Tricking them in the darkness, however, the pilot landed the aircraft at its intended destination, where one of the hijackers was killed by security personnel and the other three were captured.

5 July 1983

TWO men carrying a tape-recorder made to resemble a bomb tried to hijack an Aeroflot Tu-134A jetliner, designated as Flight 2113, during a domestic Soviet service from Moscow to Tallin. They were tricked by the pilot, who instead landed at a military airfield near Leningrad, where a military courier killed one of the assailants and wounded the other.

18 November 1983

AN Aeroflot Tu-134 jet, operating as Flight 6833 en route from Tbilisi to Batumi, Georgian SSR, one segment of a Soviet domestic service with an ultimate destination of Leningrad, got hijacked by seven assailants, three of them women. Armed with guns and training grenades, they demanded to be taken to Istanbul, Turkey. The flight engineer, a stewardess, and two passengers were shot dead. In turn, the crew killed two hijackers, while a third committed suicide.

The four captured male air pirates were later executed. An Aeroflot lounge attendant was also prosecuted for aiding in the smuggling of weapons aboard the flight.

29–30 July 1984

A Linea Aeropostal Venezolana twin-jet DC-9 was commandeered during a scheduled domestic Venezuelan service from Caracas to Curacao with 87 persons aboard. Landing at its intended destination, the airliner was stormed by commandos in the early hours of the incident's second day, and both hijackers were killed.

20 September 1986

TWO policemen were killed in a crime spree by three heavily-armed assailants in Ufa, RSFSR, USSR, and after one had run away the other two seized an Aeroflot Tu-134 jetliner at the city's airport, where it had made a scheduled en-route stop during a domestic service from Kiev to Nizhnevartovsk. Two passengers were killed in the attempted hijacking. One assailant was captured after 12 hours of negotiations, while the other was killed in a subsequent police operation. The third man, who had run away earlier, was captured.

10 March 1987

A lone assailant tried to hijack an Empresa Consolidada Cubana de Aviacion twin-engine turboprop An-24, carrying 48 persons, which was

An Aeroflot Tu-134 similar to this was involved in a violent hijacking in November 1983 that claimed several lives. (Aviation Photo News)

preparing to take off from Jose Marti Airport, serving Havana, on a scheduled domestic Cuban service to Nueva Gerona, located on the island of Pines. When the pilot refused to fly him to the US, the hijacker let loose a hand-grenade, the resulting explosion injuring 13 persons. The hijacker was then shot and killed by an off-duty police officer.

8 March 1988

A family of 11 attempted to divert to London an Aeroflot Tu-154 jetliner, operating as Flight 3739 on a domestic Soviet service from Irkutsk to Leningrad, via Kugan, with 77 persons aboard. Landing to refuel, the aircraft set down at a military airfield near Vyborg, USSR, where, seeing Soviet troops, the hijackers opened fire. An assault team then stormed aboard, and nine persons were killed, including five of the family members and a flight attendant, while 35 others were wounded and the aircraft was gutted by flames. The surviving hijackers were sentenced to prison.

29 September 1988

A Viacao Aerea Sao Paulo SA (VASP) Boeing 737 jet, operating as Flight 375 on a domestic Brazilian service from Porto Velho to Rio de Janeiro with 105 persons aboard, got hijacked by a mentally-disturbed assailant who wanted to crash the airliner into a government building in the capital city of Brasilia. He shot dead the first officer and wounded two other crew members before the aircraft landed at Santa Genoveva Airport, serving Goiania, in the state of Goias.

As he was transferring to another aircraft with the captain, police opened fire, and he then shot and wounded his hostage. Also wounded, the hijacker died two days later.

24 April 1989

A Shanghai Eastern Airline Y-7 (Chinese-built An-24) turboprop, carrying 50 persons on a scheduled domestic service from Ningbo to Xiamen, People's Republic of China, was targeted for hijack by a lone assailant who wanted to be taken to Taiwan. When he learned that the aircraft had instead landed at Fuzhou, Jiangxi, he detonated a bomb, killing himself and injuring two other passengers. A stewardess had been stabbed and wounded earlier in the hijack.

2 October 1990

THE deadliest case of aerial piracy to date occurred in China, a country that had seen relatively few hijackings in relation to its size.

Designated as Flight 8301, a Xiamen Airlines twin-jet Boeing Advanced 737-247 (B-2510) was commandeered during a domestic service from Canton to Xiamen, Fujian, by a lone assailant who claimed to have explosives strapped to his body. He demanded to be taken to Taiwan, reportedly refusing an offer by the captain to fly to Hong Kong. The dispute continued until the aircraft's fuel supply became critically low, necessitating a landing at Baiyun Airport, serving Canton.

The pilot and hijacker were alone in the flight deck when shouts and sounds of a struggle were heard, just before the aircraft landed hard, then veered off the runway. After striking a China Southwest Airlines Boeing 707, the out-of-control Xiamen aircraft slammed into a China Southern Airlines Boeing 757-21B jetliner (B-2812) that had

On 8 March 1988, during a 'family' hijacking, nine persons lost their lives in a shoot-out aboard an Aeroflot Tu-154 like this one. (Photo by Douglas Green)

been waiting to take off on a scheduled domestic flight to Shanghai. A total of 132 persons were killed in the disaster, including all but 20 of the 104 passengers and crew members of the 737, 47 of the 118 aboard the 757, and the driver of an airport service vehicle. Some 50 others suffered injuries, including the pilot (and sole occupant) of the damaged 707. The 737 and 757 were destroyed by impact and post-crash fire.

In the wake of this disaster, Chinese authorities are said to have ordered managerial restructuring, and admitted procedural deficiencies that had allowed the 757 to taxi during a hijacking.

7 January 1991

A Peruvian Compania de Aviacion Faucett SA DC-8 jet airliner with 125 persons aboard was commandeered at Trujillo, Peru, and flown to Lima, where it was stormed by police at around 21:00 local time, with the lone assailant being killed.

3 March 1991

AFTER releasing his hostages, a lone hijacker killed himself by setting off a hand-grenade aboard an Aeroflot twin-engine turboprop An-24 that was on the ground at the main airport serving Leningrad, USSR.

26–27 March 1991

A Singapore Airlines A310 wide-bodied jetliner, designated as Flight 117 and carrying 129 persons, was commandeered while en route to Singapore from Kuala Lumpur, Malaysia. The aircraft landed at Changi Airport, Singapore, where it was attacked by commandos shortly before 07:00 local time on the second day, all four Pakistani hijackers, who had been armed with explosives and knives, being killed. Two stewards had been injured when tossed from the aircraft before the commando assault, but there were no other casualties.

16 May 1992

THREE security guards were killed when thrown out while airborne by the hijackers of an Aerotaxi Casanare Ltda (Aerotaca) Twin Otter turboprop, carrying 16 persons, that had been on a Colombian domestic service originating at Bogota, with an ultimate destination of Bucaramanga. The aircraft was forced to land at Fortul, Colombia, where six passengers were released, then took off again and vanished.

8 June 1992

A man armed with a hand-grenade was killed by security forces at Vnukovo Airport, serving Moscow, after attempting to hijack an Aeroflot Tu-154 jetliner that had been on a scheduled service to Turkey from Groznyy, Russia.

24–25 April 1993

THE lone assailant who had hijacked Indian Airlines Flight 427, a twin-jet Boeing 737 on a domestic service from New Delhi to Srinagar, was killed in a commando attack at around 01:00 local

A Singapore Airlines Airbus A310, identical to the aircraft on which four hijackers were killed in a commando raid on 27 March 1991. (Photo by Douglas Green)

time on the second day of the incident at Amritsar, India, where the aircraft had set down after being denied permission to land at Lahore, Pakistan. There were no other casualties.

28 August 1993

LOADED with nearly three times its designed passenger capacity, a Tajikistan Airlines Yakovlev Yak-40 (SSSR-87995) crashed during a coerced take-off at Khorog, Tajikistan, Commonwealth of Independent States. All but four passengers among the 86 persons aboard were killed, including the crew of five.

The tri-jet transport, which had been on a scheduled domestic service to Dushanbe, was commandeered by armed men, who demanded that it take off. As disobeying them could have meant being shot, the crew chose the option that they undoubtedly felt offered the better odds for survival. But with an airfield elevation of about 7,000ft (2,000m) and the aircraft approximately 6,600 lb (3,000 kg), overweight, their action proved fatal. The aircraft never got airborne during its take-off run, overran the airport runway, and fell down a river bank. There was no post-crash fire.

25–28 October 1993

A Nigeria Airways A310 wide-bodied jetliner, carrying 153 persons, was commandeered during a scheduled domestic service from Lagos to Abuja. The four hijackers, who were armed with a gun and knives and had splashed petrol around in the passenger cabin, wanted to be taken to Frankfurt, Germany. The aircraft landed at Niamey, where 125 hostages were subsequently released. Early on the final day of the hijacking, the aircraft was stormed by security forces, and the four assailants were captured. However, one crew member was caught in the cross-fire and killed.

25–27 October 1994

A Russian Donavia Yak-40 (RA-88254) with 27 persons aboard was hijacked and forced to return to Makhachkala, Ukraine, where it had landed earlier, an en-route stop during a scheduled domestic service from Ashkhabad to Rostov-on-Don. The lone assailant demanded $2 million ransom, and negotiations went on for two days. Shortly before 07:00 local time on 27 October, when only two crew members were still being held (the rest of the hostages having been released), the hijacker set off a home-made bomb as security forces prepared to storm the aircraft and was killed. The jet airliner was destroyed in the blast.

23 November 1996

A hijacked Ethiopian Airlines Boeing 767-260ER wide-bodied jetliner (ET-AIZ) crashed in the Indian Ocean in the vicinity of the Comoro Islands, and of the 163 passengers and 12 crew members aboard 127 persons were killed. The 48 survivors, many of whom suffered serious injuries, included the captain and first officer.

Operating as Flight 961, the aircraft had been commandeered shortly after take-off from Addis Ababa, Ethiopia, bound for Nairobi, Kenya, the first segment of a service with an ultimate destination of Abidjan, Ivory Coast. Ordered to fly to Australia, despite the pilot's warning that it had insufficient range, the aircraft was ultimately forced down by fuel exhaustion at around 15:20 local time.

Banking to the left, it slammed into the sea some 300ft (100m) off shore from Grand Comore, the largest island in the Comoro chain, as the flight crew attempted to ditch in the shallow water while fighting with the assailants. The three hijackers, two men and a woman, were among those killed in the crash.

Terror from
the Middle East

Terrorism is almost synonymous with Middle Eastern affairs, the political and religious strife in that part of the world having been associated with many acts of terror over a long period of time. Aerial terrorism, however, is a relatively new phenomenon in the region, the first hijackings not occurring here until the late-1960s. Such incidents were soon joined by ground attacks on civil aircraft and, shortly afterwards, by aerial sabotage.

Some of the world's bloodiest hijackings and deadliest cases of sabotage have involved groups or individuals based in or related to the Middle East. The worst of these was the destruction of Pan Am Flight 103 over Scotland a few days before Christmas 1988, an act of terrorism which proved that even flights not originating from Middle

A BOAC Super VC-10 disappears in a cloud of dust and debris as it is blown up with two other jets in September 1970, just one of numerous terrorist attacks occurring in the Middle East. (Popperfoto)

Eastern countries were not immune. Indeed, attacks spawned in the Middle East have taken place in many different parts of the world.

The following is a list of all acts of terrorism – including hijackings, bombings, and ground attacks on airliners – either suspected or proved to be related to Middle Eastern affairs.

23 July 1968

THE first case of hijacking of a commercial flight in or out of the Middle East involved what today would be considered a most unlikely target: the national airline of Israel, El Al. Following a delay for an apparently unrelated bomb threat, Flight 426 departed from Rome, Italy, bound for Tel Aviv, Israel, the second leg of a service originating at London. Aboard the Boeing 707-458 jet were 38 passengers and a crew of 10. Less than an hour later, El Al Captain Oded Abarbanell radioed an ominous message: 'I am being forced to head for Algiers'.

Three passengers, brandishing pistols and hand-grenades and identified as members of the Popular Front for the Liberation of Palestine, had commandeered the aircraft over the Italian island of Capri. During this time the aircraft's co-pilot was wounded, though not seriously. It appeared that the intention of the air pirates was not so much to get from point A to point B, but rather to humiliate the government of Israel. Their destination was wisely chosen, as Algeria had been on hostile terms with Israel since the war in the Middle East the previous year.

Algerian complicity was suspected simply by the way the hijacking appeared to be planned – a television news crew was already on hand when the 707 arrived in the early hours of the following day at Algiers' Dar el Baida Airport. Immediately afterwards, authorities took into custody 22 Israeli nationals who had been on the flight, as either passengers or crew members. The other 26 were not only freed but were treated royally, some even being given a tour of the city! Among those released were three Jews who concealed their religion.

Five days later, 10 Israeli women and children, the former including three stewardesses, were released. The other hostages were freed some five weeks after the hijacking, despite Israel's refusal to release any of the Arab prisoners it held. The aircraft itself was later flown back by an Air France crew.

Never again would El Al be a victim of a successful hijacking, the company subsequently implementing the most rigid security measures of any carrier in the Western World. These would include the placement of plain-clothes security personnel aboard aircraft, and hand searches of all luggage. The government of Israel also adopted a policy of retaliation in response to aggressive acts against its citizens.

26 December 1968

EL Al Israel Airlines was victimized again in this ground attack on one of its aircraft at Athens, Greece. Operating as Flight 253, which had stopped at Athens airport during a service from Tel Aviv to Paris, with an ultimate destination of New York City, the Boeing 707-358B jet had been taxiing to take off when it was attacked by two terrorists armed with automatic weapons and hand-grenades. One passenger among the 47 persons aboard was killed and another wounded. Damage to the aircraft was considerable, with fire erupting in one engine, which was quickly extinguished.

Both terrorists were captured and imprisoned. Nevertheless, two days later, helicopter-borne Israeli commandos raided the international airport at Beirut, Lebanon, blowing up a dozen Lebanese-registered aircraft in retaliation for the attack at Athens.

18 February 1969

OFFICIALS at Zurich-Kloten Airport had initially enacted strict security measures following the attack on the Israeli jetliner two months earlier. That these precautions were subsequently relaxed proved unfortunate for El Al Flight 432, which had stopped in Switzerland during a service to Tel Aviv from Amsterdam, the Netherlands.

As the Boeing 720B was taxiing to its take-off position, four members of the Popular Front for the Liberation of Palestine (PFLP) suddenly appeared and sprayed the jet with machine-gun fire. At least one hand-grenade was also thrown at the aircraft but caused no damage. A trainee pilot seriously wounded in the attack later died. One of the attackers was also killed when an armed passenger opened an emergency door and returned fire. Hit some 40 times, the aircraft sustained substantial damage.

The guerrillas had driven to the centre of the airport and then hid behind a snowbank, carrying out the attack in twilight conditions. The three survivors were all captured, and later sentenced to 12 years' imprisonment each.

18 August 1969

TWO brothers, one of whom was accompanied by his wife and three children, commandeered a United Arab Airlines An-24 turboprop airliner on a scheduled Egyptian domestic service from Cairo to Luxor with 30 persons aboard, diverting the flight to El Wagah, Saudi Arabia. It was there that the assailants were arrested and returned to Egypt for prosecution, with one of the men reportedly receiving a life prison sentence.

August 1969: Its nose shattered by an explosion, a TWA Boeing 707 rests on the ground at Damascus, Syria, after its passengers and crew escaped safely. (UPI/Corbis-Bettmann)

29 August 1969

TRANS World Airlines Flight 840 was carrying 113 persons and had been en route from Rome, Italy, to Athens, Greece, with an ultimate destination of Tel Aviv, Israel, when it was hijacked over the Adriatic. Upon reaching Tel Aviv, a female hijacker used the aircraft's radio to broadcast propaganda messages. The Boeing 707-331B jetliner was then diverted to Damascus, Syria, landing at the city's international airport. Minutes after escape chutes had been deployed and an emergency evacuation accomplished, one of the hijackers tossed in a package of explosives given to him by someone on the ground; the resulting blast blew the cockpit section away from the rest of the aircraft.

The aircraft's occupants were released almost immediately, except for six Israelis. Of these, four women were freed on 1 September, and the remaining two men were released in exchange for 13 Syrian military prisoners held by Israel, but only after more than three months in captivity. The Popular Front for the Liberation of Palestine claimed responsibility for the hijack.

8 January 1970

A Trans World Airlines Boeing 707 jetliner, operating as Flight 802 on a service from Paris, France, to Rome, Italy, was hijacked to Beirut, Lebanon. After it landed, the assailant, a young Frenchman, fired about a dozen shots into the aircraft's instrument panel; he then surrendered, and was subsequently sentenced to nine months' imprisonment in Lebanon and eight months'

imprisonment in France, the sentences running consecutively.

21 February 1970

MIDDLE East-spawned terrorism took a deadly new turn with this case of aerial sabotage, involving Swissair AG Flight 330, a Convair 990A Coronado (HB-ICD), which had taken off from Zurich, Switzerland, on a service to Tel Aviv, Israel. In command was Captain Karl Berlinger; his co-pilot was First Officer Armand Etienne. Seven minutes after its departure from Zurich-Kloten Airport, the flight crew reported trouble with the aircraft's cabin pressure, and that they were returning to the airport. In a radio transmission shortly afterwards, the crew said they suspected an explosion in the 'aft compartment', and asked for immediate descent clearance. Also requested was fire-fighting equipment and a police investigation.

As the Coronado was returning to the airport, the crew announced 'fire on board'; then, having noted that their navigational instruments were not functioning properly, they asked for a ground-controlled approach (GCA). An electrical power failure was then reported. Despite navigational assistance from the approach radar controller, the aircraft deviated to the west. In the final desperate moments of the flight, one of the pilots mentioned 'smoke on board', and exclaimed 'I can't see anything!'

Out of control, the jetliner made a left turn of about 180 degrees before it slammed into a forest some 15 miles (25km) north-west of the airport at 13:34 local time and disintegrated in a fiery explosion. All 47 persons aboard (38 passengers and a crew of nine) perished. At the moment of impact,

A Swissair Convair 990A Coronado, identical to the aircraft destroyed in a suspected Arab terrorist bombing on 21 February 1970. (Swissair)

the Coronado was headed towards the east, descending at an angle of approximately 12 degrees and banked to the left. Just before that, its indicated air speed was around 485mph (780kmh). The meteorological conditions at the time and location of the crash consisted of rain, a low ceiling, with 3/8 cloud coverage at about 1,000ft (300m) and a solid overcast at approximately 2,000ft (600m), and a visibility of no more than three miles (5km). The winds were out of the south at 15 to 20 knots.

Fallen trees and bits of debris mark the crash site of the Swissair jetliner in a forest near Zurich. (Swiss Federal Aircraft Accident Investigation Bureau)

An investigation of the disaster confirmed the crew's early suspicion of foul play. The remains of an explosive device, which used an altimeter mechanism, were found in the wreckage of the aircraft. The bomb had detonated in the rear cargo hold as the jet was at an estimated height of 14,000ft (c4,300m). The resulting fire, which must have been sustained by such combustible material as the lining of the compartment, spread into the passenger cabin. Smoke from the blaze would have reduced visibility to almost zero in both the cabin and the cockpit, and there was evidence that the flight crew and passengers alike had donned emergency oxygen masks before the crash.

There was no evidence that the mechanical controllability of the aircraft had been reduced by the blaze. It was positively determined that there had been no electrical failure prior to impact. The report of such from the crew must have resulted from a short-circuit and, in turn, a loss of synchronization of the generators, after the flames spread to a bundle of wires in the cargo hold. The navigational difficulties mentioned by the crew must have been due to the effects of the blaze on the aircraft's antenna equipment, the receiving wire of which was routed near the compartment.

No arrests were ever made in connection with this terrorist act, but sabotage by Palestinian extremists was considered likely, possibly to avenge the conviction of three terrorists in a Swiss court two months earlier.

On the same day as the Swissair tragedy, and just two hours earlier, an Austrian Airlines twin-jet Caravelle suffered an in-flight explosion after taking off from Frankfurt, West Germany, but the aircraft landed safely with no injuries among the 39 persons aboard. This blast was also caused by a bomb using an altimeter trigger, which had been placed in a package being mailed to Israel.

The Swiss government reacted to the terrorist attack by requiring visas for all Arabs coming into the country. Some airlines in Europe temporarily suspended mail and freight services to Israel, while at some major airports stronger security measures were adopted, even to the point of opening luggage and frisking passengers.

14 March 1970

AN explosive device detonated in the left engine nacelle of a United Arab Airlines An-24 turboprop that was on a scheduled Egyptian domestic service from Alexandria to Cairo. The aircraft managed a wheels-up landing on the sand beside Runway 05 at Cairo airport, and there were no serious injuries among the 15 persons aboard.

21 June 1970

AN Iran National Airlines Boeing 727 jet was commandeered by three hijackers, one of them a young boy, during a scheduled domestic service from Tehran to Abadan, and diverted to Baghdad, Iraq.

22 June 1970

PAN American World Airways Flight 119, a Boeing 707 jet carrying 143 persons en route from Beirut, Lebanon, to Rome, Italy, was hijacked to Cairo, Egypt, by a lone gunman. The hijacker was arrested in Los Angeles, California, in 1973, and later sentenced to 15 years' imprisonment for interference with an aircraft crew.

12 July 1970

A Saudi Arabian Airlines Boeing 707 jet with about 140 persons aboard was commandeered during a scheduled service from Riyadh, Saudi Arabia, to Beirut, Lebanon. After landing at Damascus, Syria, the gunman fired a number of shots into the air before being detained by airport security personnel.

22 July 1970

A Boeing 727 jetliner flown by Olympic Airways of Greece and operating as Flight 255 on a service to Athens from Beirut, Lebanon, with 61 persons aboard, was commandeered by six Arab guerrillas who demanded the release by the Greek government of seven other terrorists. Upon their release, the passengers were freed and the aircraft flew from Athens to Cairo, Egypt.

6–12 September 1970

PALESTINIAN guerrillas, who had already proven their ability to use air piracy as a tool of extortion, stunned the aviation community with this multiple hijacking and mass seizure of hostages. Four jet airliners, all on transatlantic routes with an ultimate destination of New York City, were targeted.

The first victimized was Pan American World Airways Flight 93, which had stopped at Amsterdam, the Netherlands, during a service originating at Brussels, Belgium. The wide-bodied Boeing 747-121 (N752PA) carried 153 passengers and 17 crew members. The two hijackers, both of whom had been denied passage on El Al Israel Airlines for their suspicious appearance, were searched by the Pan American captain and service director for the same reason; unfortunately the men merely hid their pistols at their seats before being frisked.

Meanwhile, another US jet, operating as Trans World Airlines Flight 741, was commandeered less than 15 minutes after its departure from Frankfurt, West Germany. Aboard the Boeing 707-331B (N8715T) were 141 passengers and a crew of 10.

A British Overseas Airways Corporation Super VC-10 like the one hijacked to the Middle East with three other aircraft in September 1970. (British Aerospace)

The third aircraft hijacked was Swissair Flight 100, a McDonnell Douglas DC-8 Series 53 (HB-IDD) carrying 143 passengers and 12 crew members, commandeered after taking off from Zurich, Switzerland. Stopping briefly at Beirut, Lebanon, where several more guerrillas carrying explosives boarded, the 747 proceeded on to Cairo, Egypt. It was there that the explosives were put to use; following a short landing and emergency evacuation, the aircraft was blown up, apparently a gesture aimed at humiliating the Egyptian govern-ment for its participation in peace talks with Israel. This was the first operational loss of a 747. Fortunately, however, there were no casualties.

The 707 and DC-8 landed in the Jordanian desert, where, three days later, they were joined by another jetliner; British Overseas Airways Corporation Flight 775, a BAC Super VC-10 (G-ASGN) with 114 persons aboard, which had been hijacked shortly after leaving Bahrain during a service to London from Bombay, India. A few days later, all three aircraft were destroyed by

The Pan Am aircraft destroyed in the multiple-hijack represented the first operational loss of a Boeing 747. (UPI/Corbis-Bettmann)

explosives after all the hostages had been taken away. These were later released.

But the air pirates failed to capture their most prized target, an El Al Israel Airlines jet. Designated as Flight 219, the Boeing 707 had taken off from Amsterdam with 158 persons aboard. As it flew over the county of Essex in England, the two hijackers, a man and a woman, made their move; but the pilot, Captain Uri Bar-Lev, immediately threw the aircraft into a left bank, knocking both off balance. The male hijacker was then attacked by a steward, and in the ensuing struggle both men were shot, the hijacker fatally.

The woman, who had hijacked a TWA jet in August 1969, was meanwhile attacked by a young American. With the help of other passengers, he managed to wrestle her to the floor and then tied her with string and a necktie. During the struggle, a hand-grenade she had been holding dropped to the floor, its pin pulled, and the aircraft's occupants probably owe their lives to a faulty spring that prevented it from exploding. Subsequently, the 707 landed safely at London's Heathrow Airport.

10 September 1970

AN attempt to hijack an Egyptian airliner on a scheduled service to Cairo from Beirut, Lebanon, ended in failure when security officers subdued the three assailants. The aircraft was believed to have been operated by United Arab Airlines.

12 September 1970

AIRLINE security personnel subdued and arrested a lone hijacker after his attempt to commandeer an Egyptian airliner, believed to have been flown by United Arab Airlines, on a scheduled service to Cairo from Tripoli, Libya.

16 September 1970

A United Arab Airlines An-24 turboprop, on a scheduled Egyptian domestic service from Luxor to Cairo with 46 persons aboard, was targeted for hijacking, but the lone assailant was disarmed by a security guard aboard the airliner.

10 October 1970

A steward was wounded in the hijacking of an Iran National Airlines Boeing 727 jet during a scheduled domestic service from Tehran to Abadan with 49 persons aboard. The aircraft landed at Baghdad, Iraq, where the three air pirates were taken into custody.

9 November 1970

NINE men, six of whom were identified as petty criminals being extradited for trial, commandeered an Iran National Airlines DC-3 on a scheduled service from Dubai to Bandar Abbas, Iran, with 22 persons aboard. After a refuelling stop, the airliner proceeded on without further incident to Baghdad, Iraq.

10 November 1970

A Saudi Arabian Airlines DC-3 was commandeered by a lone hijacker while on a scheduled service to Riyadh from Amman, Jordan. It landed at Damascus, Syria.

22 August 1971

AN attempt to hijack to Israel a United Arab Airlines Il-18 turboprop that was on a scheduled service from Cairo, Egypt, to Amman, Jordan, ended when the lone assailant was overpowered by a security guard.

8 September 1971

A lone assailant commandeered an Alia Royal Jordanian Airlines twin-jet Caravelle that was on a scheduled service from Beirut, Lebanon, to Amman, Jordan. The hijacker was taken into custody after it landed at Banghazi, Libya.

16 September 1971

SECURITY personnel thwarted an attempt to hijack to Iraq an Alia Royal Jordanian Airlines Caravelle jetliner that had been on a scheduled service from Beirut, Lebanon, to Amman, Jordan, and the lone assailant was later sentenced to death.

4 October 1971

GUARDS overpowered the would-be hijacker of an Alia Royal Jordanian Airlines twin-jet Caravelle, which was on the ground at Amman, Jordan. The air pirate would later be sentenced to death.

16 October 1971

AN Olympic Airways twin-engine turboprop YS-11A on a scheduled domestic Greek service from Kalamata to Athens was hijacked to Beirut, Lebanon, by a passenger who claimed to have a bomb. He was arrested and later sentenced to prison for eight years and two months.

19 February 1972

AN attempt to hijack an Alia Royal Jordanian Airlines Caravelle jet during a scheduled service from Cairo, Egypt, to Amman, Jordan, failed when security personnel overpowered the lone assailant.

22 February 1972

A Lufthansa German Airlines Boeing 747 wide-bodied jetliner, designated as Flight 649 and carrying 189 persons on a service from New Delhi, India, to Athens, Greece, was commandeered by five air pirates who demanded, and were paid, a ransom of $5 million. The assailants were taken into custody after the aircraft had landed at Aden, but they were later released by Southern Yemen authorities.

8–9 May 1972

THE 'Black September' faction of the Palestine Liberation Organisation, which would gain notoriety with a brazen attack on the 1972 Summer Olympic Games in Munich, achieved considerably less success in this hijacking of a Belgian jetliner that was tied to an extortion plot.

Among the passengers who boarded SABENA Airlines Flight 517 at Brussels airport were two Palestinian women whose responsibility it was to smuggle aboard the weapons to be used in subsequent take-over. They hid firearms and explosives in cosmetic cases they carried and in special girdles that they wore. During the scheduled stop at Vienna, Austria, the second half of the guerrilla team, consisting of two men, went aboard. Shortly after the Boeing 707-329 had taken off on the next leg of its service to Tel Aviv, Israel, with a total of 101 persons aboard, the hijackers made their move.

Though well-planned and executed so far, the scheme contained one serious flaw: the decision to proceed on to, and land at, the flight's planned destination, Lod Airport. It was there that the terrorists announced their demands to the Israeli government, threatening to blow up the 707 unless more than 300 imprisoned Arab guerrillas were released. Israel offered to free a smaller number of prisoners, the Israeli cabinet having meanwhile already planned a military response.

Commandos, disguised as mechanics who were to prepare the aircraft for its flight out of Israel, suddenly burst into the cabin, ordering the hostages to lie down as they opened fire on the hijackers.

A blood-splattered female terrorist is taken off a SABENA 707 at Lod Airport following the Israeli commando attack on 9 May 1972. (UPI/Corbis-Bettmann)

Both men were killed, and an Israeli passenger who stood up in panic was mortally wounded; she succumbed later in hospital. The two female hijackers were captured, one of them, along with two other passengers, having been wounded. Both were later sentenced to life imprisonment.

Later that month, in retaliation for the action taken by Israeli forces, three Japanese terrorists opened fire after disembarking from a flight at Lod Airport; 26 persons were killed and 70 wounded in the attack. The sole survivor among the terrorists was later sentenced to life imprisonment.

16 August 1972

AN explosive device hidden in a record player detonated in the aft baggage compartment of a Tel Aviv-bound El Al Israel Airlines Boeing 707 jetliner shortly after it had taken off from Rome, Italy. There were no serious injuries among the 153 persons aboard the aircraft, which landed safely.

22 August 1972

TWO men and a woman commandeered an Alyemda Democratic Yemen Airlines DC-6B that was carrying 59 persons and had been on a scheduled service from Beirut, Lebanon, to Aden, South Yemen, diverting it to Banghazi, Libya.

29 October 1972

LUFTHANSA German Airlines Flight 615, a Boeing 727 jet carrying 20 persons on a scheduled service from Beirut, Lebanon, to Ankara, Turkey, was hijacked by two assailants with the intention of freeing three Arabs imprisoned for their involvement in the murder of Israeli athletes at the Olympic Games in Munich. The released prisoners boarded the aircraft at Zagreb, Yugoslavia, and it then flew on to Banghazi, Libya.

9 April 1973

ARAB guerrillas in two jeeps opened fire on an Arkia Israel Inland Airlines Viscount 800 turboprop at the airport serving Nicosia, Cyprus, after the passengers had disembarked. A security guard then stepped out of the aircraft and fired back with a sub-machine-gun, hitting one vehicle and killing one of its occupants. Sent out of control, the jeep then smashed into one of the Viscount's four engines, resulting in substantial damage to the aircraft. The surviving assailants were captured.

20–24 July 1973

IN the 87 hours between the take-over of a Japan Air Lines Boeing 747-246B (JA8109) and its fiery demise, the motive of its hijackers never became

exactly clear. The five terrorists, who included both Palestinians and members of the leftist Japanese Red Army, had commandeered the wide-bodied jetliner, operating as Flight 404, shortly after its departure from Amsterdam, the Netherlands, bound for the US. There were a total of 155 persons aboard. Just before the hijacking, a female member of the guerrilla team was killed when a grenade went off in her hand. The chief purser was wounded, and the blast also cracked a window in the aircraft, necessitating flight at a lower altitude throughout the rest of the ordeal.

The air pirates first demanded the release by Israel of Kozo Okamoto, the sole survivor of the three-man team responsible for the massacre at Tel Aviv's Lod Airport 15 months earlier. They then demanded a ransom of $5 million. However, some of the passengers were told by one terrorist that the hijacking was a protest against Israeli, German, Japanese, and American 'imperialism'. Whatever their reasoning, the surviving guerrillas and their 150 hostages finally set down at Dubai, in the United Arab Emirates, the aircraft having been denied permission to land at Beirut and Damascus (Lebanese and Syrian authorities perhaps fearful of Israeli retaliation). After 79 hours on the ground there, the 747 took off again. Libyan officials at first denied its entry into in that country too, but after the terrorists had threatened to blow it up in the air, the aircraft was cleared to land at Banghazi. Shortly after a successful evacuation, the 747 was set afire and ultimately destroyed.

A possible opportunity to stop the hijacking from ever taking place was thwarted when, despite receiving a tip-off from the Israeli secret service regarding possible terrorist activity, Amsterdam airport authorities failed to take any precautions.

Libya's leader, Colonel Muammar al-Qaddafi, later stated that the hijackers would face 'death, amputation of a foot or hand or prison' for their crime.

16 August 1973

A lone hijacker took over a Lebanese Middle East Airlines Boeing 707 jetliner that was carrying more than 100 persons on a scheduled service from Banghazi, Libya, to Beirut, Lebanon. After it had landed at Tel Aviv, Israel, security personnel boarded the aircraft and captured him; he was subsequently committed to a psychiatric facility.

25 August 1973

A Yemen Airlines DC-6B was commandeered as it was on a scheduled flight from Taiz, Yemen, to Asmara, Ethiopia. The sole hijacker surrendered after the airliner landed in Kuwait and his security had been guaranteed.

Smoke rising from a Japan Air Lines 747 on 24 July 1973 marks the beginning of the blaze that ultimately destroyed the wide-bodied transport. (Wide World Photos)

25 November 1973

TERRORISTS hijacked KLM Royal Dutch Airlines Flight 861, a Boeing 747 wide-bodied jet carrying 288 persons on a service from Beirut, Lebanon, to New Delhi, India, diverting it to Nicosia, Cyprus. The air pirates demanded the release of other terrorists jailed in Cyprus and also guarantees that the Dutch would not assist Israeli war efforts; they subsequently released their hostages when promised safe passage to an undisclosed country.

17–18 December 1973

THIS hijacking to the Middle East began with a ghastly attack on the ground at Leonardo da Vinci Airport, serving Rome, Italy. One band of terrorists, who would later identify themselves as Palestinians, took automatic weapons out of their overnight bags while still in the terminal building and opened fire shortly before 13:00 local time. They then ran out on to the flight field, where several commercial aircraft were parked, among them a Pan American World Airways Boeing 707-321B (N407PA), operating as Flight 110, which was preparing for departure on a service to Beirut,

Lebanon, with an ultimate destination of Tehran, Iran. The open front cabin door was an invitation to attack for the terrorists, who tossed incendiary bombs into the jetliner, turning its fuselage into a fiery death chamber. Of the 69 occupants of the 707, including 10 crew members, 30 persons lost their lives in the holocaust, including a stewardess and the wife of the pilot, Captain Andrew Erbeck, and another 18 suffered injuries. The aircraft itself was a total loss.

Following the assault on the American transport, the terrorists ran across the tarmac to a Lufthansa German Airlines Boeing 737 that had already been commandeered by a second band of guerrillas. They took with them 10 hostages who had been rounded up inside or outside the terminal building. In resisting, an Italian customs agent was fatally shot in the back. The jet, carrying the guerrillas, their hostages, and its crew, then took off on an odyssey that would not end until the following day.

During its 16 hours on the ground after landing at Athens airport, the hijackers demanded the release by the Greek government of two Palestinians being held in connection with a previous act of terrorism that had left four persons dead. When their demands were not met, the gunmen killed a hostage and threatened to crash the 737 into

The gutted hulk of a Pan American 707 after the terrorist attack at Rome airport in December 1973. (Wide World Photos)

the centre of Athens. Greek officials rebuffed the extortion attempt, and the aircraft finally departed.

Refused landing clearance in both Lebanon and Cyprus, the jet finally set down in Damascus, Syria, where it was refuelled before taking off again. Although Kuwait airport also denied a request to land, Lufthansa Captain Jo Kroese put the 737 down safely on a secondary runway. It was there that the terrorists surrendered, though they were released as ransom in the hijacking of a British Airways jet the following November.

3 March 1974

A British Airways Super VC-10 (G-ASGO) was commandeered during a scheduled service to London from Beirut, Lebanon, with 102 persons aboard. The jetliner landed at Schiphol Airport, serving Amsterdam, the Netherlands, where the assailants started a fire that ultimately gutted the aircraft. The passengers and crew escaped safely. The two hijackers were sentenced to five-year prison terms.

26 August 1974

TRANS World Airlines Flight 841, a Boeing 707, had a close brush with disaster when a bomb set to destroy it malfunctioned. A fire apparently caused by the device was discovered in the aft baggage compartment after the jetliner had landed at Rome, Italy, on a service from Athens, Greece. There were

no injuries this time, but just two weeks later TWA Flight 841 would again be targeted by terrorists.

8 September 1974

A Boeing Advanced 707-331B jetliner (N8734) operating as Trans World Airlines Flight 841 was apparently blown up with a bomb over the Ionian Sea some 50 miles (80km) west of the Greek island of Kefallinia and approximately 200 miles (320km) west-north-west of Athens, where it had last stopped during a service originating at Tel Aviv, Israel, with an ultimate destination of New York City. All 88 persons aboard (79 passengers and nine crew members) were killed.

The occupants of another aircraft saw the 707 pitch up, roll to the left and spiral down into the water, the depth of which was about 10,000ft (3,000m). Searchers recovered the bodies of 24 victims and a small amount of debris, and examination of the latter revealed indications of an in-flight explosion. It was later concluded that a high-explosive device had detonated in the aft cargo compartment of the aircraft at its cruising altitude of 28,000ft (c8,500m). The blast probably buckled and damaged the cabin floor in such a manner that one or more of the elevator and rudder system cables were stretched and perhaps broken, which would have resulted in the violent pitch-up and yaw and led to a loss of control.

A Palestinian organisation claimed responsibility for the mass murder, with the device apparently having been put aboard at Athens (which was notorious for its lax security). Trans World Airlines subsequently instituted a policy of ensuring the inspection of all luggage going aboard its aircraft.

6 November 1974

THREE assailants commandeered an Alia Royal Jordanian Airlines twin-jet Caravelle that had been on a scheduled domestic service from Amman to Aqaba with 21 persons aboard. They requested political asylum when it landed at Banghazi, Libya.

22–28 November 1974

THREE Palestinians commandeered British Airways Flight 870, a Super VC-10 carrying 93 persons, on the ground at Dubai airport, where the jetliner had landed during a service from London to Brunei, Borneo. The aircraft was diverted first to Tripoli, Libya, then on to Tunis, Tunisia. It was there, on the second day of the ensuing stand-off, that a German man was slain. There were threats to kill other passengers unless the demands of the hijackers were met. The authorities finally gave in, releasing 13 prisoners jailed in Egypt, and two others held in the Netherlands for hijacking another BA VC-10 the previous March; all 15 were flown to Tunis to join the others. They all surrendered on the seventh day of the siege, after their protection was assured by Tunisian officials.

2 December 1974

A Swissair DC-8 Super 62 jet carrying more than 150 persons on a scheduled service from Bombay, India, to Karachi, Pakistan, was commandeered by a teenager armed with what turned out to be a toy pistol, who demanded to be taken to the Middle East. Overpowered by the crew after the aircraft had landed for refuelling at Karachi, he was later fined and sentenced to three years' imprisonment.

13 January 1975

IN what was believed to been have a Middle East-spawned attack, a missile fired at an El Al Israel Airlines Boeing 707 jet struck a parked Jugoslovenski Aerotransport (JAT) twin-jet DC-9 at Orly Airport, serving Paris, France, leaving a hole in its fuselage. Three persons suffered minor injuries, including a steward. There were no casualties among the 148 persons aboard the 707, which was preparing to take off on a transatlantic service to New York City.

23 February 1975

A lone assailant hijacked a Yemen Airlines DC-3 that was on a scheduled domestic service from Hodeida to San'a. He was captured when the transport landed at Qizon, Saudi Arabia. His subsequent sentence of death was later commuted to life imprisonment.

1 March 1975

AN attempt to hijack an Iraqi Airways Boeing 737 jetliner, which had been on a scheduled domestic service from Mosul to Baghdad, Iraq, ended in a gun-battle between the three air pirates and security guards on the ground at Tehran, Iran. One hijacker was killed in the shoot-out and the other two were captured. On 7 April, these were executed by an Iranian firing squad.

1 January 1976

ALL 81 persons aboard (66 passengers and a crew of 15) perished when a Middle East Airlines Boeing 720B jetliner (OD-AFT) was sabotaged over north-eastern Saudi Arabia. Operating as Flight 438, the Lebanese aircraft crashed in the desert shortly before dawn some 25 miles (40km) north-west of Al Qaysumah during a service from Beirut, Lebanon, to Muscat, Oman, with an en-route stop at Dubai, United Arab Emirates. It was concluded that a high-explosive device must have detonated in its forward cargo compartment as the 720B was cruising at 37,000ft (c11,300m), causing the disintegration of the aircraft.

27 June–3 July 1976

ONE of the most daring rescue operations in modern times began with the hijack of Air France Flight 139, an A300B4-2C wide-bodied jet airliner, which was carrying 258 persons and had last stopped at Athens, Greece, during a scheduled service from Tel Aviv, Israel, to Paris.

After refuelling at Banghazi, Libya, the commandeered aircraft proceeded on to Entebbe, Uganda. About half of the hostages were released, but the hijackers held the French crew and all passengers with Israeli passports, demanding the release of more than 50 pro-Palestinian prisoners held captive in several countries.

Just before midnight on 3 July, Israeli commandos arrived by air and rescued the remaining hostages. In the assault at Entebbe airport, two passengers, one Israeli soldier, all four of the air pirates and at least 20 Ugandan soldiers were killed. In addition, an elderly woman who had earlier been taken to a hospital and was thus left behind, was reportedly murdered. A number of Ugandan MiG jet fighters were destroyed, but the A300 was later retrieved.

6 July 1976

A Libyan Arab Airlines Boeing 727 jetliner, carry-

A Trans World Airlines Boeing 707, similar to the two aircraft targeted for destruction, one successfully, in a two-week period in 1974. (Trans World Airlines)

ing 98 persons on a scheduled domestic service from Tripoli to Banghazi, was hijacked by a man armed with two knives and two replica pistols. He ordered it to Tunis, Tunisia, where it was denied entry, and then surrendered after it landed at Palma de Mallorca, Spain.

23 August 1976

THREE assailants commandeered an Egyptair twin-jet Boeing 737 that had been on a scheduled domestic flight from Cairo to Luxor with 102 persons aboard. The hijackers were overpowered after it had landed at its intended destination, and were subsequently sentenced to life imprisonment.

4 September 1976

KLM Royal Dutch Airlines Flight 366, a DC-9 jet carrying 82 persons, was hijacked during a service to Amsterdam from Nice, France, finally landing on Cyprus. There the three air pirates surrendered, and they were subsequently turned over to the Libyan embassy.

19 March 1977

TWO assailants hijacked a Turkish Airlines Boeing 727 jet that had been on a scheduled domestic

service from Diyarbakir to Ankara with 181 persons aboard. They surrendered when it landed at Beirut, Lebanon.

5 June 1977

A Lebanese Middle East Airlines Boeing 707 jet carrying 112 persons on a scheduled service from Beirut, Lebanon, to Baghdad, Iraq, got hijacked by a lone assailant who demanded a ransom. He was overpowered on the ground in Kuwait, and subsequently deported to Lebanon.

29 June 1977

CARRYING 68 persons, a VC-10 jetliner operated by the Bahrain-based airline Gulf Air was hijacked during a scheduled flight from London to the United Arab Emirates and Oman. It was diverted to Oman, where the lone assailant was taken into custody.

8 July 1977

SIX men hijacked a Kuwait Airways Boeing 707 jet that had been on a scheduled service to Kuwait from Beirut, Lebanon, demanding the release of some 300 prisoners held in various Arab countries. The assailants surrendered after landing at Damascus, Syria.

persons aboard. He demanded to be taken to Iran. During a struggle, he and the flight engineer fell down the stairway and were injured, and the former was then arrested. He was committed to a psychiatric facility the following year.

7–10 December 1981

DURING a scheduled service from Switzerland to Tripoli, Libya, a Libyan Arab Airlines Boeing 727 jet was hijacked by three men, who forced it to Beirut, Lebanon. There they demanded the release of their spiritual leader, missing in Libya for three years. This odyssey took the aircraft from Beirut to Athens, Greece, and Rome, Italy, then back to Beirut, where a mob forced airport authorities to allow its landing.

One passenger was shot and wounded, and after flying to Tehran, Iran, the 727 returned to Beirut, where the three assailants were taken into custody. Four others who had joined the original hijackers during two stops were not detained.

24 February 1982

KUWAIT Airways Flight 538, a Boeing 707 jetliner on a service to Kuwait from Tripoli, Libya, with 105 persons aboard, had landed at Beirut, Lebanon, as scheduled, when two vehicles drove up to the aircraft. From these dashed a dozen assailants, who boarded the 707 and took it over. Once again, their actions were largely to publicize and bring about the repatriation of their spiritual leader who had vanished in Libya four years earlier. They surrendered after being told that an international delegation would press for a United Nations' inquiry into the disappearance.

27 May 1982

A lone gunman commandeered a Royal Air Maroc Boeing 737 jet airliner with 100 persons aboard after its departure from Athens, Greece, an en-route stop during a scheduled service originating at Damascus, Syria, with an ultimate destination of Casablanca, Morocco. He made various demands for improved morality and the observance of strict Islamic faith in Morocco, and ordered the aircraft to be flown to Tunis, Tunisia, where he surrendered.

11 August 1982

AN explosive device detonated under a seat in the rear cabin of a Pan American World Airways Boeing 747-121 wide-bodied jetliner flying over the Pacific Ocean with 285 persons aboard, including a crew of 15. One passenger, a 16-year-old boy, was killed in the blast and 15 other persons suffered injuries.

Designated as Flight 830 and on a service from Tokyo, Japan, to Honolulu, Hawaii, the aircraft was at an approximate height of 25,000ft (7,500m), and some 150 miles (250km) west of its destination, when the explosion occurred at around 09:00 local time. Despite a hole in its cabin floor and a rapid decompression the aircraft made it there safely. Captured and prosecuted in Greece, the Palestinian responsible for the act of sabotage was released from prison in 1996, after serving about half of a 15-year sentence.

20 January 1983

AN Alyemda Democratic Yemen Airlines Boeing 707 jet with 50 persons aboard got hijacked by three men during a scheduled service from Aden, Democratic Yemen, to Kuwait. After forcing the aircraft to land in Djibouti, the hijackers surrendered, and subsequently received suspended prison sentences.

20–23 February 1983

TWO men hijacked a Libyan Arab Airlines Boeing 727 jet carrying 158 persons on a scheduled domestic service from Sabha to Tripoli, forcing it to land at Valletta, Malta. They then demanded to be taken to Morocco, but the government of that country refused the aircraft entry. Negotiations went on for three days at Valletta, until the hijackers surrendered.

22 June 1983

A Libyan Arab Airlines Boeing 727 jetliner was commandeered by two men during a scheduled flight to Tripoli from Athens, Greece. Low on fuel, the aircraft finally landed at Larnaca, Cyprus, where the hijackers were later sentenced to seven years' imprisonment for hijacking and possession of explosives.

6 July 1983

SIX men armed with pistols, sub-machine-guns, and explosives hijacked an Iran Air Boeing 747 wide-bodied jet that had been on a scheduled domestic service from Shiraz to Tehran with nearly 400 persons aboard. The aircraft landed in Kuwait, where about half of the passengers were released. Though the air pirates wanted to be flown to Iraq, they agreed to go instead to Paris, France, where they subsequently surrendered. They were sentenced to prison terms, which were suspended, and were then granted political asylum by the French government.

19 August 1983

SHORTLY before it was scheduled to depart for

Damascus, Syria, a Syrian Arab Airlines Boeing 727 jet was severely damaged by an incendiary device while on the ground at Rome, Italy. All the occupants were evacuated safely, and there were no injuries.

27 August 1983

AN Air France Boeing 727 jet with 119 persons aboard was commandeered during a scheduled service to Paris from Vienna, Austria. After three stops, the aircraft landed safely at Tehran, Iran, where the five assailants surrendered after three days of negotiations.

23 September 1983

DESIGNATED as Flight 771, a Boeing Advanced 737-2P6 jet transport (A40-BK) operated by Gulf Air, the joint airline of Bahrain, Oman, Qatar and the United Arab Emirates, crashed and burned in the desert about 30 miles (c50km) north-east of Abu Dhabi as it was preparing to land at the city's airport, an en-route stop during a service from Karachi, Pakistan, to Manama, Bahrain. All 111 persons aboard (105 passengers and a crew of six) perished.

The disaster took place at about 15:30 local time. There were indications of an in-flight explosion having occurred in a cargo hold that resulted in a fire, and evidence pointed to an act of sabotage rather than an electrical or fuel blaze. Some articles of luggage assigned to the flight had been checked in by a ticket-holder who did not board the aircraft.

7 March 1984

A knife-wielding hijacker commandeered an Air France twin-jet Boeing 737 which was on a scheduled service to Paris from Frankfurt, West Germany, demanding to be taken to Libya. The aircraft instead landed at Geneva, Switzerland, where he was overpowered by police.

5 April 1984

A Syrian national being returned to his country hijacked a Saudi Arabian Airlines L-1011 wide-bodied jet, operating as Flight 287 on a service to Damascus, Syria, from Jiddah, Saudi Arabia. He was overpowered by the flight crew after the aircraft had landed for refuelling at Istanbul, Turkey, and was taken into custody.

26–27 June 1984

TWO men commandeered an Iran Air Boeing 727 jet airliner that was carrying 136 persons on a scheduled domestic service from Tehran to Bushehr, forcing it first to Qatar, where the passengers were released. It then landed at Cairo, Egypt,

and the following day proceeded on to Baghdad, Iraq, where the hijackers surrendered and requested political asylum. One of them later returned to Iran, where he was arrested and subsequently executed.

21 July 1984

A lone assailant carrying a Molotov cocktail tried to hijack a Lebanese Middle East Airlines Boeing 707 jet with 146 persons aboard, demanding that it return to Abu Dhabi, from where it had taken off earlier on a scheduled service to Beirut. Due to its low fuel, the aircraft proceeded on to its intended destination, where, after giving a press conference, the hijacker was taken into custody.

31 July–1 August 1984

THREE men armed with pistols, sub-machine-guns, and explosives hijacked Air France Flight 747, a Boeing 737 jet that was on a service to Paris from Frankfurt, West Germany, with 64 persons aboard. Stopping along the way in Switzerland, Lebanon and Cyprus, the aircraft landed at Tehran, Iran, where the air pirates allowed the passengers and crew to disembark before setting off explosives in the cockpit and surrendering.

7 August 1984

AN Iran Air A300 wide-bodied jetliner that had taken off earlier from Tehran, carrying 315 persons on a scheduled service to Jiddah, Saudi Arabia, got hijacked by two assailants using a knife and a fake bomb. Refused entry into French airspace, the aircraft landed at Rome, Italy, where the hijackers surrendered. One of them was sentenced to 7$\frac{1}{2}$ years' imprisonment for air piracy; the other was released.

28 August 1984

A man and a woman commandeered an Iran Air A300 wide-bodied jetliner that had been on a scheduled domestic service from Shiraz to Tehran with 206 persons aboard, diverting it to Baghdad, Iraq, where they requested political asylum.

8 September 1984

AN Iranian policeman and a family of four commandeered an Iran Air Boeing 727 jet that was carrying 123 persons on a scheduled domestic flight from Bandar Abbas to Tehran. They were promised asylum after it landed at an undisclosed military airfield in Iraq.

12 September 1984

FOUR men failed in an attempt to hijack an Iran

An Airbus A300, three of which, operated by Iran Air, were targeted for hijack during a five-week period in 1984. (Airbus Industrie)

Air A300 wide-bodied jet that was on a scheduled domestic service from Tehran to Shiraz, two of them being wounded by security guards.

12 September 1984

AN Iraqi Airways Boeing 737 jetliner with 110 persons aboard on a scheduled flight from Larnaca, Cyprus, to Baghdad, Iraq, was targeted for an attempted hijacking by Iranian terrorists, but all three men were killed by security guards.

5 November 1984

A Saudi Arabian Airlines L-1011 wide-bodied jetliner was diverted to Tehran, Iran, by two assailants during a scheduled service from London to Riyadh with 131 persons aboard. Their demands included improved treatment of North Yemenis in Saudi Arabia and aid to the government of North Yemen. They were overpowered by other passengers and taken prisoner by Iranian troops, one of the hijackers later being sentenced to 12 years' imprisonment in Iran.

4–8 December 1984

A Kuwait Airways Airbus A310, operating as Flight 221 and carrying 161 persons, was commandeered after it took off from Dubai, an en-route stop during a service from Kuwait to Karachi, Pakistan. The wide-bodied jetliner was forced to land at Tehran,

Iran, where more than a third of the occupants were released. On the same day, however, an American passenger was killed in a scuffle and his body was tossed out on to the runway.

The hijackers were demanding the release of 17 prisoners held in Kuwait, three of whom were under sentence of death. On the second day of the siege, they reported planting explosives in the A310 and said they would detonate them if their demands were not met. About 30 more hostages were freed before another American passenger was slain, his body also being thrown out of the aircraft.

Over the next couple of days, more hostages were released. Then, shortly before midnight local time on 8 December, the hijackers asked that a generator be attached to the aircraft and also requested a doctor and two cleaning men. Disguised as the latter, Iranian security men entered the jetliner and subsequently overpowered the assailants, freeing the remaining seven hostages.

5 January 1985

AN attempt to hijack an Iran Asseman Airlines F.27 Friendship turboprop was made during a scheduled domestic service from Khorrambad to Tehran, but the three assailants were overpowered by security guards.

7 February 1985

FOUR men drove up to and forcefully boarded a

An American hostage, in white shirt, is removed from the hijacked Kuwaiti Airbus moments before being shot by terrorists, 7 December 1984. The man on the stairs with his arms raised is an Iranian negotiator. (Wide World Photos)

Cyprus Airways Boeing 707 jet at the international airport serving Beirut, Lebanon, beginning a five-hour siege aboard the aircraft. They surrendered on being told that their demand for the release of two Lebanese being held in Cyprus would be considered.

23 February 1985

A Middle East hijacking not related to either politics or religion was the commandeering of a Lebanese jetliner out of Beirut international airport by an apparently disgruntled security guard. Designated as Flight 203, the Middle East Airlines Boeing 707-320C had been on a service to Paris and London.

After shots were fired by the hijacker, the 104 passengers and crew members began to evacuate via the emergency chutes, but the aircraft started to move. One passenger, a 65-year-old man, was killed as he tried to exit and was slammed to the ground by engine exhaust. Another 13 persons also suffered injuries.

Following the fatality, which occurred at about 11:30 local time, the 707 took off and proceeded to Larnaca, Cyprus, where it landed twice before

returning to Beirut. As negotiators waited, the hijacker slipped away and vanished.

17 March 1985

A lone assailant commandeered a Saudi Arabian Airlines Boeing 737 jet that had been on a scheduled domestic service from Jiddah to Riyadh with 97 persons aboard. The aircraft landed for refuelling at Dhahran, where the hijacker released all his hostages except the captain and first officer. Security forces subsequently boarded, and killed him when he tossed a hand-grenade. There were no other casualties, and the blast caused only minor damage.

27 March 1985

A Lufthansa German Airlines Boeing 727 jet with 151 persons aboard, on a scheduled service from Munich to Athens, Greece, was hijacked by a lone man armed with a knife and a broken bottle. Demanding to be taken to Libya, he allowed the aircraft to land for refuelling at Istanbul, Turkey, where security personnel disguised as airline employees went aboard and overpowered him. He was sentenced in Turkey to a prison term of eight years and four months.

1 April 1985

A lone assailant who claimed to have a gun and a bomb commandeered a Lebanese Middle East Airlines Boeing 707 jetliner that was on a scheduled service from Beirut to Jiddah, Saudi Arabia, carrying 76 persons. He first demanded financial aid for the anti-Israel resistance movement in southern Lebanon, but was persuaded to give himself up and was taken into custody after the aircraft had landed at its intended destination.

4 April 1985

THERE were no injuries when a rocket was fired into an Alia Royal Jordanian Airlines Boeing 727 jet that was taxiing to take off at Athens, Greece, on a scheduled service to Amman, Jordan. The device failed to explode, and the aircraft sustained only minor damage.

11–12 June 1985

AN Alia Royal Jordanian Airlines Boeing Advanced 727-2D3 (JY-AFW) was seized by five assailants shortly before it was to have taken off from Beirut, Lebanon, on a scheduled service to Amman, Jordan, with 74 persons aboard. The jetliner flew to Cyprus, but was denied entry into either Tunisia or Syria, and it eventually returned to Beirut, where the hijackers released their hostages and then blew up the aircraft. The leader of the hijackers would later be sentenced to 30 years' imprisonment.

12 June 1985

IN apparent retaliation for the Alia hijacking, a lone assailant armed with a hand-grenade commandeered a Lebanese Middle East Airlines Boeing 707 jetliner that was on a scheduled service from Beirut to Larnaca, Cyprus. He soon gave himself up and was returned to Amman, Jordan.

14–30 June 1985

THE United States found itself bogged down in a major Middle East crisis with the hijacking of Trans World Airlines Flight 847. Operating on a service from Athens to Rome and carrying 153 persons, the Boeing Advanced 727-231 jetliner was commandeered by two terrorists while in Italian airspace.

Landing at Beirut, Lebanon, the hijackers demanded the release by Israel of some 800 prisoners, mostly Lebanese (31 were ultimately freed).

Some of the passengers are released from a hijacked TWA jetliner following its landing at Beirut, Lebanon, June 1985. (Reuters/Corbis-Bettmann)

After 19 hostages, consisting of 17 women and two children, had been released, the 727 proceeded on to Algiers, Algeria, where it was first refused, then granted, permission to land. Here another 22 passengers were freed.

Early the next morning, the aircraft returned to Beirut, the crew pleading that the airport lights be turned on in the darkness. It was here that US Navy diver Robert Stethem, a passenger, was murdered. More hijackers then boarded the 727 and additional food was brought aboard before the jetliner

The intact but gutted hulk of an Egyptair Boeing 737 at Malta is examined following the disastrous Egyptian commando attack of 24 November 1985. (UPI/Corbis-Bettmann)

departed again, returning to Algiers, where the terrorists threatened to kill Greek passengers unless the authorities released a 21-year-old Lebanese arrested in Athens, who was accused of planning this hijacking. Facing more killings and the destruction of the aircraft, the Greek government complied, and the suspected terrorist was flown to Algiers.

Two days into the hijacking, more hostages were let go, and the jetliner returned a final time to Beirut. The remaining 39 hostages were taken into Beirut city, where 29 of them signed a letter to President Ronald Reagan asking him to negotiate their release and refrain from direct military action. All were freed 17 days later, and the aircraft was subsequently retrieved.

A US Navy ship commissioned 10 years after the TWA incident was named in honour of Petty Officer Stethem. The terrorist convicted of his murder was sentenced to life imprisonment in West Germany in 1989.

5 August 1985

AN attempt by two men to hijack an Iran Air Boeing 727 jet during a scheduled domestic service from Tehran to Bandar Abbas ended with one being killed by security guards and the other arrested.

2 November 1985

A lone assailant was overpowered by security guards after trying to hijack an Iran Air Boeing 707 jet that had been on a scheduled domestic service from Bandar Abbas to Tehran.

23–24 November 1985

THIS hijacking was believed to have been carried out by a pro-Libyan Palestinian splinter group hostile to Egyptian President Hosni Mubarak and Palestine Liberation Organization (PLO) Chairman Yasser Arafat. An Egyptair Advanced Boeing 737-266 (SU-AYH) jet airliner, operating as Flight 648 and carrying 98 persons, including a crew of six and four security guards, was commandeered while en route to Cairo from Athens, Greece. The aircraft was diverted to Malta, landing at Luqa International Airport, serving Valletta.

At 20:20 local time on 24 November, following a siege lasting more than 20 hours, Egyptian commandos who had arrived earlier on a C-130 transport stormed the aircraft, blasting their way in through a cargo door. Immediately thereafter, the hijackers lobbed hand-grenades into the cabin, touching off a fire that gutted the interior of the aircraft. Among the 62 persons killed were a guard shot in an exchange of gunfire while the 737 was still airborne, two female passengers slain after it had landed, and four of the five hijackers. Nearly all the survivors suffered injuries, although 11 women who had been released before the assault escaped unscathed. A Maltese court of inquiry would later blame all but two of the fatalities on the commandos.

Despite being sentenced to 25 years in prison on Malta, the surviving terrorist was released in February 1993. Five months later he was arrested by FBI agents in Lagos, Nigeria.

23 December 1985

ONE hijacker was killed during an attempt to take over an Iran Air jetliner that was on a scheduled domestic service from Sirri Island to Shiraz.

27 December 1985

A reportedly 'mentally unbalanced' man armed with a razor blade tried to hijack a Saudi Arabian Airlines Boeing 747 wide-bodied jet that was on a scheduled service to Riyadh from Karachi, Pakistan, with 213 persons aboard. He was subdued and arrested by a security guard.

4 March 1986

AN attempt to hijack to Libya an Olympic Airways Boeing 737 jet, which was on a scheduled domestic service with 76 persons aboard, ended with the aircraft landing at Santorini, Greece, its intended destination, where the lone assailant was arrested.

2 April 1986

IN apparent retaliation for the sinking of two Libyan gunboats in a skirmish with US Navy forces in the Gulf of Sidra the previous week, a Trans World Airlines Advanced Boeing 727-231 jetliner, designated as Flight 840, was bombed over southern Greece, in the vicinity of Corinth. Four passengers among the 121 persons aboard, including a mother, daughter and baby granddaughter, lost their lives when the explosive device detonated on the cabin floor between the tenth and eleventh rows. Nine other passengers suffered injuries. The blast occurred at around 14:30 local time, as the aircraft was at an approximate height of 15,000ft (5,000m) and descending for a landing at Athens airport, an en-route stop during a service that had originated (as a Boeing 747) in Los Angeles, California, with an ultimate destination of Cairo, Egypt. The 727 got down safely despite a hole measuring about 10ft by 3ft (3m by 1m) in the right side of its fuselage, just forward of the wing. Those killed had been ejected from the aircraft by the blast and all but one had died in their fall to earth.

The primary suspect in this act of sabotage was a Lebanese woman who was thought to have planted the bomb the previous day during a flight from Cairo to Athens, but further investigation revealed the charge to be unfounded.

17 April 1986

A vigilant security guard probably made the difference in this attempt to sabotage an El Al Israel Airlines Boeing 747 wide-bodied jetliner, designated as Flight 16, which was to have departed from London's Heathrow Airport, bound for Tel Aviv, with 375 persons aboard. A plastic explosive had been placed in a suitcase being carried by an Irish woman, believed to have been an innocent dupe. A man who planned to take another airline was subsequently arrested; he was later sentenced to 45 years' imprisonment.

The bomb had passed through the airport's security X-ray but was caught by the guard, who

The large hole in the fuselage of a TWA Boeing 727 through which four victims were ejected in a terrorist bombing over Greece, 2 April 1986. (Wide World Photos)

thought the bag seemed unusually heavy. The British government said it had evidence that the Syrian ambassador had been involved in the plot and as a result broke off diplomatic relations with Syria.

26 June 1986

A bomb hidden in a suitcase exploded on the conveyor belt before it was to have been loaded on to a Tel Aviv-bound El Al Israel Airlines Boeing 747 wide-bodied jet at Barajas Airport, serving Madrid, Spain, and 13 persons were injured, three seriously.

6 September 1986

NO aerial hijacking, this seizure of Pan American World Airways Flight 73 occurred after the Boeing 747-121 had landed at Karachi, Pakistan. Dressed as security guards and armed with automatic weapons, the four terrorists responsible, who were identified as Palestinians, boarded the wide-bodied jetliner via stairs after it had arrived from Bombay, India, one segment of a service originating at Frankfurt, West Germany, with an ultimate destination of New York City.

The three-member flight crew escaped after hearing shots; the other 375 persons aboard, including the cabin crew, were held hostage as negotiations continued all day. They finally broke off in the evening, around 21:00 local time, when a power generator ran out of fuel oil, causing the failure of the aircraft's lights, air conditioning, and radio. About an hour later, after they had herded their hostages into the centre part of the cabin, the terrorists opened fire and detonated hand-grenades.

Among the 21 persons killed was a stewardess and an American passenger who had been shot and thrown out on the tarmac earlier. More than 100 others were wounded or otherwise injured. The hijackers were captured alive following the 17-hour ordeal and were subsequently condemned to death, though the sentences would later be commuted. Although the aircraft sustained some damage in the attack, it remained structurally intact.

25 December 1986

IRAQ found itself on the receiving end of this terrorist attack, a hijacking attempt involving the country's national airline. The Iraqi Airways twin-jet Boeing Advanced 737-270C (YI-AGJ), designated as Flight 163 and en route from Baghdad to Amman, Jordan, was carrying 107 persons, including 15 crew members and a security guard.

After the aircraft had entered Saudi Arabian airspace, cruising at a height of 28,000ft (c8,500m), one of the hijackers took out a hand-grenade and forced his way into the cockpit. Shooting between the terrorists and the guard then erupted as the 737 was at an altitude of about 15,000ft (5,000m), and at least two hand-grenades exploded, one near the cockpit, which injured the flight crew.

The jetliner diverted and attempted an emergency landing at Arar, Saudi Arabia, located some 250 miles (400km) south-west of Baghdad, under partial control and engine thrust; however, at about 12:30 local time it slammed into the desert and burst into flames, about half-a-mile (0.8km) from the airstrip. The final death-toll was 71, the fatalities resulting from the explosions, gunfire, or the crash; all the survivors were injured, many seriously.

Four underground groups claimed responsibility for the attempted hijacking, but none said they had planned to destroy the aircraft.

24 July 1987

IN an apparent attempt to compel the release by West Germany of the Lebanese convicted of killing US Navy Petty Officer Robert Stethem in a TWA hijacking two years earlier, a lone assailant commandeered Air Afrique Flight 56, a DC-10 wide-bodied jet airliner en route from Rome to Paris, one segment of a service originating at Brazzaville, Congo, with 163 persons aboard.

After the aircraft had landed for refuelling at Cointrin Airport, serving Geneva, Switzerland, the hijacker shot dead a male passenger; immediately thereafter security personnel stormed the aircraft and captured the gunman. About 30 persons were injured in the emergency evacuation of the DC-10, and the hijacker would later be sentenced to a life prison term.

5–20 April 1988

A Kuwait Airways Boeing 747 wide-bodied jetliner, designated as Flight 422 and carrying 112 persons, was commandeered by a group of hijackers during a service to Kuwait from Bangkok, Thailand. The aircraft first landed at Mashhad, Iran, where more terrorists boarded with additional weapons, and then proceeded to Beirut, Lebanon, where it was denied entry. It was there that a merciless ground controller engaged in a tense radio conversation with the Kuwait Airways pilot and one of the hijackers. In a plea for assistance, the pilot stated, 'They are forcing me to land . . . we request to land . . . if we don't they will shoot us . . . I have a gun pointed at me . . . please help me . . . I don't have fuel . . . please give permission to land'; but the controller only responded, 'It is not our problem . . . the fuel in Lebanon is polluted . . . go away'.

The aircraft finally diverted to Larnaca, on Cyprus, where it was allowed to land after permission was initially refused. Only after two Kuwaiti passengers were murdered over a period of three days was a request to refuel granted. The 747 then flew on to Algiers, Algeria, landing at Houari Boumedienne Airport. The hijackers, who were demanding the release by Kuwait of 17 prisoners convicted of bombings there five years earlier, now reported that they had rigged the aircraft with explosives.

Over the next 15 days, the hijackers freed a number of other hostages, releasing the last few after Kuwait commuted the death sentences on three of the prisoners they held.

21 December 1988

THE worst case of aerial sabotage believed spawned in the Middle East was the destruction of Pan American World Airways Flight 103 over Scotland. A little more than two weeks earlier, an anonymous telephone message had been received at the American Embassy in Helsinki, Finland, warning that a sabotage attempt would be made against a Pan Am aircraft flying between Frankfurt, West Germany, and the US. This threat was made known to various American embassies, but not to the general public. The rationale behind this policy was simple: why give the perpetrators the publicity they were seeking and in the process do financial harm to the airline industry? Besides, some authorities had dismissed the threat as a hoax.

Flight 103 did originate at Frankfurt, stopping at London, where the continuing passengers were joined by nearly 200 others and transferred from a Boeing 727 to a wide-bodied 747-121 (N739PA). Baggage, already theoretically security-checked at Frankfurt, was also transferred, without further screening.

Having taken off almost half-an-hour late from Heathrow Airport, the jetliner was cruising at flight level 310 on its way to New York City when it was ripped apart by an explosion. A high-explosive substance, believed to have been Semtex that was probably hidden in the shell of a radio-cassette player, had detonated in a suitcase placed in the left side of the forward cargo hold. The blast had caused catastrophic structural failure almost immediately, with the cockpit and forward fuselage section separating from the rest of the aircraft. As the main portion fell to earth, all four engines broke away, and the rear fuselage disintegrated.

Wreckage and victims were scattered over a wide area, but the greatest damage was done in the Sherwood Crescent residential district of Lockerbie, where the wings and centre fuselage section ploughed a huge crater and exploded in flames. All 259 persons aboard perished, including 16 crew members. Eleven more were killed on the ground, five others were injured, and more than 20 houses destroyed outright or damaged beyond repair.

The body of a second hostage killed at Cyprus airport is dropped from Kuwait Airways Flight 422, April 1988. (Wide World Photos)

A huge crater marks the main fuselage impact site of the Pan Am 747 destroyed over Lockerbie, Scotland, on 21 December 1988. (Wide World Photos)

Initially, the bombing was believed to have been carried out with financial assistance from the government of Iran, this in retaliation for the accidental downing of an Iran Air Airbus A300 by a US warship the previous July. In late 1991, however, the US Justice Department announced its indictment of two alleged Libyan intelligence agents in connection with the Pan Am tragedy. They were suspected of planting the bomb in a suitcase that was carried from Malta to Germany on an Air Malta flight, then interlined on to Flight 103. The mass murder was probably intended to avenge the US bombing of Tripoli, Libya, which, in the 'eye-for-eye' world of Middle East hostilities, had itself been in retaliation for a terrorist attack. Nearly a decade after the Lockerbie disaster, and despite concerted pressure from the West, Libya had yet to turn over the two suspected saboteurs for prosecution.

23 August 1989

IN an attempted hijacking apparently related to Middle Eastern matters, an Air France A300 wide-bodied jet with more than 100 persons aboard was targeted by a lone assailant during a scheduled service from Paris to Algiers, Algeria. Denied clearance to land at three cities, the aircraft finally set down at its intended destination, where the hijacker, who had been carrying a fake explosive device, surrendered.

19 September 1989

FRANCE'S backing of elements opposed to the government of Libya and/or its support of anti-Syrian forces in Lebanon were thought to have been the motivating factors behind this, the worst case of sabotage involving a European airline. Operating as Flight 772, the Union de Transports Aeriens (UTA) McDonnell Douglas DC-10 Series 30 (N54629) had taken off from Ndjamena, Chad, bound for Paris, the second segment of a service originating at Brazzaville, in the Congo. About an hour later, or around 14:00 local time, the wide-bodied jet was shattered by an explosion whilst cruising at 35,000ft (c10,500m) over Niger, in the vicinity of Bilma. Wreckage was scattered over an area of nearly 50 square miles (80 sq km) in the Tenere Desert, a region of the Sahara. All 170 persons aboard, including a crew of 14, perished.

Traces of the explosive pentharite were identi-

A French UTA DC-10 Series 30, identical to the transport blown up over the Sahara in September 1989. (Photo by Douglas Green)

fied, confirming that the aircraft had been destroyed by a bomb. The device was apparently hidden in a suitcase and detonated in the forward baggage compartment, resulting in the in-flight disintegration of the DC-10. The Libyan/Syrian connection was revealed by a subsequent French investigation. The bomb was believed to have been carried aboard by a Congolese man, who boarded the flight as a passenger at Brazzaville and then disembarked at Ndjamena.

23 November 1989

A loose wire probably prevented the detonation of a bomb in the luggage compartment of a Saudi Arabian Airlines Boeing 747 wide-bodied jet, operating as Flight 367, which had been over the Arabian Sea on a service from Islamabad, Pakistan, to Riyadh, Saudi Arabia, with 339 persons aboard. Ten passengers were subsequently arrested for their part in what appears to have been a suicide mission.

25 January 1990

FOUR men armed with pistols and hand-grenades attempted to hijack Iran Air Flight 133, a Boeing 727 jet airliner that had been on a domestic service from Shiraz to Bandar Abbas, but all were killed in a shoot-out with security guards.

2 August 1990

A British Airways Boeing 747-136 wide-bodied jetliner (G-AWND), operating as Flight 149 on a service from London to Kuala Lumpur, Malaysia, was caught in the Iraqi invasion after landing in Kuwait, an en-route stop. During the attack on Kuwait airport an emergency evacuation of the aircraft was carried out by the 385 persons aboard. All the passengers and crew members were held hostage by Iraq, only being eventually released in December. The 747 was blown up by retreating Iraqi forces the following February.

14–15 August 1993

A KLM Royal Dutch Airlines Boeing 737-400 jet with 139 persons aboard was commandeered during a scheduled service to Amsterdam from Tunis, Tunisia, landing at Dusseldorf, Germany. On the second day, police entered the aircraft and arrested the lone hijacker, who had demanded the release of the prime suspect being held in connection with the bombing of the World Trade Center in New York City earlier in the year.

29 November 1993

AN Iranian domestic flight, possibly one of Iran Air, was commandeered by a couple who were accompanied by their five children. They asked for political asylum when the airliner landed at Al Basrah, Iraq.

8 March 1994

A Saudi Arabian Airlines jetliner with 153 persons aboard, on a scheduled flight from Jiddah, Saudi Arabia, to Addis Ababa, Ethiopia, was hijacked to Nairobi, Kenya. There, the lone assailant, who had been carrying a toy gun, was wounded and captured.

19 July 1994

IN what was suspected to be a Middle East-spawned act of terrorism, a Compania Alas Chiricanas SA EMBRAER EMB-110P1 Bandeirante (HP-1202AC) plummeted into a wooded area about five miles (10km) from Colon, Panama, from where it had taken off shortly before, on a scheduled domestic service to Panama City. Including a crew of three, all 21 persons aboard were killed in the crash, which occurred at about 18:30 local time.

Metal fragments that were believed to have come from an explosive device were found in the wreckage and in some of the victims' bodies. A number of passengers on the flight were reported to have been Jewish businessmen, and a Lebanese group was said to have 'hinted' that they were responsible for the attack.

11 December 1994

WHILE at a height of 30,000ft (c10,000m) over the Pacific Ocean, a bomb exploded under a seat in the cabin of a Philippine Airlines Boeing 747-283B Combi wide-bodied jet, which was operating as Flight 434 on a service from Manila, the Philippines, to Tokyo, Japan. The passenger occupying that seat was killed and 10 of the other 292 persons aboard suffered injuries in the blast, which occurred at around 11:30 local time some 185 miles

Bullet holes in the windscreen of an Air France Airbus illustrate the violent end of a hijacking at Marseille airport on 26 December 1994. (Wide World Photos)

(300km) east of Okinawa, where the aircraft landed safely.

This was reportedly the 'trial run' for a planned attempt to blow up a dozen US airliners on trans-pacific flights, designed to punish the United States for its continued support of Israel. The principal saboteur in the plot was later convicted in an American court.

24–26 December 1994

AIR France Flight 8969, an Airbus A300B2-101 wide-bodied jet bound for Paris carrying 283 persons, was seized by four Muslim extremists as it prepared to take off at Houari Boumedienne Airport, serving Algiers, Algeria. Three passengers were killed there before the aircraft proceeded on to Marignane Airport, located near Marseille, France. Here, on the third day of the ordeal, shortly after 06:00 local time, an elite unit of French commandos stormed the aircraft, killing all four hijackers. Injured in the raid were 13 other passengers, three members of the crew, and nine commandos.

19 September 1995

A Kish Air Boeing 707 jet airliner carrying 174 persons on a scheduled domestic Iranian service was commandeered by a steward, landing safely at a military base in southern Israel.

27 March 1996

AN Egyptair Airbus A320 jetliner with 152 persons aboard was hijacked during a scheduled service to Cairo from Jiddah, Saudi Arabia, and landed at Martubah, Libya, where the three assailants surrendered.

26 July 1996

IN what may have been a Middle East-spawned hijacking, a Spanish Iberia DC-10 wide-bodied jet airliner, designated as Flight 6621 and en route from Madrid to Havana, Cuba, with 232 persons aboard, was commandeered to Miami, Florida. There the lone hijacker, a Lebanese man who had claimed to have a bomb that was actually a fake, surrendered to American authorities.

A few days later, two Palestinians were arrested in Germany and admitted helping plot the hijacking, but said they backed out of the plan after arriving in Madrid from Beirut, Lebanon.

Blood for Money

The cracking of the 1949 Quebec Airways bombing case and the subsequent hanging of the three perpetrators should have taught all potential airline saboteurs that such crimes would be dealt with firmly. Nevertheless, half-way through the next decade such 'get-rich-quick' (or make somebody else rich quick) crimes, involving the in-flight destruction of an aircraft with a view to making a sizeable insurance claim, would reach critical proportions, becoming as much of a menace to safe air travel in North America as mid-air collisions and bad weather conditions. The first such incident, in 1955, saw the saboteur pay for his crime with his life, but subsequent bombers would become more ingenious, destroying aircraft over water or mountainous terrain, in order to hamper attempts to solve the crime.

Such attacks would take place periodically over a period of nearly a decade. Interestingly, in only one case – that involving the National Airlines DC-7B over the Gulf of Mexico in 1959 – would insurance money actually be collected. But with over 200 lives being lost and a number of aircraft destroyed, the saboteurs would succeed in injecting a new element of fear and risk into the air travel business.

1 November 1955

UNITED Air Lines Flight 629, a Douglas DC-6B

Completely intact, the empennage of the United Air Lines DC-6B sabotaged in November 1955 rests in a field some distance from where the main wreckage fell. (The Denver Post)

(N37559), took off from Stapleton Airfield, serving Denver, Colorado, bound for Portland, Oregon, one segment of a domestic transcontinental service originating at New York City, with an ultimate destination of Seattle, Washington. Approximately 10 minutes later, or shortly after 19:00 local time, while climbing in visual meteorological conditions and at an estimated height of 5,000ft (c1,500m) above the ground, the transport was shattered by an explosion. The loud blast was confirmed by eye-witnesses; tower controllers reported seeing lights in the sky, then a flash on or near the ground that illuminated the base of the clouds, some 10,000ft (c3,000m) above. Burning wreckage was scattered over a wide area in the vicinity of Longmont, about 40 miles (65km) north-west of Denver. All 44 persons aboard (39 passengers and five crew members) perished.

In the first hours following the crash, definite clues were uncovered indicating an explosion within, but foreign to, the aircraft. Chemical analysis revealed the residue of dynamite in the wreckage, while other pieces found could have originated from a dry cell battery, these being the two main components of a bomb. The blast had taken place in the No 4 baggage compartment, with a disintegrating force that tore the aft fuselage section to pieces. During its fall to earth, a more complete break-up of the aircraft occurred, including the separation of the wings and forward fuselage.

A criminal investigation conducted by the FBI was launched about a week into the Civil Aeronautics Board (CAB) probe, leading to the arrest on 14 November of John G. Graham, whose mother had been a passenger on the flight. He thereafter confessed to the mass murder. Before the aircraft had taken off, he took out $37,500 in life insurance on her – six policies purchased for 25 cents apiece from an airport vending machine (these would later be banned in the state of Colorado). He had planted the bomb, fashioned from 25 sticks of dynamite, in her suitcase.

Convicted of the crime, John Graham was executed in the Colorado gas chamber in 1957.

25 July 1957

BEFORE proceeding on towards its ultimate destination of Los Angeles, California, Western Air Lines Flight 39 landed at McCarran Field, serving Las Vegas, Nevada, its final en-route stop during a service that had originated at Rochester, Minnesota. It was here that Saul Binstock boarded, becoming one of the 13 passengers on the twin-engine Convair 240.

About 15 minutes after take-off, the 62-year-old retired jeweller entered the lavatory, located in the rear of the aircraft's cabin. Some 20 minutes later, or around 03:40 local time, as it was cruising at 10,000ft (c3,000m) over the Mojave Desert of Southern California, the Convair was rocked by an

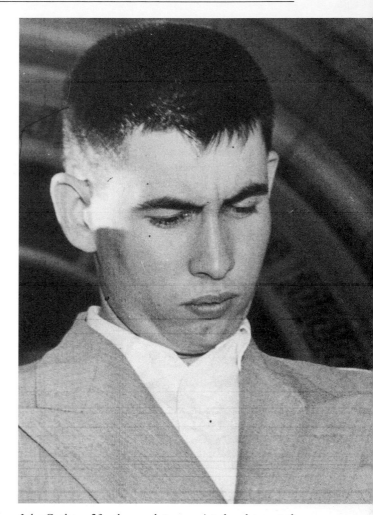

John Graham, 23, who was later convicted and executed for the bombing of United Air Lines Flight 629, in which 44 lives were lost. (Wide World Photos)

explosion, which resulted in an immediate decompression of the cabin and left a hole measuring approximately 6ft by 7ft (1.8 m by 2m) near the tail assembly. The victim's body, which had been blasted out into the pre-dawn darkness, would later be found along the route of the flight.

In what was believed to have been a suicide-for-insurance scheme on his part, he had set off dynamite, after spending considerable time trying to ignite the blasting cap. There were no injuries among the other 15 persons aboard, who included a crew of three, and the damaged aircraft managed a safe emergency landing at a military air base.

16 November 1959

THIS aviation mystery was widely believed to have been an act of aerial sabotage that could not be proven due to a lack of evidence.

Originating at Miami, National Airlines Flight 967 had landed at Tampa, Florida, before proceeding on towards New Orleans, Louisiana, its next scheduled stop during a transcontinental domestic US service with an ultimate destination of Los Angeles, California. Last reported cruising at 14,000ft (c4,300m) in darkness and good weather conditions, the Douglas DC-7B (N4891C) had been about 120 miles (190km) east-south-east of New Orleans when radio and radar contact was lost shortly before 01:00 local time.

Search vessels combing the Gulf of Mexico subsequently recovered a small amount of debris, mostly cabin furnishings, as well as the bodies of nine victims, and the remains of a tenth. There were

Dr Robert Spears, suspected but never convicted in the destruction of a National Airlines DC-7B in November 1959. (Wide World Photos)

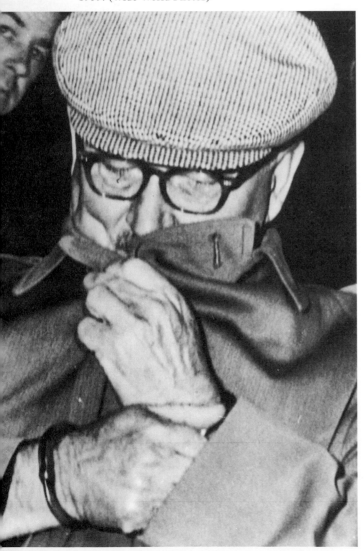

no survivors among the 42 persons aboard the aircraft, including six crew members. Attempts to locate the main wreckage, which lay in water more than 200ft (60m) deep, were unsuccessful, preventing the US Civil Aeronautics Board (CAB) from being able to determine of the cause of the crash.

The sabotage theory gained credibility two months later when Robert Vernon Spears, a naturopathic doctor first listed as a passenger on the downed DC-7B, showed up alive in Arizona. He reportedly told his wife that another man had taken his seat on the flight, leading to speculation that the aircraft had been sabotaged with some type of explosive device in an elaborate insurance swindle.

Dr Spears died in 1969, perhaps taking the solution to the mystery with him to the grave.

6 January 1960

NATIONAL Airlines had been using Boeing 707 jetliners on its New York to Florida route for more than a year, in a lease agreement with the major US international carrier Pan American World Airways. This time, however, the trip would take a little longer; the 707 being used had to be removed from service due to a cracked cockpit window. Two other aircraft were brought in as replacements, a turboprop Lockheed Electra, which boarded most of the 105 passengers, and an older piston-engine Douglas DC-6B (N8225H), to which the rest were assigned. Designated as Flight 2511, the latter had taken off from New York International Airport for Miami late the previous night.

Nearly three hours later, or around 02:40 local time, an explosion occurred in its passenger cabin as the transport was cruising at 18,000ft (c5,500m) in darkness over south-eastern North Carolina. The blast, beneath the far right seat in row No 7, impaired the structural integrity of the DC-6B, which made a descending right turn before it disintegrated and plummeted to earth. All 34 persons aboard, including a crew of five, were killed.

The main wreckage had fallen in a field near the town of Bolivia, located some 15 miles (25km) south-west of Wilmington, but additional debris and the body of one passenger was found on Kure Beach, some distance to the east of the main crash site. The mutilated body, in which was embedded wire fragments and foreign particles, was that of Julian A. Frank, a 33-year-old New York attorney who was known to be in serious financial trouble and who had taken out more than $1 million in insurance. His wounds could only have resulted from the detonation of an explosive in close proximity to the victim. Amid the wreckage of the aircraft, there was further conclusive evidence of destruction by a foreign substance. Sodium nitrate found in the cabin air vent is a typical residue of dynamite; there were also traces of manganese dioxide, commonly found in a dry cell battery,

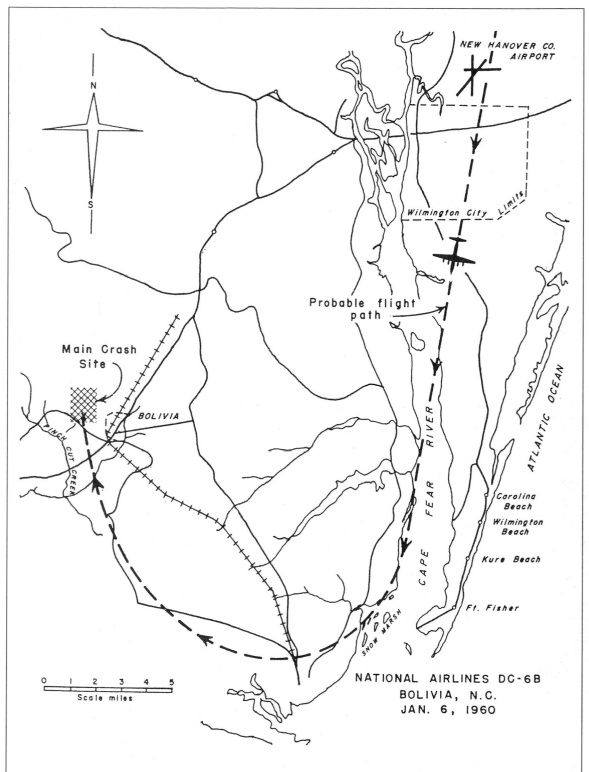

The flight path of the National Airlines DC-6B sabotaged on 6 January 1960 included a descending turn after the detonation of the bomb in its passenger cabin. (Civil Aeronautics Board)

which could have been used to set off the explosive.

The break-up of the DC-6B could not be attributed to any mechanical malfunction or structural failure, nor to the weather (although winds of 100 kts at the cruising altitude were responsible for the wide dispersion of many light pieces of cabin material; at the crash site there was rain and fog at the time).

22 May 1962

THE first successful sabotage of a commercial jet airliner, which could easily have occurred two years earlier, involved Continental Air Lines Flight 11, which was en route from Chicago, Illinois, to Kansas City, Missouri, the first segment of a domestic US service scheduled to terminate at Los Angeles, California. The Boeing 707-124 (N70775) crashed along the Iowa/Missouri border, killing all 45 persons aboard (37 passengers and eight crew members). One victim was actually removed alive from the wreckage but succumbed to his injuries about 1½ hrs later.

Although the main wreckage fell into a field approximately five miles (10km) north-north-west of Unionville, Missouri, pieces were found over a path 40 miles (65km) long in a north-easterly direction, and some light debris was located up to 120 miles (c190km) from the crash site. This evidence of an in-flight break-up could not be disputed. Early suspicions of sabotage were soon proven by the FBI, which established that dynamite had been detonated aboard the 707, apparently in the used towel bin underneath the wash basin in the right rear lavatory.

Flying in darkness and clear weather conditions at a height of around 37,000ft (11,300m), the jetliner had just circumnavigated some thunderstorm activity when the bomb exploded, causing severe structural damage. Subsequently, and after the flight crew had initiated an emergency descent, donned smoke masks, and lowered the undercarriage, the aircraft broke up at a high altitude. Losing the aft 38ft (11.5m) of its fuselage, the 707 pitched down, causing most of its left wing, the outer portion of its right wing, and all four engines to separate.

The explosive device was believed to have been carried aboard by a passenger in a suicide-for-insurance plot.

7 May 1964

AMONG the passengers who boarded Pacific Air Lines Flight 773 at Reno, Nevada, was 27-year-old Francisco Gonzales. Deeply in debt and fraught with personal problems, he was also bent on self-destruction.

Following a scheduled stop at Stockton, California, the twin-engine turboprop Fairchild F-27A (N2770R) continued on towards its ultimate destination, San Francisco. It was last observed by ground radar while on a south-westerly heading and cruising at an altitude of 5,000ft (c1,500m) before the Oakland approach control centre received a frantic, unintelligible message from the flight. Deciphered through laboratory analysis, the message, sent by co-pilot Ray Andress, was believed to have been, 'Skipper's shot! We've been shot! I was trying to help . . .'

At around 06:50 local time, the aircraft crashed

A Fairchild F-27 of the type flown by Pacific Air Lines that crashed on 7 May 1964 after its two pilots were shot. (Fairchild Aircraft)

Little remained of the twin-engine turboprop following its high speed plunge to earth. (Wide World Photos)

on a hill and disintegrated in a ball of fire some 15 miles (25km) east of Oakland. All 44 persons aboard, including a crew of three, perished. In the wreckage was found the remains of a recently-fired .357 Magnum revolver. This was the weapon the suspect had purchased the day before his trip to Reno. A cardboard carton that had contained the weapon was found in a trash can at San Francisco International Airport, where he had also purchased two insurance policies worth a total of $105,000. Found elsewhere in the remains of the aircraft was a piece of tubing from the pilot's seat containing a bullet indentation, evidence that a shooting had taken place in the cockpit.

The manner in which the gunman must have shot the two pilots could not be determined due to the condition of their remains, but it was believed that Captain Ernest Clark had been killed immediately. First Officer Andress may then have tried to save the aircraft and managed to pull up before the F-27 went into its final plunge from an approximate height of 3,000 feet (1,000m). Ironically, a rule requiring that the cockpit door be locked at all times in flight, which in this case might have protected the crew, was introduced only a week before the disaster, but was not to take effect until August.

Francisco Gonzales, who had reportedly told others throughout the previous week of his intention to kill himself, was thus easily able to carry out his threat in a horrifying act of suicide and mass murder.

8 July 1965

A suicide-for-insurance scheme was suspected in the destruction of a Canadian Pacific Air Lines Douglas DC-6B (CF-CUQ). All 52 persons aboard (46 passengers and six crew members) perished when the transport exploded and plummeted to earth vertically near the Canadian town of 100 Mile House, in British Columbia.

Operating as Flight 21 and en route from Vancouver to Prince George, the first segment of a service with an ultimate destination of Whitehorse, Yukon Territory, the aircraft was observed cruising in clear weather conditions at an approximate height of 15,000ft (c5,000m) when witnesses reported a mid-air explosion that tore off its empennage. Its crew managed three 'May Day' distress messages before the DC-6B crashed and burned in a wooded area.

The unknown saboteur was believed to have ignited a mixture of acid and gunpowder, which may have been poured into the toilet bowl in the left rear lavatory.

Skyjack by Parachute

When the man known as D.B. Cooper leapt from a 727 into the darkness over the American Pacific North-west, he opened a bizarre new chapter in the world of aerial piracy. The idea was actually quite ingenious, for it tackled the dilemma that had always faced the hijacker: where to go after the aircraft lands?

However, the success rate of the parachuting hijacker was very, *very* low – in fact, none of those who employed this daring gimmick escaped, with the single exception of D.B. Cooper (and there were indications that even he didn't make it). Subsequent air pirates generally displayed less creativity than Cooper, in some cases not even realizing that only certain types of aircraft had a rear stairway from which such a jump could be made with relative safety.

Skyjacking by parachute virtually disappeared after the early-1970s, and with such a high rate of failure it is easy to understand why. But whether he is seen as an almost-heroic figure, one who 'got away with it', or just another ruthless criminal, D.B. Cooper and the legend associated with him will probably remain an indelible part of aviation history.

The following is a list of actual or would-be parachuting hijackers, excepting those involving fatalities, which appeared in a previous chapter.

12–13 November 1971

CONTRARY to popular belief, 'D.B. Cooper' was not the first air pirate to attempt a parachute escape from a hijacked airliner. That distinction goes to the lone assailant who commandeered Air Canada Flight 812, a DC-8 jet carrying 125 persons on a domestic service from Vancouver, British Columbia, to Toronto, Ontario. The hijacker, who claimed to be a member of the Irish Republican Army, was armed with a sawn-off shotgun, and had threatened to destroy the aircraft with dynamite.

The DC-8 landed twice at Great Falls, Montana, the first time for refuelling and the acquisition of $50,000 – only a small part of the $1.5 million he was demanding – and the second time to release all of the passengers. Originally the gunman asked to be taken to Ireland, but he then had the aircraft zig-zagging all over southern Canada and the northern US. He also demanded and was provided with a parachute, which he prepared to use as the jet neared Calgary, Alberta.

It was not known exactly how he planned to jump from one of the DC-8's side doors, but it never came to that anyway. As he bent over to put on the parachute, he was hit over the head with the blunt end of a fire axe, wielded by the captain. Seriously injured, he was arrested, and later sentenced to life imprisonment.

24 November 1971

ONE of the passengers who boarded Northwest Airlines Flight 305 at Portland, Oregon, was about to make history; the other 41 persons aboard were to become a part of history. Claiming to have a bomb, the lone assailant, known only by the alias 'D. B. Cooper', took over the Boeing 727 jet as it proceeded to Seattle, Washington, the final destination of the flight, which had originated at Washington, DC. He demanded $200,000 and four parachutes. A ransom request was rare in the history of US hijackings, but the demand for parachutes was a novelty.

The aircraft landed at Seattle, where all the passengers and two of the three cabin attendants were released, and the 727 then proceeded back south, followed by two military jet fighters. The aircraft had been ordered to Reno, Nevada, with the flight crew being asked to maintain a height of not over 10,000ft (3,000m), and a low air speed, with the undercarriage and flaps extended. When the aircraft landed at Reno, the air pirate, the money,

Artist's concept of D. B. Cooper, the most famous of the parachuting air pirates. (Wide World Photos)

and two of the parachutes were gone. He had obviously opened and jumped out from the rear stairway over the Cascade Mountains in the area of southern Washington and northern Oregon.

Interest in the mystery waned until 1980, when it was renewed after some of the ransom money was unearthed along the bank of the Columbia River, near Vancouver, Washington. This find led many to believe that the hijacker had been killed in the jump. There were other reasons to believe this as well, for one of the two parachutes he took with him was a ground training model, and could not be opened.

The case of 'D. B. Cooper' may forever remain a mystery; somewhat easier to understand was the ensuing spate of copy-cat hijackings, none of which would succeed.

24 December 1971

A lone hijacker armed with a revolver and an alleged bomb, which turned out to be a fake, commandeered Northwest Airlines Flight 734, a Boeing 707 jetliner en route to Chicago from Minneapolis, Minnesota, with 35 persons aboard. He demanded a ransom of $300,000 and two parachutes, but later surrendered. He was committed to

a psychiatric facility and charges against him were dropped.

12 January 1972

DEMANDING $1 million and 10 parachutes, a lone assailant hijacked Braniff International Airways Flight 38, a Boeing 727 jet carrying 101 persons on an intrastate service from Houston to Dallas, Texas. He subsequently surrendered and was sentenced to 20 years' imprisonment.

20 January 1972

A Hughes Airwest twin-jet DC-9, designated as Flight 800 and carrying 73 persons, was commandeered during an intrastate service from Las Vegas to Reno, Nevada. The hijacker, who had demanded half-a-million dollars and two parachutes, jumped from the aircraft in the vicinity of Denver, Colorado. He was captured, however, and later sentenced to prison for 40 years.

7 April 1972

A lone assailant armed with a pistol and an alleged bomb hijacked United Air Lines Flight 885, a

20 January 1972: A stewardess picks up the money in a hijack-for-ransom involving a Hughes Airwest DC-9. (Wide World Photos)

Boeing 727 jet that had been on a domestic service from Denver, Colorado, to Los Angeles, California, with 91 persons aboard. Demanding $500,000, he parachuted from the aircraft near Provo, Utah, and was captured shortly thereafter. He was sentenced to 45 years in prison, and after escaping was killed resisting capture in 1974.

9 April 1972

PACIFIC Southwest Airlines Flight 942, a Boeing 727 jet on an intrastate service from Oakland to San Diego, California, with 92 persons aboard, was hijacked by a lone assailant who, claiming to have a hand-grenade, demanded $500,000 and four parachutes, which he never used. He was subsequently captured and placed in a psychiatric facility for a year.

5 May 1972

AN Eastern Airlines Boeing 727 jet, designated as Flight 175 and carrying 55 persons on a domestic service from Allentown, Pennsylvania, to Washington, DC, was commandeered by a passenger who was armed with a pistol and also said he had a bomb. Carrying a ransom of more than

$300,000, he parachuted from the aircraft over Honduras, but was later captured. He was sentenced to life imprisonment that September; the money was recovered about a year after the crime.

2 June 1972

IN the first of two US airline hijackings in a single day, a man and a woman commandeered a Western Air Lines Boeing 727 jetliner, operating as Flight 701, which had been on a domestic service from Los Angeles, California, to Seattle, Washington, with 97 persons aboard.

The hijackers received $500,000 in ransom money, which would later be recovered, and five parachutes, which would not be used. Switching to a longer-range Boeing 720 jet at San Francisco, the couple were flown to Algiers, Algeria, where they surrendered. Arrested in France three years later, the man was given a prison sentence of five years, but his accomplice remained a fugitive.

2 June 1972

THE second hijacking of the day involved a United Air Lines Boeing 727 jet, designated as Flight 239, which a lone gunman forcefully boarded at Reno,

Nevada, as it was preparing for a domestic service to San Francisco, California. He parachuted from the aircraft in the vicinity of Lake Washoe, Nevada, some 25 miles (40km) south of Reno, with about three-quarters of the $200,000 ransom he had obtained, but was captured within two hours and subsequently sentenced to 30 years' imprisonment.

23 June 1972

ARMED with a sub-machine-gun, a hijacker commandeered American Airlines Flight 119, a Boeing 727 jet carrying 101 persons on a domestic US service from St Louis, Missouri, to Tulsa, Oklahoma. Demanding more than half-a-million dollars in ransom, he parachuted from the aircraft in the vicinity of Peru, Indiana. He got caught five days later, and was subsequently sentenced to life imprisonment.

30 June 1972

A Hughes Airwest DC-9 twin-jet airliner, which was operating as Flight 775 on a domestic US service from Seattle, Washington, to Portland, Oregon, was targeted for hijack by a lone assailant who turned out to be unarmed. His demand was for $50,000 and a parachute, though he was captured on the ground at the aircraft's intended destination. He was committed to a psychiatric facility five days later.

6 July 1972

A lone gunman hijacked Pacific Southwest Airlines (PSA) Flight 389, a Boeing 727 jet carrying 58 persons on a domestic intrastate service from Oakland to Sacramento, California. He demanded a ransom of $455,000 and a parachute, but later surrendered after the aircraft had returned to its point of origin. He was subsequently sentenced to prison for 30 years.

10 July 1972

A Lufthansa German Airlines twin-jet Boeing 737 was hijacked during a scheduled domestic service from Cologne to Munich, with the lone assailant demanding a ransom and a parachute. He was overpowered and captured by police.

12 July 1972

THE first of two US hijacks-for-ransom on the same day involved a National Airlines Boeing 727 jet, operating as Flight 496 on a domestic service to New York City from Philadelphia, Pennsylvania, with 120 persons aboard. The two assailants demanded three parachutes and $600,000, but they subsequently surrendered. They were sentenced to 50 and 60 years' imprisonment respectively.

12 July 1972

A lone hijacker took over American Airlines Flight 633, a Boeing 727 jet carrying 57 persons on a domestic US service from Oklahoma City, Oklahoma, to Dallas, Texas. He demanded a ransom of more than half-a-million dollars and a parachute, but then surrendered. He would later be sentenced to life imprisonment.

12 March 1974

A Japan Air Lines Boeing 747 wide-bodied jetliner was hijacked during a scheduled service from Tokyo to Okinawa by a lone assailant who also demanded $55 million, 200 million yen, 15 parachutes, and mountain-climbing gear. He was captured on the ground at Naha, Okinawa, by police dressed as food handlers.

11 July 1980

SKYJACKINGS by parachute had faded into distant memory when a 15-year-old boy commandeered Northwest Airlines Flight 608 on a domestic US service from Seattle, Washington, to Portland, Oregon. He demanded $100,000, a parachute, and a light aeroplane, but was captured on the ground. A prison sentence of 20 years was later deferred, and he underwent psychiatric treatment and vocational training.

18 January 1983

THREE men hijacked a Thai Airways Shorts 330 twin-engine turboprop that had been on a scheduled domestic service from Phitsanulok to Chiang Mai, and their demand for three parachutes was refused. They escaped from the aircraft as it was on the ground, but two were subsequently captured.

Shot Up and Shot Down

Not all violent acts against commercial aircraft are committed by greedy individuals or amoral terrorist groups. A number of aircraft have simply been shot down, even by established and democratic governments.

Commercial airliners have, on occasion, been mistaken for combat or other types of military aircraft, or have simply been victims of haste and faulty judgement. Israel, which lost a transport to hostile action in 1955, repeated the mistake itself with the downing of an off-course Libyan jetliner nearly two decades later. A navigational error apparently precipitated the downing of Korean Air Lines Flight 007 by the Soviet Union in 1983. The event sparked harsh criticism by the United States, which would find itself at the opposite end of a similar controversy five years later, after shooting down a wide-bodied transport flying along a prescribed airway.

Occasionally, aircraft have been targeted for destruction by ground forces, though sometimes it has simply been a matter of being in the wrong place at the wrong time.

As might be expected, all such events are more likely to occur during wartime, but they have occurred in peacetime too, especially during the uneasy era of the 'Cold War'.

Although arguably falling outside of the technical definition of 'aerial terrorism', the following is a list of all air-to-air and surface-to-air attacks by military or quasi-military forces on commercial aircraft that were in operation at the time or which resulted in

A Korean Air Lines Boeing 747-200B of the type involved in history's most notorious incident of a commercial airliner being shot down, that of Flight 007 in September 1983. (Photo by Douglas Green)

human casualties, excepting ground assaults by terrorist groups, which have been dealt with elsewhere.

24 August 1938

A China National Aviation Corporation Douglas DC-2 on a scheduled service from Hong Kong to Chungking was attacked by five Japanese military fighters, then strafed after it had ditched in the Pearl River near Wangmoon, China, located some 225 miles (360km) north-west of Macao. Of the 17 persons aboard, only one passenger and two members of its crew of four (the pilot and radio operator) survived. The wreckage was later salvaged, and the bodies of all but three of the victims were recovered.

6 May 1939

A Chinese Eurasia Aviation Corporation Junkers Ju.52/3M (XVII) was reportedly shot down near Hanchung, China, by Japanese aircraft. The number of casualties is not known.

14 June 1940

A Junkers Ju.52/3m (OH-ALL) flown by the Finnish carrier Aero O/Y was shot down near Kar, Estonian SSR, USSR, by a Soviet military aircraft, and all nine persons aboard the trimotored transport were killed.

20 June 1940

AN Air France Dewoitine D.338 three-engine airliner (F-ARTD) was inadvertently shot down by French anti-aircraft fire near Ouistreham, Normandy, France, and its pilot was killed.

7 July 1940

AN Air France Dewoitine D.338 (F-AQBA) was shot down by a Japanese fighter over the Gulf of Tonkin, off French Indo-China. The number of casualties is not known.

27 October 1940

A Eurasia Junkers Ju.52/3m airliner *(XXV)* was attacked by a Japanese aircraft and crash-landed near Kunming, Yunnan, China. Among its four occupants, both crew members were injured but the two passengers escaped unscathed.

29 October 1940

NINE persons aboard were killed when a China National Aviation Corporation Douglas DC-2 on a scheduled domestic flight from Chungking to Kunming was attacked by Japanese fighters, then strafed on the ground after crash-landing some 75 miles (120km) north-east of its destination. Three passengers and two crew-members, one of them the co-pilot, survived.

27 November 1940

AN Air France Farman F-224 four-engine airliner (F-AROA) was shot down by an Italian aircraft over the Mediterranean. The number of casualties is not known.

3 June 1941

A Great Western and Southern Air Lines de Havilland Dragon (G-ACPY), on a domestic British service from the Isles of Scilly to Penzance, Cornwall, was lost over the Atlantic with six persons aboard (five passengers and the pilot). The twin-engine commercial biplane was believed shot down by German military aircraft shortly after its departure at around 17:00 local time.

24 January 1942

A Dutch Koninklijke Nederlandsch-Indische Luchtvaart Maatschappij (KNILM) Douglas DC-3 airliner (PK-AFW) was reportedly shot down by the Japanese near Samarinda, on the island of Borneo. The number of casualties is not known.

26 January 1942

ANOTHER transport flown by the Dutch airline Koninklijke Nederlandsch-Indische Luchtvaart Maatschappij (KNILM), this one a Grumman Goose twin-engine amphibian (PK-AFS), was shot down by Japanese military aircraft near Kupang, on the Western Pacific island of Timor. The number of casualties is unknown.

30 January 1942

A British Overseas Airways Corporation (BOAC) Short S.23 'Empire Class' flying boat (G-AEUH), on a scheduled service for the Australian carrier Qantas Empire Airways from Darwin, in the Northern Territory of Australia, to Kupang, on the island of Timor, was reportedly shot down at sea by Japanese aircraft near its destination. Five survivors were rescued from among the 18 persons aboard, including two of the transport's crew of five.

15 February 1942

A British Overseas Airways Corporation (BOAC) Consolidated Liberator four-engine transport (G-AGDR) was apparently shot down by accident and crashed in the English Channel south of Plymouth, England, in the vicinity of the

Eddystone Lighthouse. All nine persons aboard (four passengers and a crew of five) were killed.

28 February 1942

A British Overseas Airways Corporation (BOAC) Short S.23 (G-AETZ) with 20 persons aboard (16 passengers and a crew of four) was lost over the Indian Ocean some 150 miles (250km) from Java, in the Dutch East Indies, from where it had taken off earlier on a scheduled flight to Broome, Western Australia. The four-engine flying boat was believed shot down by Japanese aircraft during a service undertaken by BOAC on behalf of the Australian carrier Qantas Empire Airways.

3 March 1942

FOUR persons aboard were killed and eight others survived when a Dutch Koninklijke Nederlandsch-Indische Luchtvaart Maatschappij (KNILM) DC-3 airliner (PK-AFV) was shot down by Japanese fighters near Wyndham, Western Australia.

28 March 1942

A Linee Aeree Transcontinentali Italiane SA (LATI) Savoia-Marchetti SM 82 (I-BURA) was shot down, apparently at sea, near Sicily. The number of casualties aboard the Italian trimotored airliner is not known.

13 August 1942

AN Air France Liore et Olivier H.246 (F-AREJ) on a scheduled service from Marseille, France, to Algiers, Algeria, was attacked by Royal Air Force Hurricane fighters some 50 miles (80km) from its destination. The four-engine flying boat actually reached Algiers, but sank after landing in the water, four passengers losing their lives.

15 November 1942

THE number of casualties and the location of the shooting-down of a Linee Aeree Transcontinentali Italiane SA (LATI) Savoia-Marchetti SM 75 tri-motor airliner (I-TELO) are not known. It was probably on an Italian domestic flight.

10 April 1943

A Linee Aeree Transcontinentali Italiane SA (LATI) Savoia-Marchetti SM 75 (I-BONI) was shot down, although the location and the number of casualties aboard the Italian trimotor airliner are not known.

1 June 1943

ONE of the commercial air routes not disrupted by the Second World War was the one between Portugal and England. It was while on this service that one civil airliner met with a violent end.

The twin-engine Douglas DC-3 in question was operated by KLM Royal Dutch Airlines but, owing to the German occupation of the Netherlands, it was registered to the UK as G-AGBB. Designated as Flight 2L272, the transport departed from Portela Airport, serving Lisbon, bound for an airfield at Whitchurch in Somerset, England. It was to follow the coasts of Portugal and Spain, staying clear of occupied France.

During its flight, eight Luftwaffe Junkers Ju.88 twin-engine fighters took off from France. Perhaps it was fate, or perhaps it was German intelligence gathering combined with good timing, but the paths of the fighters and G-AGBB intersected over the Bay of Biscay at around 13:00 local time.

Soon after visual contact with the airliner was established, an attack commenced. The radio operator of the DC-3 was able to transmit a message before the fighters struck; moments later, the airliner, which had been set afire, plummeted into the sea. All 17 persons aboard perished, including a crew of four and British actor turned Hollywood star Leslie Howard. The German pilots reported seeing four parachutes, but this could not be explained as the airliner was not known to have been carrying such emergency equipment.

The German attack on an unarmed commercial transport may have been ruthless, but it was not unprecedented; twice in the previous six months aircraft flying along the same route had come under attack, though on both earlier occasions they had managed to escape.

27 August 1943

A Douglas DC-3 (SE-BAF) flown by the Swedish carrier Aktiebolaget Aerotransport (ABA) was apparently shot down by German aircraft over the North Sea during a scheduled service to Sweden from England. There were no survivors among the seven persons (three passengers and four crew members) aboard the transport.

22 October 1943

AN Aktiebolaget Aerotransport (ABA) DC-3 (SE-BAG) was shot down by German aircraft near Halla, Vasterbotten, Sweden, located about 60 miles (100km) north-west of Ornskoldsvik, possibly during a scheduled domestic service. All but two of the 15 persons aboard the airliner were killed in the incident.

21 April 1945

IN the closing days of the Second World War, Allied forces shot down a Deutsche Luft Hansa AG

Focke-Wulf Fw.200 Condor (D-ASHH) near Piesenkofen, Germany. The German four-engine airliner was capable of carrying about two dozen passengers, but the casualties resulting from this incident are not known.

25 July 1950

AFTER refusing its order to land, a DC-3 flown by the Lebanese carrier Compagnie Générale de Transport was attacked by an Israeli Air Force Spitfire fighter over Israeli territory north of Rosh Pinna, near the Sea of Galilee. Among the 28 persons aboard the airliner, one passenger and the radio operator were killed by the Spitfire's guns, while seven others suffered injuries.

Following the attack, which occurred at around 19:15 local time, the DC-3 flew back across the border and the fighter gave up the pursuit. Lebanese officials insisted that their aircraft never entered Israeli airspace and had been flying three miles (5km) north of the border when attacked.

27 July 1953

IN what proved to be the last military action of the Korean War, a twin-engine Ilyushin Il-12 operated by the Soviet airline Aeroflot was shot down by a US Air Force F-86 jet fighter, about 10 miles (15km) south of the Yalu River, North Korea. All 21 persons aboard (15 passengers and six crew members) were killed. The Soviet Union claimed the attack had occurred over China.

According to the US Air Force, the Il-12, which it identified as a transport 'assigned to Communist Air Forces in China', was flying in an easterly direction when spotted some 35 miles (55km) north-east of Kanggye. The Soviets identified it as a regular commercial flight to the USSR from Lushun, Liaoning, China.

After one firing pass by the F-86, both engines of the Ilyushin transport caught fire, and soon afterward, at about 12:30 local time, the aircraft exploded and plummeted to earth.

3 June 1954

A Belgian Airlines (SABENA) DC-3 cargo transport carrying a load of pigs was attacked by a MiG jet fighter in Soviet markings whilst flying at 11,500ft (c3,500m) just inside the Yugoslav border, over the town of Murska Sobata. Its radio operator was killed and two of its other three crew members were wounded, though the damaged DC-3 managed a forced landing near Graz, Austria.

The transport had been on a scheduled service from London to Belgrade, Yugoslavia, when the fighter reportedly dived out of the clouds and tried to force it towards Hungarian airspace at around 10:00 local time. When the airline crew ignored the action, the MiG opened up with cannon fire.

23 July 1954

AT about 09:45 local time, a Cathay Pacific Airways Douglas DC-4 (VR-HEU) on a scheduled service from Singapore to Hong Kong was shot down by two Communist Chinese MiG jet fighters, ditching off Hainan Island in the South China Sea. Ten persons aboard the British-operated airliner lost their lives, including two of its six crew members. A US Navy amphibious aircraft rescued the eight survivors.

27 July 1955

THE risks of breaching the 'Iron Curtain' surrounding Eastern Europe were fully realised in this disastrous incident. El Al Israel Airlines Flight 402/26, a Lockheed 049 Constellation (4X-AKC), had stopped at Vienna, Austria, as scheduled, before proceeding on toward Tel Aviv, the second segment of a service originating at London.

After passing over Belgrade, Yugoslavia, the aircraft began to stray to the east of the prescribed airway. An Israeli investigative commission attributed the deviation to an incorrect radio compass indication, the instrument apparently having been affected by thunderstorm activity in the area. This must have misled the crew into believing that they had reached the reporting point at Skopje, Yugoslavia, when in fact the flight was seven minutes from that position. The course would then have been altered to a heading of 142 degrees in order to stay within the airway. Considering the heavy cloud coverage, westerly winds of 70 kts – 50 kts above those forecast – and the absence of navigational aids between Belgrade and Skopje, the crew could not have been aware of their drift.

The Constellation entered Bulgarian airspace some 40 miles (65km) east of the proper track. Shortly thereafter, it radioed the distress message 'SOS DE 4X-AKC'. The first attack by two jet fighters was at the cruising altitude of 18,000 (c5,500), and set the airliner afire. As it was descending, the crew apparently looking for a place to land, a second attack occurred at approximately 8,000ft (2,500m), and a third at about 2,000ft (600m), whereupon an explosion occurred in the right wing, and the aircraft then broke up and plummeted to earth near Petrich, Bulgaria. All 58 persons aboard (51 passengers and a crew of seven) perished. The disaster took place around 07:40 local time.

Israel rejected Bulgaria's contention that the Constellation had been notified within the established regulations but refused to land before the fighters opened fire. Bulgaria maintained it had flown much deeper into its airspace, though this contradicted the

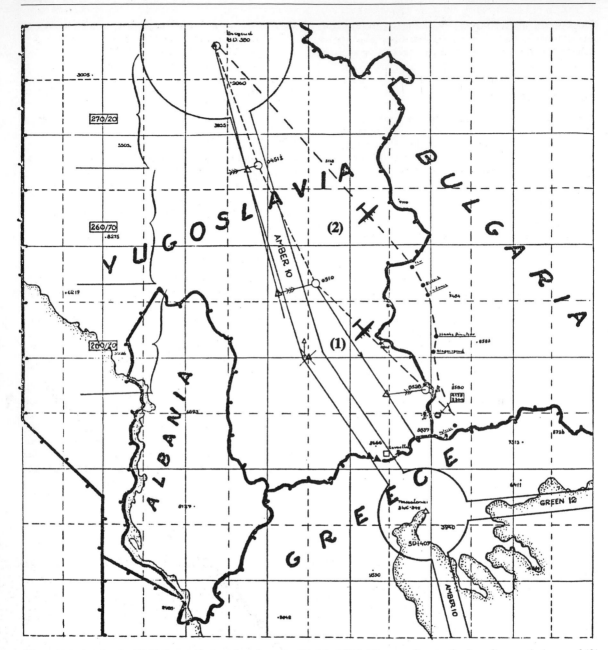

The route taken by the El Al Constellation shot down on 27 July 1955, (1) according to the Israeli commission, and (2) according to the Bulgarian authorities. (International Civil Aviation Organisation)

accounts of ground witnesses in both Yugoslavia and Greece. It also expressed regret over the incident, admitting that its defence forces had exhibited 'a certain haste' in downing the aircraft.

1 June 1959

A twin-engine Curtiss Wright C-46 (TI-1022) flown by the Costa Rican carrier Aerolineas Nacionales SA crashed and burned in Nicaragua after report-

edly being 'forced down' by Nicaraguan Air Force fighters. There were an estimated 50 to 60 persons aboard the airliner, all of whom were killed.

16 September 1965

AN Air Vietnam Douglas DC-3 airliner (XV-NIC) crashed and burned in a rice paddy immediately after it had taken off from Quang Ngai, South Vietnam, on a scheduled domestic service to

Saigon, apparently having been hit by ground fire. Including a crew of three, 39 persons aboard were killed; the one passenger who survived was seriously injured.

10 April 1969

THE three crew members (and only occupants) of an Ethiopian Airlines DC-3 (ET-AAQ) were killed when the cargo transport, being operated for United Arab Airlines on a non-scheduled cargo flight, was reportedly shot down near Suez, Egypt.

26 June 1970

IT was a lucky day for the 104 persons aboard Alitalia Flight 713, a DC-8 Series 43 jet airliner that had been on a service from Tehran, Iran, to Beirut, Lebanon.

Whilst cruising at an approximate height of 30,000ft (10,000m) over Syria, about five miles (10km) east of Damascus, the Italian-registered aircraft experienced a heavy jolt, dropping some 3,000ft (1,000m). Its No 1 power plant having been shut down, the DC-8 landed safely at its intended destination. There were no casualties, but damage to the aircraft was frighteningly serious. In its left wing was found a hole approximately 2ft (0.6m) in diameter, and both port engines were peppered with hundreds of metal fragments. It was concluded that the aircraft had miraculously survived being struck by a missile.

11 February 1972

A Royal Air Lao DC-4 (XW-TDE) was apparently shot down near Vientiane, Laos, where it was to have landed during a scheduled service originating at Saigon, South Vietnam. All 23 persons aboard (17 passengers and a crew of six) were killed. In its last radio transmission, received at 13:20 local time, the airliner was reported to be flying at 10,000ft (3,000m).

2 October 1972

NINE persons aboard, including two pilots, were killed when a Cambodia Air Commercial DC-3 (XW-TDA) was hit by a mortar shell and crashed while approaching to land at Kampot, Cambodia, during a scheduled domestic passenger service. There were no survivors.

21 February 1973

A number of intentional acts of aggression had soured Arab-Israeli relations even before this deadly blunder over the Sinai Peninsula.

Operating as Flight 114, a Libyan Arab Airlines Boeing 727-224 jetliner (5A-DAH) had taken off from Tripoli and stopped at Banghazi before proceeding on towards its ultimate destination, Cairo, Egypt.

Although the aircraft generally assumed the correct heading, its track was displaced to the east, then to the south, of the normal route, leading to its passage of the Egyptian capital. Significantly, a low cloud cover obscured the ground during much of the trip, and it was only when they were over the Sinai, and the terrain had become visible, that the crew realised their incorrect position. By now, however, the 727 had already been spotted on radar

A Libyan Arab Airlines Boeing 727-224 like the one downed over the Sinai by Israeli fighters in February 1973. (Photo by Douglas Green)

by Israeli defence forces, which sent up two F-4 Phantom II jet fighters.

Using hand gestures, rocking their wings and, eventually, by firing their cannons across the nose of the intruder, the military pilots tried to get the commercial transport to land. The airline crew apparently did not understand the actions of the fighter pilots, and when they turned back and raised the undercarriage, which had been lowered, this was construed by the Israelis as an attempt to escape. At an approximate height of 5,000ft (1,500m), 5A-DAH was attacked and hit with tracers, touching off a fire. The jetliner subsequently crashed and exploded some 10 miles (15km) to the east of the Suez Canal, while attempting a belly-landing in the desert, 108 persons aboard being killed, including eight crew members. Four passengers and the aircraft's co-pilot survived with injuries.

The navigational error that led to the shooting down of the 727 probably resulted from a strong tail-wind, and in its report on the tragedy the International Civil Aviation Organisation (ICAO) ruled it 'probable' that the Cairo non-directional beacon had not been functioning properly at the time. In addition, the Cairo approach control radar was out of order, making it impossible for controllers to detect the deviation.

Israeli Defence Minister Moshe Dayan admitted an 'error in judgement' in the downing of the Libyan transport, and his country agreed to compensate the families of the victims.

4 May 1973

THREE persons aboard were killed and eight injured when a Khmer Hansa aircraft, possibly a DC-3, was hit by a mortar shell and crashed as it was taking off from Kampot, Cambodia, about 100 miles (150km) south-west of Phnom Penh.

19 May 1973

A Cambodia Air Commercial DC-3 airliner (XW-TDM) was apparently hit by ground fire shortly after it had taken off from Svay Rieng, Cambodia, crashing some 80 miles (130km) south-east of Phnom Penh. All 11 persons aboard (nine passengers and two pilots) were killed.

28 November 1974

AN Air Cambodge Douglas DC-4 cargo transport on a service from Cambodia to Hong Kong was apparently shot down near An Loc, South Vietnam, some 60 miles (100km) north of Saigon, around 15:00 local time. All five persons aboard were killed.

16 December 1974

A Korean Air Lines DC-8 Super 63 jetliner that had accidentally strayed into restricted airspace was fired at by South Korean anti-aircraft units near Seoul. The aircraft was not hit, but shrapnel falling into the city killed one person and injured 27.

12 March 1975

AN Air Vietnam Douglas DC-4 (XV-NUJ) was apparently shot down by North Vietnamese or Viet Cong forces over the Central Highlands of South Vietnam, approximately 15 miles (25km) south-west of Pleiku, and all 26 persons aboard (20 passengers and a crew of six) were killed.

The airliner was last reported cruising along a prescribed airway at 11,000ft (c3,400m) on a scheduled service to Saigon from Vientiane, Laos, when it was believed to have been hit by anti-aircraft fire or a hand-held surface-to-air missile at around 18:30 local time.

8 April 1975

A South African Airways Boeing 747 wide-bodied jetliner carrying about 300 persons on a scheduled service from Johannesburg to London was hit by ground fire and damaged while landing at Luanda, Angola, an en-route stop. There were no injuries.

11 April 1975

TWO of its three crew members (and only occupants) lost their lives when a Sorya Airlines DC-3 crashed in flames when hit by ground fire as it took off from Phnom Penh, Cambodia, on a domestic flight to Kompong Chnang.

27 June 1976

A Middle East Airlines Boeing 720B jetliner (OO-AGE) that was parked, sans passengers, at the international airport serving Beirut, Lebanon, was destroyed by a rocket hit and shell fire. One member of its flight crew was killed and two others injured.

26 November 1977

AN African Lux C-54B cargo transport (9Q-CAM), on a non-scheduled service from Rhodesia to Zaire, was shot down by Mozambique ground forces over Tete Province, Mozambique. Its two crew members (and only occupants) were reportedly captured.

20 April 1978

THOUGH overshadowed in history by the Soviet

downing of KAL Flight 007 five years later, the following was a headline-grabbing incident in its own right.

The bizarre saga of Korean Air Lines Flight 902 began at Orly Airport, serving Paris, from where the Boeing Advanced 707-321B jetliner (HL-7429) took off, bound for Seoul, South Korea. This polar trip would include an en-route stop at Anchorage, Alaska. Built more than a decade earlier, the aircraft lacked a modern inertial navigational system, and as a magnetic compass is useless in this part of the world, and with a scarcity in ground aids, the crew would have to rely upon the older but well-proven method of celestial navigation.

Trouble first arose in the vicinity of Iceland, when atmospheric conditions prevented the aircraft from communicating with the corresponding ground station. Approximately over Greenland, and following the instructions of the navigator, the 707 inexplicably initiated a turn of 112 degrees, heading in a south-easterly direction toward the USSR. A while later, the pilot, Captain Kim Chang Kyu, sensed something was amiss by the rather obvious fact that the sun was on the wrong side of the aircraft!

Before the crew could take any corrective action, the transport was intercepted by at least two Soviet Su-15 jet fighters, one of which flew just off its starboard wing for 10 to 15 minutes before veering away. (The Soviets would later claim that the fighter pilots had tried in vain to contact the jetliner, though this was refuted by the Korean crew.) Moments later, the 707 was under attack; one of the fighters raked it with cannon fire, blasting away its left wing tip and causing a rapid decompression of its cabin.

Descending rapidly from 35,000 to 5,000ft (c10,700–1,500m), the damaged aircraft was kept under control, the pilot then skilfully crash-landing it on a frozen lake in the twilight, at about 18:45 local time. Among the 109 aboard, two passengers were killed and 13 other persons seriously wounded, all during the aerial attack. Numerous minor injuries were also reported.

The passengers and most of the crew were released two days afterwards, the captain and navigator about a week later. It was learned in 1991 that the Soviet pilot had ignored orders to destroy the 707.

3 September 1978

AIR Rhodesia Flight 825, a four-engine turboprop Vickers Viscount 782D (VP-WAS), had taken off shortly after 17:00 local time from Kariba, on a domestic service to Salisbury. About five minutes later it sent a distress message, reporting the failure of both starboard power plants, the airliner having been struck near the right in-board engine by a heat-seeking missile fired by nationalist guerrillas.

September 1978: Rhodesian security forces recover the remains of victims from a Viscount airliner shot down by Joshua Nkomo's guerrilla forces. (Wide World Photos)

The following day, its wreckage was located in bush country some 35 miles (55km) south-east of Kariba. Eight passengers were found alive among the 56 persons, including a crew of four, who had been aboard the Viscount. The world also learned with horror that 10 others who had survived the crash-landing were murdered, being allegedly shot by the guerrillas.

12 February 1979

FOR the second time in less than six months, an Air Rhodesia airliner was destroyed by nationalist guerrilla forces. All 59 persons aboard (54 passengers and a crew of five) perished when the Vickers Viscount 748D turboprop (VP-YND), designated as Flight 827, was hit by two surface-to-air missiles. It crashed shortly before 17:00 local time approximately 30 miles (50km) east of Kariba, from where it had taken off about five minutes earlier after making an en-route stop during a domestic service originating at Victoria Falls, with an ultimate destination of Salisbury.

The downing was described as a 'mistake' by a guerilla spokesman, resulting from an erroneous belief that the Rhodesian Army commander had been aboard.

8 June 1980

HAVING been reportedly misidentified as a foreign aircraft, a Lineas Aereas de Angola (TAAG-Angola Airlines) Yakovlev Yak-40 (D2-TYC) was accidentally brought down by anti-aircraft fire at around 15:30 local time near Matala, Huila,

Angola, during a scheduled domestic service from Jamba to Lubango. All 19 persons aboard the tri-jet airliner (15 passengers and a crew of four) perished.

23 September 1980

ALL four crew members (its only occupants) were killed when an Iraqi Airways Ilyushin Il-76T (YI-AIO) was apparently shot down during an Iranian air raid as the four-engine cargo jet was approaching to land at Baghdad, Iraq.

16 May 1981

A Lineas Aereas de Angola (TAAG-Angola Airlines) Lockheed 382G (L-100 Series 20) Hercules (D2-EAS) was shot down near Menogue, Angola, its four crew members (and only occupants) being killed. The four-engine turboprop cargo aircraft was approaching to land when hit by a heat-seeking missile in its No 4 power plant at an approximate height of 4,000ft (1,200m).

1 September 1983

THE Cold War never experienced any direct exchanges between the Super Powers, although there were a number of 'flashpoints', during which tensions reached the brink. The most infamous of these was the Cuban missile crisis in 1962, but also standing out in history was the downing by Soviet defence forces of Korean Air Lines Flight 007.

This international incident began as a routine trip from New York City to Seoul, South Korea. Making the flight would be a Boeing 747-230B (HL7442), which made its departure from John F. Kennedy International Airport on the evening of 31 August. Stopping for refuelling and a change of crew at Anchorage, Alaska, the wide-bodied jetliner proceeded on the second leg of its transpacific service. Aboard were 240 passengers, 20 cabin attendants, six off-duty company personnel and three flight crewmen.

Only 10 minutes out of Anchorage, the aircraft began to stray from the prescribed airway, assuming a track that would ultimately take it into the restricted airspace of the Soviet Union. A military radar recording captured this deviation, but it was of little use, since at the time there was no interaction between military and civilian air traffic control services; furthermore, such a deviation was not considered abnormal.

Entering Soviet territory while at a point some 250 miles (400km) north of assigned route R-20, the 747 passed over the southern Kamchatka Peninsula, then the location of both a missile and a submarine base. Fighters that were scrambled into action failed to locate the transport, and it proceeded out over the Sea of Okhotsk. Defence

forces would get a second opportunity as the jetliner again entered Soviet territory, this time over the southern tip of Sakhalin Island, another militarily sensitive area.

Shortly after 06:00 local time, the pilot of a Soviet Air Force Sukhoi Su-15 jet fighter radioed that in the pre-dawn darkness he had made visual contact with what he referred to as the 'target'. During the ensuing pursuit, which lasted some 20 minutes, the Russian was believed to have implemented the IFF (identification friend or foe) code procedure, and then to have fired his cannon in an attempt to get the attention of the airline crew. Unable to make contact with the 747, he ultimately launched two air-to-air missiles, at least one of which struck the transport, possibly in the area of the left wing. The first officer was able to transmit a distress message, reporting cabin decompression and that the aircraft had initiated a descent. Moments later, at about 06:35, the 747 plummeted into the Sea of Japan an estimated 50 miles (80km) south-west of Sakhalin, near the island of Moneron, in international waters, possibly after a mid-air explosion. There was no chance of survival for the 269 persons aboard the aircraft. A small amount of debris was later recovered, as were the remains of several victims.

A report on the tragedy released in 1993 by the newly-established Commonwealth of Independent States (CIS) largely supported the actions of the Soviet defence forces a decade earlier. Using information from the aircraft's digital flight data recorder (DFDR) and cockpit voice recorder (CVR), this new inquiry was able to determine that the crew of Flight 007 had either left the autopilot in the heading mode, or switched it to the inertial navigation system (INS) when already too far off course to capture the desired track. (This was one of two plausible explanations considered by the International Civil Aviation Organisation in its own investigation, the second being the faulty programming of the INS as the 747 sat on the ground at Anchorage.)

Flying with the autopilot in the heading mode should have caused the illumination of lights on the instrument panel indicating that the INS was not engaged. Furthermore, there would have been other ways for the crew to determine the position of the aircraft, even by using the ground-mapping mode of the weather radar installed on HL7442. Nevertheless, the ICAO admitted that such inattentiveness was not 'unknown in international civil aviation'.

The CIS report further stated that the aircraft had been misidentified as an RC-135 reconnaissance jet, one of which the US Air Force had been operating in the area before Flight 007 came along (but which had returned to its base more than an hour before the latter was attacked).

It can be said that the North Pacific route, still

On 10 September 1983, more than a week after its destruction, police officers continue to search for debris from KAL Flight 007, some of which was washed ashore on beaches in northern Japan. (Wide World Photos)

widely used by commercial air traffic, is a lot safer today, not just because of what has subsequently happened within the Russian bloc, but also due to the establishment of a long-range radar system designed to monitor the region, which went into operation in December 1984.

8 November 1983

A Lineas Aereas de Angola (TAAG-Angola Airlines) Boeing Advanced 737-2M2 (D2-TBN) which crashed near Lubango, Huila, Angola, was thought to have been a victim of hostile action. All 130 persons aboard (126 passengers and a crew of four) were killed when the twin-jet transport crashed at around 15:20 local time, immediately after it had taken off on a scheduled domestic service to the capital, Luanda.

Climbing to an approximate height of 200ft (60m), the aircraft made a steep turn to the left before it plummeted to the ground about half-a-mile (0.8km) beyond the end of the airport runway, exploding on impact.

The cause of the disaster given by Angolan authorities was a 'technical failure' during weather conditions described as 'very bad', but it was widely believed that the 737 had been shot down by guerrillas fighting the government at the time, probably by means of a surface-to-air missile.

4 September 1985

A Bakhtar Afghan Airlines Antonov An-26 (YA-BAM) was shot down over western Afghanistan, about 12 miles (20km) east of Kandahar, from where it had taken off minutes earlier on a scheduled domestic service to Farah province. All 52 persons aboard (48 passengers and a crew of five) were killed in the crash, which occurred shortly after 11:00 local time.

According to the Afghan government, the Soviet-built twin-engine turboprop was hit at an approximate height of 13,000ft (4,000m) by a surface-to-air missile fired by guerrillas.

20 February 1986

AN Iran Asseman Airlines Fokker F.27 Friendship Mark 600 twin-engine turboprop (EP-ANA), on a non-scheduled domestic service from Tehran to Ahwaz, in the province of Khuzestan, was shot down about 20 miles (30km) north-east of its destination by an Iraqi jet fighter. All 49 persons aboard (44 passengers and a crew of five) were killed when the aircraft was hit by at least one air-to-air missile at about 12:25 local time, some 330 miles (530km) south-west of the Iranian capital.

16 August 1986

A Sudan Airways Fokker F.27 Mark 400M Friendship turboprop airliner (ST-ADY) was shot down at around 10:30 local time shortly after it had taken off from Malakal, Sobat, on a scheduled domestic service to the Sudanese capital of Khartoum. It plunged to earth in flames, and all 60 persons aboard (57 passengers and three crew members) perished.

The aircraft was reportedly struck by a SAM-7 surface-to-air missile fired by Sudanese rebels. The airline subsequently suspended flights to the southern part of the country.

15 October 1986

IRAQI warplanes attacked an Iran Air Boeing Advanced 737-286 (EP-IRG) as the jet airliner was discharging passengers on the ground at Shiraz airport in Iran's Fars Province at about 17:00 local time. Of the estimated 80 persons aboard, three passengers lost their lives in the attack and some 30 other persons were injured. The 737 was destroyed.

31 December 1986

A United Airlines Boeing 737 jet, operating as Flight 1502, was hit by ground fire while approaching to land at the Raleigh-Durham airport, North Carolina. A male passenger was wounded, but the aircraft reached its intended destination safely. An

FBI investigation indicated that the gunman responsible for the attack was aiming at the pilot; the assailant was later sentenced to prison for 20 years.

9 March 1987

ALL three occupants were killed when an Aero Express DC-3 (N49454) was shot down by Honduran forces over southern Honduras, near El Paraiso, while on a suspected drug-smuggling operation.

14 October 1987

A Zimex Aviation Lockheed 382G (L-100-30) Hercules four-engine turboprop cargo transport (HB-ILF) was hit by a heat-seeking surface-to-air missile about five minutes after take-off from Cutato, Bie, Angola. Struck in its No 3 power plant at an approximate height of 2,000ft (600m), which resulted in an uncontrollable fire, the Swiss-registered aircraft crashed while trying to return to its point of departure, killing its six occupants (four crew and two passengers) as well as two persons on the ground.

6 November 1987

TEN persons (eight passengers and two pilots) were killed when an Air Malawi Shorts Skyvan Series 3 (7Q-YMB) was shot down near Ulonque, Tete, Mozambique. There were no survivors. The twin-engine turboprop had been on a domestic charter service from Blantyre to the capital city, Lilongwe. Mozambique military forces had received no advance information about the flight, and destroyed the aircraft at around 08:30 local time.

It was subsequently recommended that aircraft intending to fly over or land in Mozambique should first apply for authorisation from competent government authorities to avoid a repetition of this tragedy.

21 April 1988

BOTH crew members (its only occupants) lost their lives when an African Air Carriers DC-3 (N47FE) crashed near Quelimane, Mozambique. The cargo transport was believed to have been shot down.

3 July 1988

FIVE years after the downing of KAL Flight 007, for which it had verbally lashed the USSR, the United States found itself on the opposite side of a similar controversy after one of its navy ships destroyed an Iranian wide-bodied jetliner over the Persian Gulf.

The genesis of this tragedy dated back more than a year, when US Naval forces began convoying Kuwaiti oil tankers to counter the attacks on civilian ships that had grown out of the Iran-Iraq War. The risks soon became apparent when, in May 1987, a missile, fired supposedly 'accidentally' by an Iraqi jet fighter, struck the frigate *Stark*, killing 37 American sailors.

In the wake of the *Stark* incident, a new set of 'rules of engagement' were formulated in order to clarify the authority of US commanders to take protective measures when facing 'hostile intent'.

American forces were alerted to the probability of significant Iranian military activity during the weekend that encompassed the American Independence Day holiday. On the morning of Sunday 3 July, the US Navy cruiser *Vincennes* and the frigate *Elmer Montgomery* had become involved in a skirmish with some Iranian gunboats in the Strait of Hormuz. During this time, Iran Air Flight 655, a twin-jet Airbus A300B2-203 (EP-IBU), took off from the Bandar Abbas international airport, which was used by both civilian and military aircraft, bound for Dubai in the United Arab Emirates. In the confusion of the moment, i.e. with the surface battle continuing and with an Iranian P-3 patrol aircraft in the vicinity, conceivably providing targeting information, the Airbus was misidentified as an F-14 jet fighter. As the commercial jet proceeded on a heading of 200 degrees, its flight path generally along the prescribed airway but slightly to the right of its centreline, the crew was given a number of warnings from the *Vincennes* and the American frigate *John Sides*. Faced with the potential of another disaster such as that suffered by the *Stark*, the commanding officer of the *Vincennes*, Captain Will Rogers III, ordered the launch of two Standard surface-to-air missiles. At a position about 10 miles (15km) from the vessel, the aircraft was hit at around 10:25 local time and at an approximate altitude of 13,500ft (4,100m). One wing and its tail having been broken off, it plummeted into the water near the island of Henqam. All 290 persons aboard (274 passengers and 16 crew members) perished.

Conducting its own inquiry into the tragedy, the US Navy revealed the underlying factor in the misidentification. The atmospheric conditions in the Persian Gulf at the time, with a high level of evaporation, were conducive to radar ducting, or the bouncing of the signal. The ship had apparently picked up a Mode II signal emanating from a military aircraft, perhaps an F-14 or even a C-130 transport, that was on the ground at the same airport from which EP-IBU had taken off.

Interestingly, tape recordings of the ship's defence system clearly indicated a Mode III transponder code, normally associated with a civilian aircraft. Pivotal in the decision to destroy the A300 was a report that the target was descending toward the ship, when in reality its altitude was

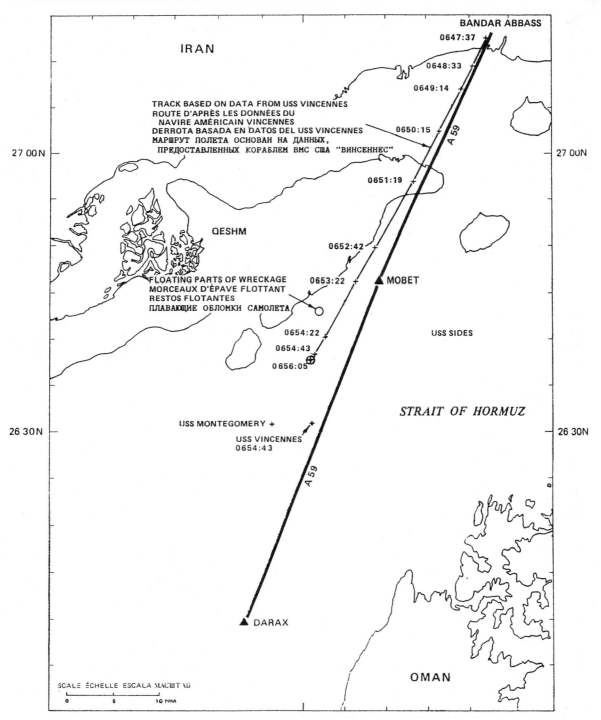

A map showing the slight displacement from the airway centreline of the Iran Air A300 destroyed on 3 July 1988, and its position relative to the Vincennes, *which shot it down, and other US Navy ships.* (International Civil Aviation Organisation)

increasing. This could have happened had the tactical information co-ordinator passed on only range values, which were interpreted as height, or if he misread his read-out and interchanged altitude and range. Also, due to the weather conditions, actual visual contact with the airliner was never made.

Radio challenges had been made to Flight 655, including the threat of defensive action, on both military air defence (MAD) and international air defence (IAD) frequencies. Although EP-IBU was not equipped to receive the MAD frequency, its pilots should have been monitoring IAD when flying in the Gulf area. They either may not have been doing so, or perhaps did not identify theirs as the challenged aircraft.

The Navy report referred to the downing as a 'tragic and regrettable accident', placing some of the blame on Iran itself for allowing an airliner to operate in a 'war zone'. Conceding to its error, the US would some eight years later agree to pay more than $60 million in damages to the families of those killed aboard Flight 655.

8 April 1989

DURING its approach to land at Luena, Moxico, Angola, the No 2 power plant of a Lockheed 382E (L-100-20) Hercules (S9-NAI) cargo transport, operated by the Sao Tome and Principe-based airline Transafrick Corporation Ltd, caught fire. The four-engine turboprop landed in scrub approximately one mile (1.5km) from the airfield, where it burnt out. Its crew of three escaped unscathed.

The wreckage showed evidence of small arms fire, but it could not be determined whether the aircraft had been struck before or after its forced landing.

28 June 1989

A Somali Airlines Fokker F.27 Friendship Mark 600RF (60-SAZ) was believed shot down by rebels near Borama, Woqooyi Galbeed, Somalia, all 30 persons aboard (24 passengers and a crew of six) being killed. Apparently hit by a surface-to-air missile, it crashed shortly before 09:30 local time, about 10 minutes after the twin-engine turboprop had taken off from Hargeysa on a scheduled domestic service to Mogadiscio.

5 January 1990

A Lineas Aereas de Angola (TAAG-Angola Airlines) Lockheed 382B (L-100) Hercules (D2-THB) was hit in its No 4 power plant by a heat-seeking missile after taking off from Menongue, Cuando Cubango, Angola. The four-engine turboprop cargo aircraft, its right wing ablaze, managed to return to its point of origin, but on landing ran off the airfield runway on to rough terrain and was destroyed. There were no serious injuries among the seven persons aboard.

12 June 1990

AN Aeroflot Ilyushin Il-76T jet freighter (SSSR-

86905) was hit by a surface-to-air missile over Afghanistan, and subsequently belly-landed at Kabul. The aircraft was destroyed and two of the 10 persons aboard were seriously injured.

2 October 1990

AN Iraqi Airways Il-76 jet transport, believed to have been carrying military personnel, was shot down near Kuwait City, Kuwait, killing approximately 130 persons aboard. There were no survivors. The aircraft was hit by a surface-to-air missile fired by Kuwaiti resistance fighters, the downing occurring during the occupation of Kuwait by Iraqi forces.

16 March 1991

NINE persons aboard (five passengers and a crew of four) perished when a Lockheed 382G (L-100-30) Hercules (CP-1564), flown by the Sao Tome and Principe-based Transafrick Corporation Ltd, was shot down near the town of Malanje, Angola, apparently by rebel forces. There were no survivors. The four-engine turboprop cargo aircraft was reportedly hit by a surface-to-air missile at a height of 17,000ft (c5,200m) while on an internal Angolan service from Luanda to the province of Lunda Norte.

10 July 1991

AN Aeroshasqui SA CASA 212-200 Aviocar (OB-1218) was shot down by members of Peru's national police force near Bellavista, Loreto. All 15 persons aboard the Peruvian-registered twin-engine turboprop (13 passengers and two pilots) were killed.

The police officers, who reportedly had been drinking, had tried to stop the airliner from taking off from the local airport so that it could be searched, and opened fire when it returned to land. Both pilots were shot and the aircraft then plummeted to the ground at around 16:50 local time.

28 January 1992

ALL 47 persons aboard were killed when a turbine-engine Mil MI-8 believed flown by Aeroflot, the airline of the newly-established Commonwealth of Independent States, was shot down about five miles (10km) south of Stepanakert, Azerbayzhan. The aircraft, en route from Agdam to Shusha, was hit by a surface-to-air missile, exploded, and crashed near its destination, resulting in the highest death toll ever in a commercial helicopter disaster.

27 March 1992

AN Aeroflot Yak-40 jet airliner was hit by a heat-seeking missile shortly after it took off from

Stepanakert, Azerbayzhan, on a scheduled service to Yerevan, Armenia. The damaged aircraft landed safely despite a fire that was subsequently extinguished. Ten passengers suffered minor injuries.

29 May 1992

AN Ariana Afghan Airlines Tu-154 jetliner, on a non-scheduled service, was hit by a missile near Kabul, Afghanistan. One of the pilots was wounded but the aircraft landed safely. The Tu-154 had been hit at an approximate height of 600ft (200m) above the ground during its final approach to land at the city's airport.

26 April 1993

A Komiavia Kontsem An-12 cargo aircraft (RA-11121) was hit in its No 4 power plant by a surface-to-air missile at a height of around 15,000ft (c5,000m) over Angola. The four-engine turboprop crash-landed in a field near Luena, in the province of Moxico, from where it had taken off earlier on an internal Angolan service to Catumbela. Although there had been no fatalities as a result of either the missile-strike or the crash, one crew member was killed when he stepped on a land-mine; a second suffered injuries.

21 September 1993

A Transair Georgia Airlines twin-jet Tupolev Tu-134A (SSSR-65893) was allegedly shot down by Abkhazi separatist forces over the Black Sea near Sukhumi, Georgia, CIS. All 27 persons aboard (22 passengers and a crew of five) were killed. The aircraft had been on a non-scheduled service from Sochi, Russian Federation, and was on its approach when reportedly hit at an altitude of around 1,000ft (300m) by a missile fired from a patrol boat, which sent it plunging into the water about 2¹/₂ miles (4km) from Babusheri Airport, serving Sukhumi, where it was to have landed.

22 September 1993

WHILE landing at the Babusheri Airport, serving Sukhumi, Georgia, CIS, a Transair Georgia Airlines Tupolev Tu-154B jetliner (SSSR-85163), which had been on a Defence Ministry of Georgia domestic charter service from Tiblisi and was carrying mostly military personnel, was hit by a missile apparently fired by Abkhazi separatists. Of the 132 persons aboard the aircraft, 106 were killed in the subsequent crash, including half of its 12 crew members. All the survivors suffered serious injuries. The Tu-154 was just about to touch down in twilight conditions when the missile-strike occurred at about 18:30 local time.

23 September 1993

THE pilot was killed when a Transair Georgia Airlines Tupolev Tu-134A (SSSR-65001), which was on the ground boarding soldiers and refugees at Babusheri Airport, serving Sukhumi, Georgia, CIS, was hit by a mortar or artillery shell that had apparently been fired from offshore in the Black Sea. Numerous passengers suffered injuries and the twin-engine jet, which was on a non-scheduled domestic service to Tiblisi, was destroyed.

27 July 1994

ALL seven occupants were killed when a Russian-built and registered Kiev Airlines Antonov An-26 twin-engine turboprop cargo aircraft was shot down near Bihac, in Bosnia-Herzegovina, as it approached to land, crashing in a minefield.

28 January 1995

A twin-engine turboprop Beechcraft Super King Air 200 (D2-ECH), flown by the Angolan operator Aviacao Ligeira, crashed shortly after take-off from Cafunfo, Angola, apparently when hit by a missile. Two of the aircraft's six occupants were killed.

28 April 1995

OPERATED by the Sri Lankan carrier Helitours, a British Aerospace BAe 748 Series 2A (4R-HVB) crashed near Jaffna, Sri Lanka, killing all 45 persons aboard (42 passengers and a crew of three). The twin-engine turboprop had just taken off from Palay Air Force Base, on a non-scheduled domestic trooping flight to Colombo, when the pilot requested permission to return due to a fire in its left power plant. However, the flames spread to its wing before a safe landing could be made, and the aircraft crashed some 700ft (200m) short of the runway. A surface-to-air missile was believed responsible for bringing down the airliner.

29 April 1995

ANOTHER Helitours aircraft, a British Aerospace BAe 748 Series 2B (4R-HVA), was shot down near Jaffna, Sri Lanka, and all 52 persons aboard (49 passengers and a crew of three) were killed. The twin-engine turboprop, on a domestic military charter service from Anuradhapura, crashed and burned some five miles (10km) from Palay Air Force Base, where it was to have landed, after reportedly being struck by a surface-to-air missile while descending from a height of 3,000ft (c1,000m).

Miscellaneous Acts of Terror

Through advances in procedures and security equipment, commercial aviation has made great strides forward in the war against aerial terrorism. It is now possible, for example, to detect firearms and explosives going aboard aircraft. Consequently, in 1995 only three hostile acts against airlines were recorded throughout the world, compared to more than 80 such incidents in 1970.

There has also been progress in the diplomatic arena in dealing with such terrorism. Nations have become far less receptive to the concept of 'good' versus 'bad' hijackings, and have been returning perpetrators for punishment regardless of political sympathies, and in some cases prosecuting them on their own behalf.

But no security system is infallible, and hijackers and saboteurs alike continue to demonstrate originality in their *modus operandi*. Thus, even with sophisticated preventative measures in place, a bomb was allowed to go aboard a jumbo jet crossing the Atlantic in 1985, resulting in history's worst act of aerial sabotage. And despite the screening of

A hijacked Polish Airlines (LOT) Il-18 prepares to take off following its diversion to West Berlin in October 1969. (Wide World Photos)

its regular passengers, one airline was shocked in 1987 when one of its own employees was able to bring down an aircraft using a weapon that had been smuggled past detection equipment.

The following is a list of miscellaneous acts of terror that have occurred since 1966 which do not fall into any of the categories previously dealt with.

23 April 1967

FIVE men commandeered a Nigeria Airways Fokker F.27 turboprop that was carrying 29 persons on a scheduled domestic service from Benin City to Lagos, diverting it to Enugu, Nigeria. A few days after the hijacking, new security procedures, consisting of guards aboard aircraft and hand-searches of luggage, were introduced by the airline.

29 May 1967

A DC-4 operated by the Colombian airline Aerocondor, on a scheduled domestic service from Barranquilla to Bogota, was sabotaged with a time bomb, which blew a hole in its rear fuselage. There were no injuries among the 22 persons aboard the transport, which landed safely.

12 October 1967

ALL 66 persons aboard (59 passengers and a crew of seven) were killed when a British European Airways (BEA) de Havilland Comet 4B jetliner (G-ARCO) was blown up with an explosive device over the Mediterranean Sea off the south-western coast of Turkey.

Designated as Flight 284, which had originated at London, the aircraft stopped at Athens, Greece, before proceeding on towards Nicosia, Cyprus. The second half of the service was being conducted by BEA on behalf of Cyprus Airways. The last radio contact with the Comet was heard around 07:20 local time; three hours later, its wreckage was spotted floating some 100 miles (150km) east-south-east of the island of Rhodes. The bodies of all but seven of the victims were recovered, but most of the aircraft's wreckage sank in water that was more than 6,000ft (1,800m) deep and could not be recovered.

The indications of a high-explosive device were discovered in one of the seat cushions plucked from the sea, which contained many small particles of metal and fibres as well as about 20 perforations. The bomb had detonated in the cabin, probably on or above the floor and near to the side support of a seat that was believed to have been occupied by a passenger. Never determined was the type of explosive used in the device. An analysis of how the debris was distributed indicated that the structural break-up of the Comet did not occur at the cruising altitude of 29,000ft (c9,000m). The blast must have caused severe damage and sent the aircraft out of control, with the fuselage snapping into at least two major sections at an approximate height of 15,000ft (c5,000m).

Although at first thought to have been an assassination attempt on the leader of Greek forces in Cyprus, who had been incorrectly identified as being among the passengers, this was quite possibly some kind of insurance scam. Two of the passengers were found to be carrying abnormally high coverage, with one of the policies having been taken out shortly before the departure from Athens. But neither suspects nor motive were ever positively identified.

12 November 1967

A crude, home-made explosive device detonated in the rear baggage compartment of an American Airlines Boeing 727 as the jetliner was on a scheduled domestic service from Chicago, Illinois, to San Diego, California. Despite substantial damage, the aircraft reached its intended destination safely, and there were no injuries among the 78 persons aboard. A minor executive had planted the bomb in a suitcase belonging to his wife, who was a passenger; he was convicted and sentenced to prison.

9 February 1968

AN American serviceman armed with a pistol forced his way aboard a Pan American World Airways DC-6B that was on the ground at Da Nang, South Vietnam, preparing for a US military charter service to Hong Kong. He was captured and later court-martialled, but was subsequently diagnosed as a schizophrenic and given a medical discharge.

4 July 1968

AN attempt to hijack to Mexico a Trans World Airlines Boeing 727 jet, which was designated as Flight 329 and on a service from Kansas City, Kansas, to Las Vegas, Nevada, with 71 persons aboard, ended with the capture of the lone assailant, who claimed to be carrying a gun and dynamite but was actually unarmed. He was sentenced to prison and subsequently received additional time for an escape attempt.

30 October 1968

A Servicios Aereos Especialies SA (SAESA) C-46 airliner on a scheduled domestic Mexican service from Tampico to Reynosa with 32 persons aboard was hijacked to the US, landing at Brownsville, Texas. The lone assailant was extradited back to Mexico for prosecution.

2 November 1968

DEMANDING to be taken to South Vietnam, a 17-year-old boy armed with a shotgun boarded Eastern Airlines Flight 224 at the airport serving Birmingham, Alabama, as the DC-9 jet was preparing for a domestic service to Chicago with 54 persons aboard. He was disarmed by the pilot while the aircraft was still on the ground. Because of his youth he was placed on probation, and given psychiatric treatment.

5 November 1968

FOUR men armed with guns and hand-grenades seized a Philippine Air Lines Fokker F.27 Friendship on a scheduled domestic service from Mactan to Manila, and shooting broke out between them and a security guard at around 21:00 local time. One passenger was killed and two others wounded. Also injured were the guard and one of the gunmen; he and the other three fled when the twin-engine turboprop landed at Manila international airport.

8 November 1968

A Greek Olympic Airways Boeing 707 jetliner with 130 persons aboard was commandeered by two Italians, who passed out handbills and ordered the aircraft to return to Paris, France, from where it had taken off earlier on a scheduled service to Athens, Greece. The hijackers were sentenced to six months' and eight months' imprisonment respectively.

19 November 1968

AN explosion and fire occurred in the lavatory of a Continental Air Lines Boeing 707 jet, designated as Flight 18, as it was descending through an altitude of 24,000ft (c7,300m) in the vicinity of Gunnison, Colorado, preparing to land at nearby Denver while on a domestic US service from Los Angeles, California. The blaze was extinguished by the crew, and the 707 landed safely with no injuries among the 70 persons aboard. A passenger who was seen leaving the lavatory before the blast was arrested by the FBI and charged with the attempted destruction of the aircraft.

2 January 1969

A lone assailant hijacked Olympic Airways Flight 944, a DC-6B carrying 102 persons on a domestic service to Athens from the Greek island of Crete, diverting it to Cairo, Egypt. The hijacker spent eight months in an Egyptian jail before being sent to Sweden, where he was imprisoned for another one year and 10 months. Extradition to Greece for further prosecution was denied.

11 March 1969

IN an apparent act of sabotage, two explosions in the passenger cabin severely damaged an Ethiopian Airlines Boeing 707 jet that had landed at Frankfurt, West Germany, and was parked and unoccupied. There were no casualties.

4 June 1969

A DC-3 operated by the Angolan airline Direccao de Exploracao dos Transportes Aereos, on a scheduled domestic service from Ambrizete to San Antonio with 11 persons aboard, was commandeered by three hijackers, landing at Pointe Noire, Congo.

11 August 1969

SEVEN students hijacked an Ethiopian Airlines DC-3 that was carrying 19 persons on a scheduled domestic service from Bahir Dar to Addis Ababa, with the transport landing at Khartoum, Sudan.

16 August 1969

A Greek doctor who was accompanied by his wife and their two children hijacked an Olympic Airways DC-3 during a scheduled domestic service from Athens to Agrinion, Greece, with 28 persons aboard. Disarmed by soldiers after the airliner had landed in Albania, the air pirate was sentenced to 3 1/2 years' imprisonment in Sweden in 1971.

6 September 1969

A Philippine Air Lines twin-engine turboprop Hawker Siddeley HS 748 Series 2 on a scheduled domestic service to Zamboanga City, on Mindanao, from Mactan, via Dipolog City, was the target in this act of sabotage. At around 15:30 local time, or some 15 minutes before the planned landing, an explosion occurred in the aircraft's lavatory, on its right side, at an approximate height of 2,000ft (600m). The suspected saboteur, a passenger who had entered the lavatory about five minutes earlier, either fell out or, according to some eyewitness accounts, jumped to his death through the hole created by the blast; his body was later found in a rice field some five miles (10km) north of the flight's destination.

Among the other 30 persons aboard, including a crew of three, five were injured, none seriously. The aircraft managed a safe landing at Zamboanga airport.

13 September 1969

AN Ethiopian Airlines DC-6B carrying 66 persons on a scheduled flight from Addis Ababa, Ethiopia, to Djibouti, French Somaliland, was hijacked by three men, one of whom was shot and wounded by a police official. The other two were taken into custody upon landing at Aden, South Yemen.

13 September 1969

A lone hijacker commandeered a Servicio Aereo de Honduras SA (SAHSA) DC-3 that was on a scheduled domestic service from La Ceiba to the Honduran capital of Tegucigalpa with 35 persons aboard. He was taken into custody when the airliner landed in El Salvador.

16 September 1969

A Turkish Airlines Viscount turboprop, designated as Flight 124, on a domestic service from Istanbul to Ankara with 63 persons aboard, was diverted to Sofia, Bulgaria, where the lone hijacker, who was reportedly protesting about Turkish travel restrictions, was taken into custody. He would later be committed to a psychiatric facility.

19 October 1969

A Polish Airlines (LOT) Il-18 turboprop carrying 74 persons on a scheduled service to East Berlin from Warsaw, Poland, was hijacked by two armed defectors, landing in West Berlin. Both assailants spent two years in a German prison.

31 October 1969

A hijacking that set a record for distance travelled involved Trans World Airlines Flight 85, a Boeing 707-131 jetliner that had last stopped at Los Angeles, California, on a service which had originated at Baltimore, Maryland, with an ultimate destination of San Francisco. The aircraft first landed at Denver, Colorado, where the 40 passengers and all but one of the three cabin attendants disembarked. It also landed for refuelling at New York City; Bangor, Maine; and Shannon, Ireland; before reaching Rome, Italy, a total distance of 6,800 miles (c11,000km).

Responsible for the diversion was Raffaele Minichiello, one day short of his 20th birthday. A member of the US Marine Corps, he was absent-without-leave from Camp Pendleton, California, and also faced a court-martial on charges of breaking and entering a post exchange. He was armed with an M-1 carbine, with which he fired one shot in anger as the aircraft was on the ground at John F. Kennedy International Airport, New York. (The captain of the 707 blamed his behaviour largely on the actions of FBI agents, who gathered around the aircraft as it was being refuelled.) After forcing an Italian policeman to drive him away from the airport at gunpoint, he was captured south of Rome.

He served 18 months in prison in his native Italy, but remained a fugitive from US charges.

10 November 1969

A knife-wielding 14-year-old boy took a girl hostage and then forced his way aboard Delta Air Lines Flight 670 at Greater Cincinnati Airport, located near Hebron, Kentucky, where the twin-jet DC-9 was preparing for a domestic service to Chicago with 75 persons aboard. He later surrendered. Declared as mentally incompetent, the youth was held in juvenile detention for about 1½ years.

20 November 1969

TWO hijackers 'armed' with toy pistols and a fake bomb took over a Polish Airlines (LOT) twin-engine turboprop An-24 that was carrying 20 persons on a scheduled service from Wroclaw, Poland, to Bratislava, Czechoslovakia. The aircraft landed in Austria, where the two assailants were sentenced to prison for two years and 27 months respectively.

11 December 1969

A South Korean Air Lines YS-11 turboprop, on a scheduled domestic service from Kangnung to Seoul with 51 persons aboard, was hijacked to North Korea, landing near Wonsan. Despite protests, the North Korean authorities did not release any of the hostages for more than two months. The airline subsequently began placing armed security personnel aboard its aircraft.

22 December 1969

AN Air Vietnam Douglas DC-6B (B-2005) on a scheduled domestic flight over South Vietnam, from Saigon to Da Nang, sustained substantial damage when an explosive device detonated in its cabin as it was descending for a landing at Nha Trang, an en-route stop located some 200 miles (320km) north-east of the capital. The blast created a hole about 5ft (1.5m) in diameter in the fuselage and knocked out most of the aircraft's systems, including its hydraulics.

After the undercarriage had been lowered by gravity, a nose-high flapless landing was made at Nha Trang airport, with the DC-6B becoming airborne briefly before touching down again. The throttles were closed, but the pneumatic brakes could not be applied, and the airliner overran the runway, ploughed into houses and a school and caught fire. Most of the 34 persons killed were on the ground; among the 77 aboard the aircraft, including a crew of seven, all but 10 passengers survived. About 35 others suffered injuries in the crash, which occurred around 14:30 local time. The bomb had exploded in the vicinity of the front left lavatory, slightly ahead of the engines.

6 January 1970

THE would-be hijacker of a Delta Air Lines DC-9 jet, operating as Flight 274 on an intrastate service from Orlando to Jacksonville, Florida, with 65 persons aboard, was overpowered and captured after demanding to be taken to Switzerland. He spent five years in prison, part of a 25-year sentence for air piracy, before his deportation in 1975.

7 January 1970

A twin-engine Convair 440 flown by the Spanish airline Iberia on a scheduled domestic service from Madrid to Zaragoza with 46 persons aboard was commandeered by a lone assailant using a toy pistol, who wanted to go to Albania. He surrendered when the aircraft landed at its intended destination and was subsequently sentenced to a prison term of six years and one day.

12 March 1970

A man committed suicide aboard a United Air Lines Boeing 727 as the jetliner was in flight over Nebraska, on a scheduled domestic service from San Jose, California, to Chicago, Illinois. The victim's automatic pistol, triggered by a reflex, fired a second time, seriously wounding another passenger.

31 March–3 April 1970

NINE Japanese student radicals armed with swords, members of the infamous 'Red Army', commandeered Japan Air Lines Flight 351, a Boeing 727 jet carrying 138 persons on a domestic service from Tokyo to Fukuoka, demanding to be taken to North Korea. The aircraft instead landed at Kimpo airport, Seoul, South Korea, where a stand-off went on for 79 hours. The hijackers finally agreed to release the passengers and four cabin attendants in return for Japan's Deputy Minister of Transport, and the aircraft flew on to Pyongyong, North Korea.

Two men not directly involved in the hijacking later received prison sentences in Japan, one for conspiracy and the other for providing the weapons used.

21 April 1970

A Philippine Air Lines Hawker Siddeley 748 Series 2 (PI-C-1022), operating as Flight 215 on a domes-

A Philippine Air Lines Hawker Siddeley 748 of the type destroyed by an explosive device during an intra-island flight on 21 April 1970. (British Aerospace)

tic service to Manila from Cauayan, Isabela, was blown up with a bomb about 100 miles (150km) north-north-east of the capital. The twin-engine turboprop crashed and burned in a mountainous region near Pantabangan, on Luzon, and all 36 persons aboard, including four crew members, perished.

The aircraft was last reported at 10,500ft (c3,200m), and was awaiting clearance to begin its descent when the explosion in the cargo compartment ripped away its tail assembly shortly after 11:30 local time.

The bombing may have been a suicidal act by one of the passengers, or was perhaps aimed at the assassination of Colonel Filemon Lagman, who had been leading the drive to stop illegal logging and mining operations in Isabela province and was on the flight.

23 April 1970

A lone assailant with a toy pistol and an alleged bomb, which was also a fake, commandeered a bus to the airport at Pellston, Michigan, where he forced his way aboard a North Central Airlines twin-jet DC-9, operating as Flight 945, and demanded to be taken to Detroit. He was subdued by the crew and subsequently committed to a psychiatric facility.

11 May 1970

A bomb exploded aboard a DC-9 of the Spanish carrier Iberia after the jetliner had landed at Geneva, Switzerland, and after its passengers and crew members had disembarked. There were no injuries.

14 May 1970

AN Ansett Airlines of Australia DC-9 jet was commandeered by a man with a cap pistol while it was on the ground at Sydney international airport, preparing for a scheduled domestic service to Brisbane, Queensland. The 60 passengers escaped and the hijacker then surrendered; he was sentenced to a prison term of five years.

30 May 1970

USING a real-looking toy pistol, an otherwise unarmed hijacker commandeered an Alitalia DC-9 jetliner that had been on a scheduled domestic Italian service from Genoa to Rome with 35 persons aboard. It landed at Cairo, Egypt.

2 June 1970

THE third bombing of a Philippine Air Lines aircraft in less than a year involved Flight 537, which was on a domestic service from Manila to Bacolod, on the island of Negros. The twin-engine turboprop Fokker F.27 Friendship Mark 100 had been cruising at an altitude of 13,000ft (c4,000m) near Roxas, located on Panay, when it was rocked by an explosion shortly after 06:00 local time. The detonation of a fragmentation grenade between rows 4 and 5 on the left side of the aircraft created a hole in the fuselage about 3ft (1m) in diameter. One of the 44 persons aboard – the suspected saboteur – was killed, succumbing in hospital later that morning.

Twelve other passengers and one of the four crew members assigned to the flight suffered injuries. Following the blast, the pilot initiated an emergency descent and landed the Friendship safely at Roxas airport.

4 June 1970

TRANS World Airlines Flight 486, a Boeing 727-231 jet carrying 58 persons on a domestic service from Phoenix, Arizona, to St Louis, Missouri, was hijacked by a lone assailant armed with a revolver, a razor blade, and a bottle of gasoline, who demanded a ransom of $100 million. He was given about $100,000 when the aircraft landed at Dulles International Airport, near Washington, DC. On discovering that he had been short-changed, he ordered the 727 to return to Dulles. After wounding the pilot in a scuffle while on the ground, the assailant was himself shot by an FBI agent. Charges against the hijacker were later dropped, and he was committed to a psychiatric facility.

5 June 1970

A Polish Airlines (LOT) An-24 turboprop with 23 persons aboard was commandeered during a scheduled domestic service from Stettin to Gdansk, landing at Copenhagen, Denmark. The hijacker was sentenced to 3^1/2 years in prison by a Danish court.

8 June 1970

A group of nine Czechs, including an infant, took control of a Ceskoslovenske Aerolinie (CSA) Il-14 that was carrying 27 persons on a scheduled domestic flight to Prague from Karlovy Vary, diverting it to Nuremburg, West Germany, where the hijackers asked for political asylum. The adult members of the band were instead tried and convicted in a German court, receiving prison terms ranging from eight months to 2^1/2 years.

9 June 1970

TWO hijackers were foiled by the crew in an attempt to take over a Polish Airlines (LOT) aircraft that was on a scheduled domestic service from Katowice to Warsaw. They were sentenced to four and five years' imprisonment respectively.

22 July 1970

AFTER it had landed at Tan Son Nhut Airport, serving Saigon, South Vietnam, during a scheduled domestic service from Pleiku, an American servicemen held the pilot of an Air Vietnam DC-4 at knifepoint for two hours. He subsequently surrendered.

3 August 1970

A lone assailant armed with a starter pistol tried to hijack to Hungary a Pan American World Airways Boeing 727 jetliner, designated as Flight 742, which was on a service from Munich, West Germany, to West Berlin, with 125 persons aboard. The crew convinced him that the aircraft did not have enough fuel to make the trip, and he subsequently surrendered. Charges against him were dropped, and he was committed to a psychiatric facility.

7 August 1970

ARMED with a hand-grenade, a lone assailant tried to hijack a Polish Airlines (LOT) twin-engine turboprop An-24 to West Germany. It instead landed in East Berlin. The hijacker was sentenced to eight years' imprisonment for the hijacking and additional time for the crimes of rape and blackmail.

8 August 1970

TWO brothers, one of them accompanied by his son, hijacked a Ceskoslovenske Aerolinie (CSA) Il-14, which was on a scheduled domestic flight from Prague to Bratislava, Czechoslovakia, with 27 persons aboard. Having landed at Vienna, Austria, two of the assailants were sentenced to a year's imprisonment and the other to 15 months.

19 August 1970

A lone assailant armed with what would later be found out to be only a toy pistol commandeered an All Nippon Airways Boeing 727 jetliner during a domestic Japanese service from Nagoya to Sapporo. He ordered the aircraft to land at a military base and demanded a rifle and ammunition in what may have been a suicide plot. During the confusion brought about by the feigned pregnancy pains of a passenger he was overpowered by police, and was subsequently sentenced to seven years' imprisonment.

19 August 1970

THREE men accompanied by two women commandeered a Polish Airlines (LOT) Il-14 that was on a scheduled domestic service from Gdansk to Warsaw. The transport landed on the Danish island of Bornholm, where the hijackers asked for asylum. Their leader was expelled back to Poland nearly a decade later.

26 August 1970

A would-be hijacker and 10 other persons aboard were injured when a bomb he was carrying accidentally exploded during an attempt to commandeer a Polish Airlines (LOT) An-24 turboprop. The aircraft returned safely to Katowice, Poland, from where it had taken off earlier on a scheduled domestic flight to Warsaw with 31 persons aboard. The assailant was sentenced to 25 years' imprisonment.

31 August 1970

THREE hijackers armed with pistols and waving a Molotov cocktail commandeered an Air Algerie twin-engine turboprop Convair 640 that had been on a scheduled domestic service from Annaba to Algiers. After landing on Sardinia, where 11 passengers were released, and then at Brindisi, Italy, the aircraft proceeded on to Albania, where it was refused permission to land. They instead went on to Yugoslavia, where they asked for asylum.

14 September 1970

FOUR hijackers accompanied by two children took over a Romanian Airlines (TAROM) BAC One-Eleven jetliner that was on a scheduled service from Bucharest, Romania, to Prague, Czechoslovakia, with 89 persons aboard. The aircraft landed in West Germany, where one of the assailants was acquitted and the other three were sentenced to 2 1/2 years' imprisonment.

15 September 1970

A lone assailant who attempted to hijack to North Korea a Trans World Airlines Boeing 707-131B jetliner was shot and wounded by a private security guard on the ground at San Francisco International Airport, where the aircraft, operating as Flight 15 an carrying 59 persons, had just arrived from Los Angeles, California, on an intrastate segment of a domestic transcontinental service originating at New York City. He would later be sentenced to 12 1/2 years imprisonment for kidnapping.

27 October 1970

TWO students commandeered an Aeroflot L-200 Morava that was on a scheduled domestic Soviet service from Kerch to Krasnodar with a total of four persons aboard. After the twin-engine light aircraft landed at Sinop, Turkey, the authorities

The light twin-engine L-200 flown by Soviet airline Aeroflot, which was commandeered to Turkey by two students in October 1970. (Wide World Photos)

returned both hijackers to the USSR, where they received prison sentences of 10 and 12 years respectively.

13 November 1970

A married couple, reportedly drunk at the time, tried to commandeer an Aeroflot Il-14 airliner that was on a scheduled domestic service from Vilnius to Palanga, USSR. They were overpowered by the crew and other passengers and the flight landed safely at its intended destination. The husband subsequently received a death sentence, which, largely due to world reaction, was later commuted to 15 years' imprisonment; his wife was given three years.

10 December 1970

AN attempt to hijack a Czechoslovak Aero Taxi Morave on a domestic service from Bratislava to Brno ended when the other passengers overpowered the lone assailant while in the air. One person was wounded but the aircraft returned safely to Brno.

21 December 1970

A Puerto Rico International Airlines Heron, operating as Flight 157 on an intra-island service from San Juan to Ponce with 21 persons aboard, got hijacked by a lone assailant who was overpowered

by the crew. He would later spend more than two years in a psychiatric facility.

22 January 1971

AN Ethiopian Airlines DC-3 was hijacked during a scheduled domestic flight from Bahir Dar to Gondar with 23 persons aboard and diverted to Banghazi, Libya, where the trio of assailants were taken into custody.

30 January–2 February 1971

IN India's first case of airline hijacking, two young Kashmiris commandeered an Indian Airline Corporation Fokker F.27 Friendship Mark 100 (VT-DMA), designated as Flight 422, during a domestic service from Srinagar to Delhi, forcing it to Lahore, West Pakistan. It was there that the other 30 persons aboard were released unharmed and the twin-engine turboprop destroyed by flames. The two assailants, who suffered minor injuries in sabotaging the aircraft, would later be deported to the US.

8 March 1971

AT the airport serving Mobile, Alabama, a 16-year-old boy armed with a pistol forced his way aboard National Airlines Flight 745, which was en route to New Orleans, Louisiana, with 46 persons aboard. He ordered the Boeing 727 jet to Miami, Florida, where he surrendered. Due to his age, he was sentenced to a correctional facility.

30 March 1971

HALF-A-DOZEN young men commandeered a Philippine Airlines twin-jet BAC One-Eleven jet carrying 45 persons on a scheduled domestic service from Manila to Davao. Landing for re-fuelling in Hong Kong, where more than half of the passengers were released, the aircraft proceeded on to Canton, China. Two of the hijackers returned to the Philippines six years later and both were subsequently indicted in a military court.

21 April 1971

A single assailant who said he had a pistol and a hand-grenade but was in fact unarmed failed in his attempt to hijack to Italy an Eastern Airlines DC-8 jet, which had been operating as Flight 403 en route from Newark, New Jersey, to Miami, Florida, with 59 persons aboard. He was sentenced to three years, although the prison sentence was suspended.

8 May 1971

A DC-4 of the Colombian airline AVIANCA, on a scheduled domestic flight from Monteria to Cartagena, was hijacked by a lone assailant, who was detained when the transport landed at Maracaibo, Venezuela.

13 May 1971

AN All Nippon Airways YS-11 turboprop was commandeered and forced to return to Tokyo, Japan, from where it had taken off earlier on a scheduled domestic service to Sendai. The lone assailant offered no resistance and was arrested by police.

17 May 1971

THE attempted hijacking of a Scandinavian Airlines System (SAS) DC-9 jetliner, on a scheduled domestic service to Stockholm, was averted on the ground at Malmö, Sweden, with the lone assailant being taken into custody.

27 May 1971

A Romanian Airlines (TAROM) Il-14 on a scheduled domestic service from Oradea to Bucharest with 24 persons aboard was commandeered by six hijackers, all of whom were taken into custody when the transport landed in Vienna, Austria. They were sentenced to prison terms ranging from two years to 30 months.

28 May 1971

A former policeman who claimed to have wrapped himself in explosives hijacked Eastern Airlines Flight 30, a Boeing 727 jetliner carrying 138 persons en route to New York City from Miami. The aircraft was flown to Nassau, in the Bahamas, where, after landing, the assailant was overpowered by an airline pilot and taken into custody. Deported to the US, he was later committed to a psychiatric facility.

4 June 1971

A United Air Lines Boeing 737 jet designated as Flight 796, on a domestic service from Charleston, West Virginia, to Newark, New Jersey, was commandeered by a lone gunman who wanted to be taken to Israel. Stopping at Dulles International Airport, serving Washington, DC, to switch to a longer-range aircraft, the hijacker was captured. He was later sentenced to concurrent 20 year prison terms for air piracy and interference with an airline crew.

29 June 1971

A woman who tried to hijack a Finnair DC-9 jet airliner that was on a scheduled service from Helsinki, Finland, to Copenhagen, Denmark, was overpowered by the crew.

2 July 1971

TWO assailants, a man and a woman armed with four pistols and alleged explosives, hijacked a Braniff International Airways Boeing 707 jet, operating as Flight 14, en route from Mexico City to San Antonio, Texas, one segment of a service originating at Acapulco, Mexico, with an ultimate destination of New York City. They were demanding a ransom of $100,000 and to be taken to Algeria.

Landing at Lima, Peru, and Rio de Janeiro, Brazil, the US aircraft, with 110 persons aboard, later touched down at Buenos Aires, Argentina, where the authorities refused to refuel it for the transatlantic trip. The passengers were released and, following a stand-off, the two hijackers gave themselves up. Both of them were sentenced to prison in Argentina and in 1975 were extradited to Mexico, where they served additional time.

24 August 1971

AN Alia Royal Jordanian Airlines Boeing 707 jetliner was extensively damaged by a bomb that detonated in an aft lavatory as the aircraft was parked on the ground at Madrid, Spain. There were no injuries.

24 September 1971

WITH the intention of freeing two prisoners and escaping with them to Algeria, a woman commandeered an American Airlines Boeing 727 jetliner, operating as Flight 124, en route to New York City from Detroit, Michigan, with 76 persons aboard. Armed with a pistol and dynamite, she was captured by police and subsequently given probation for assaulting a federal officer.

26 October 1971

AN Olympic Airways aircraft on a scheduled domestic service from Athens to the Greek island of Crete was hijacked to Rome, Italy, where the lone assailant was overpowered and captured.

20 November 1971

SABOTAGE with an explosive device was suspected in the crash of a China Airlines Sud-Aviation Caravelle III (B-1852), which occurred in the Formosa Strait. Designated as Flight 825 and en route to Hong Kong from T'ai-pei, Taiwan, the second leg of a service that had originated at Osaka, Japan, the Taiwanese-registered twin-engine jet was last reported cruising in darkness at 26,000ft (c8,000m) when it vanished from radar contact at around 21:50 local time, at a position some 200 miles (320km) from its intended destination and in the vicinity of the Pescadores.

Subsequently, a small amount of debris washed ashore on one of the islands, but no survivors or bodies were found. There had been 25 persons aboard the aircraft (17 passengers and a crew of eight).

3 December 1971

A lone assailant attempted to hijack a Pakistan International Airlines Boeing 707 jetliner on a scheduled service to Karachi, Pakistan, but she was overpowered by police on the ground at Orly Airport, serving Paris. She received a five-year prison sentence, which was suspended.

22 December 1971

AN attempt to commandeer a twin-engine Islander operated by the Dominican Republic carrier Alas Del Caribe Air, during a scheduled domestic service from Santiago to Santo Domingo, was foiled when the lone assailant was overpowered by the pilot and other passengers after the aircraft had landed at Dajabon, Dominican Republic.

26 December 1971

AMERICAN Airlines Flight 47, a Boeing 707 jet carrying 85 persons on a domestic service from Chicago, Illinois, to San Francisco, California, was taken over by a lone assailant, who demanded $200,000. The hijacker, who had used a knife, a pistol that turned out to be a toy, and a fake bomb, was overpowered and subsequently served three years' imprisonment for air piracy and interference with an airline crew.

26 January 1972

A Jugoslovenski Aerotransport (JAT) McDonnell Douglas DC-9 Series 32 (YU-AHT) was blown up

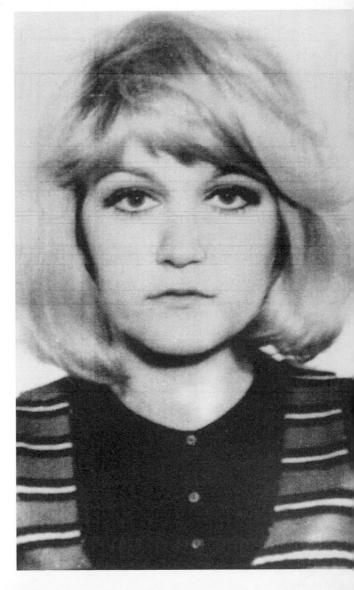

In January 1972, 22-year-old stewardess Vesna Vulovic miraculously survived the bombing of a Yugoslav DC-9 over Czechoslovakia. (UPI/Corbis-Bettmann)

by a bomb over north-western Czechoslovakia, falling into a mountainous region near the town of Hermsdorf. All but one of the 28 persons aboard (22 passengers and five crew members) were killed.

Originating at Stockholm, Sweden, Flight 364 had stopped at Copenhagen, Denmark, before proceeding on towards Zagreb, and ultimately Belgrade, both in Yugoslavia. The jet airliner had been cruising in clear weather conditions at an approximate altitude of 33,000ft (10,050m) when the explosion occurred in its forward baggage compartment, shortly after 17:00 local time. Croatian Nationalist activists were suspected of the act of sabotage.

The one remarkable aspect of the tragedy was the almost miraculous survival of 22-year-old stewardess Vesna Vulovic, who remained in the aircraft's tail assembly as it spun to earth like a falling leaf, and tumbled out when it struck the ground. It was theorized that the impact on sloping terrain was similar to a ski-jumping effect, with deceleration forces within human tolerance. She would later recover from the critical injuries suffered in the crash, which included brain damage, a fractured spine and paralysis from the waist down.

29 January 1972

DESIGNATED as Flight 2, a Trans World Airlines Boeing 707 jet was on a transcontinental service from Los Angeles to New York City with 101 persons aboard when it was commandeered by a gunman who demanded some $300,000 in ransom and the release of prisoners. He was shot and wounded by an FBI agent on the ground at John F. Kennedy International Airport, and subsequently sentenced to life imprisonment on multiple charges.

7 March 1972

ARMED with a pistol, a teenage boy three weeks short of his 15th birthday forced his way aboard a National Airlines Boeing 727 jetliner, operating as Flight 67 on an intrastate service to Miami, which was on the ground at Tampa, Florida. He was overpowered by a US federal marshal, and charges against him were later dismissed.

7–8 March 1972

IN an extortion plot, Trans World Airlines was informed that bombs were on four of its aircraft. One bomb was actually found, aboard Flight 7, a domestic transcontinental service from New York City to Los Angeles, California, and at about 04:00 local time on 8 March another exploded in the cockpit of a Boeing 707-331 (N761TW) jetliner that was on the ground at McCarran Airport, serving Las Vegas, Nevada. There were no injuries, but the aircraft was damaged, beyond repair.

Although $2 million were demanded, no money was ever collected and no suspects were apprehended.

11 March 1972

A female assailant hijacked an Alitalia Caravelle that had been carrying 38 persons on a scheduled Italian domestic service from Rome to Milan, with the jetliner landing at Munich, West Germany.

13 April 1972

A lone gunman tried to hijack to Mexico a Frontier Airlines twin-jet Boeing 737, designated as Flight 91, on a US domestic service from Albuquerque, New Mexico, to Tucson, Arizona, with 33 persons aboard. Surrendering at Los Angeles International Airport after a six hour stand-off, he was sentenced to life imprisonment for air piracy, but was paroled after serving six years.

16 April 1972

AN attempt to hijack a Puerto Rico International Airlines Heron, operating as Flight 179 on a domestic service from Ponce to San Juan, failed when the lone assailant, allegedly carrying a bomb but actually unarmed, was overpowered on the ground by another passenger and a mechanic. He served two years in prison after being convicted of conveying false information concerning attempted air piracy.

17 April 1972

AN unarmed assailant who claimed to have a pistol forced his way aboard an Alaska Airlines Boeing 727 jetliner, designated as Flight 1861, at Seattle, Washington, but was later captured. He was committed to a psychiatric facility for approximately a year.

17 April 1972

A Swissair DC-9 carrying 20 persons was hijacked during a scheduled service from Geneva, Switzerland, to Rome, Italy, but the lone assailant was captured after the jetliner had landed at its intended destination. He was sentenced to more than two years' imprisonment in 1973, but was released six days later after posting bail.

17 April 1972

A lone assailant who said he had a pistol but was in fact unarmed commandeered Delta Air Lines Flight 952, a Convair 880 jet carrying 78 persons, in an extortion plot. He surrendered at Chicago, Illinois, after a service from West Palm Beach, Florida, and was later sentenced to 20 years' imprisonment for air piracy.

18 April 1972

THE co-pilot of a Slovair Let 410 twin-engine turboprop was shot and wounded during the hijacking of a scheduled Czechoslovakian domestic service from Prague to Marienbad. The aircraft landed in West Germany, where the two assailants were sentenced to seven years' imprisonment. One of them would later commit suicide.

3 May 1972

WITH the intention of releasing three imprisoned members of the Turkish Liberation Army, four assailants hijacked a Turkish Airlines twin-jet DC-9 that was on a scheduled domestic service from Ankara to Istanbul with 61 persons aboard. They surrendered after landing at Sofia, Bulgaria, and later in the year were sentenced to three years' imprisonment.

24–26 May 1972

A South African Airways Boeing 727 jetliner carrying 64 persons was hijacked during a scheduled service from Salisbury, Rhodesia (Zimbabwe), to Johannesburg, South Africa, landing at Blantyre, Malawi, where, the following day, the passengers and crew escaped. The two assailants were overpowered by troops and subsequently sentenced to prison; both were deported to Zambia in 1974.

25 May 1972

A home-made pipe bomb exploded in the ice water service compartment of a LAN-Chile Boeing 727 as the jetliner was on a scheduled service from Panama to Miami, Florida, with 60 persons aboard. The blast, which occurred around 01:20 local time at an approximate height of 30,000ft (c10,000m), caused extensive damage and a rapid depressurization of the cabin, but there were no injuries, and the aircraft landed safely at Montego Bay, Jamaica.

28 May 1972

A lone assailant with the objective of receiving medical treatment in London commandeered an Olympic Airways Boeing 707 jetliner that was on a scheduled domestic service from Crete to Athens, Greece, with 130 persons aboard. After landing at its intended destination, police rushed the aircraft and captured the hijacker, who was later sentenced to two years' imprisonment.

15 June 1972

FIRST thought to have been an incidental act of war, the destruction of Cathay Pacific Airways Flight 700Z turned out to be an act of sabotage, possibly motivated by personal profit. The Convair 880M jetliner (VR-HFZ) flown by the Hong Kong-based carrier had stopped at Bangkok, Thailand, before proceeding on towards Hong Kong, one segment of a service originating at Singapore. Shortly after a loss of radio contact with the aircraft, just before 14:00 local time, its burning wreckage was located in the Central Highlands of South Vietnam, near Pleiku. All 81 persons aboard (71 passengers and a crew of 10) perished.

The sudden and catastrophic nature of the disaster, coupled with the fact that it had occurred in a war-torn region, led to early speculation that VR-HFZ had been shot down. But the metallic particles found in the debris and in some of the victims' bodies were too small and light to be associated with military missiles or projectiles. The outward travel of the fragments also indicated an internal rather than external explosion, pointing to a bomb.

Its flight data recorder (FDR) read-out showed the aircraft had been cruising at 29,000ft (c9,000m) at an indicated air speed of approximately 350mph (560kph) and on a heading of about 70 degrees when the high-explosive device detonated within its passenger cabin, in or near the centre section. The vertical stabiliser broke off after being hit by at least one victim who had been ejected from the cabin and, possibly, by some seats, also blown out. In-flight fire also occurred when the blast ruptured a right wing fuel tank. Damage probably inflicted on the flying controls routed beneath the cabin floor together with the loss of the vertical tail fin must have caused erratic, high-speed manoeuvres that led to the progressive break-up of the jetliner, with the various components striking the ground after a vertical descent. Those occupants not killed in the initial blast were probably rendered unconscious in the resulting explosive decompression.

Suspected of the mass murder was a Thai police lieutenant whose fiancée and daughter by a previous marriage were passengers on the flight. Both had been insured prior to their departure, prompting the investigative board to recommend that the sale of such insurance at airports be discouraged. Owing to insufficient evidence, the suspect was acquitted of the charges two years later.

5 July 1972

A knife-wielding assailant who had already seriously wounded his estranged wife boarded an American Airlines Boeing 707 jet that was parked at Buffalo, New York, international airport, holding

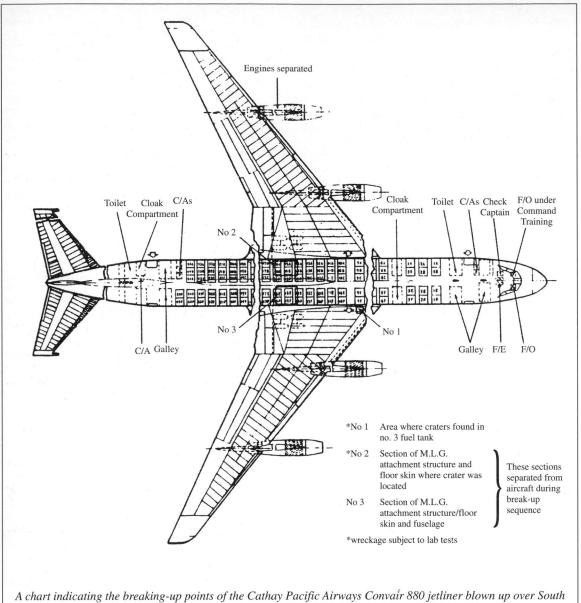

A chart indicating the breaking-up points of the Cathay Pacific Airways Convair 880 jetliner blown up over South Vietnam on 15 June 1972. (International Civil Aviation Organisation)

hostage his 14-month-old daughter and demanding to be flown out of the area. He surrendered after three hours and, the following year, was given five years' probation.

12 July 1972

AN attempt to hijack a DC-8 jetliner operated by the French carrier Union de Transports Aeriens (UTA), which was on a scheduled service to Paris from Abidjan, Ivory Coast, was foiled, the gunman being shot and captured after wounding his wife.

18 July 1972

AN Aerolineas TAO Viscount 785D, designated as Flight 511 and carrying 51 persons, was on a domestic Colombian service from San Andres Island to Cartagena, with an ultimate destination of Bogota, when a passenger went berserk. Forcing his way into the cockpit of the turboprop airliner, he shot both pilots, the captain fatally. He was subdued by others aboard after emptying his gun, the shooting taking place around 18:00 local time.

Though wounded in the face and bleeding, the first officer managed to land the aircraft safely at

Crespo Airport, serving Cartagena, where the assailant was taken into custody.

31 July 1972

FIVE assailants commandeered Delta Air Lines Flight 841, a DC-8 jetliner carrying 101 persons, during a domestic US service to Miami, Florida, from Detroit, Michigan. Their demands for a million dollars and a trip to Algeria were met. Three children who accompanied them were returned to the US, as was the money. Four of the hijackers were arrested in Paris, and although extradition to the US was denied, all spent between three and five years behind bars in France.

17–18 August 1972

A lone assailant rode up on a bicycle to the airport serving Reno, Nevada, and then, armed with a shotgun, commandeered United Air Lines Flight 877, a Boeing 727 jet bound for San Francisco, California.

He forced the aircraft to fly to Vancouver, British Columbia, and demanded an assortment of weapons, 15 gold bars, and $2 million, which he said was destined for children crippled in the Vietnam War. He released the passengers and cabin staff and ordered the 727 on to Seattle, Washington, where an FBI agent, using a weapon smuggled through a cockpit window, shot and wounded him. He was later sentenced to 30 years' imprisonment.

15 September 1972

WHAT was believed to have been a hand-grenade detonated aboard an Air Manila Fairchild F-27 as the twin-engine turboprop, which had taken off minutes earlier from Romblon on a scheduled domestic service within the Philippines with 42 persons aboard, was cruising at an altitude of 11,000ft (c3,400m). The blast occurred at 18:45 local time, the lightly damaged aircraft landing safely at Roxas. Two unexploded hand-grenades were found on the floor of the cargo compartment.

15 September 1972

A Scandinavian Airlines System (SAS) twin-jet DC-9 carrying more than 80 persons on a scheduled service from Göteborg to Stockholm, Sweden, was commandeered by three terrorists, who demanded a ransom and also secured the release of six Croatian nationalists. All nine were then flown to Madrid, Spain, where the three responsible for the hijacking were sentenced to 12 years' imprisonment.

11 October 1972

A lone assailant who claimed to have a bomb commandeered a Lufthansa German Airlines Boeing 727 jetliner that was on a scheduled service to Frankfurt from Lisbon, Portugal, with 58 persons aboard. He was shot and wounded by a sharpshooter while walking towards a getaway car.

22 October 1972

A Turkish Airlines Boeing 707 jet, carrying 81 persons, was hijacked during a scheduled domestic service from Istanbul to Ankara, landing at Sofia, Bulgaria. The four air pirates threatened to blow up the aircraft unless the Turkish government released 13 prisoners and instituted reforms; the pilot and a passenger were wounded and, the following day, the hijackers surrendered. They were sentenced to terms of 2 to 2½ years' imprisonment in Bulgaria, and the 'ringleader' was later sentenced to 20 years in Turkey.

14 December 1972

A Quebecair twin-jet BAC One-Eleven, carrying 62 persons on a scheduled domestic Canadian service to Montreal from Wabush, Newfoundland, was hijacked by a lone assailant armed with a rifle. He required the pilot to proceed on to his intended destination, then shuttle between Montreal and Ottawa. He released the passengers and later surrendered, being subsequently sentenced to 20 years' imprisonment.

2 January 1973

ARMED with a pistol, a lone assailant who wanted to be taken to Canada boarded a Piedmont Airlines twin-engine turboprop YS-11, operating as Flight 928, which had just landed at Baltimore, Maryland. He surrendered after several hours of negotiations and was later sentenced to 20 years' imprisonment.

4 January 1973

DEMANDING $2 million and passage to North Vietnam, a lone assailant commandeered a Canadian Pacific Western Airlines twin-engine turboprop Convair 640 at the airport serving Vancouver, British Columbia. After releasing the passengers he was arrested by police.

19 March 1973

AN Air Vietnam Douglas DC-4 (XV-NUI) was sabotaged while on a scheduled domestic service from Saigon to Ban Me Thuot, crashing in the Central Highlands of South Vietnam near its destination and some 150 miles (250km) northeast of the capital. All 59 persons aboard, including a crew of five, perished. The airliner had been on its landing approach when, at about 10:05

local time, it plunged to earth from an approximate altitude of 2,000ft (600m) after an explosive device detonated in its cargo hold near the main wing spar.

30 May–June 3 1973

A Sociedad Aeronautica de Medellin Consolidada SA (SAM) Electra turboprop airliner was hijacked during a scheduled domestic Colombian service from Pereira to Medellin, with the two assailants demanding a ransom plus the release by the government of 140 prisoners. None were released and the hijackers received only a quarter of the amount requested.

The Electra landed several times, where passengers were either released or escaped, and four days into the siege the hijackers themselves escaped. Both were captured about a week later.

10 June 1973

A Royal Nepal Airlines Twin Otter turboprop was commandeered during a scheduled domestic service from Biratnagar to Kathmandu. It landed at Forbesganj, Bihar, India, where the three assailants escaped into the jungle with three million rupees that were being transported on the flight by a Nepalese bank.

8 July 1973

A lone assailant sent a note to the captain of an Aeroflot Il-18 turboprop, which had earlier taken off from Moscow on a scheduled international service, stating that he wanted the aircraft to proceed directly to its ultimate destination of Hanoi, North Vietnam, without landing as planned at Tashkent, USSR. Claiming to have an explosive device, he locked himself in a lavatory. The crew tricked him into believing they were setting down in Afghanistan for refuelling when in fact they landed at Tashkent, where the man was arrested. Found to be mentally disturbed, he was committed to a psychiatric facility.

26 July 1973

WHILE on a scheduled domestic service originating at Vilnius, with an ultimate destination of Palanga, USSR, a passenger rushed into the cockpit of an Aeroflot Il-14 and, striking the captain in the head with a screwdriver, demanded to be flown to Sweden. He was overpowered by members of the crew. Exempted from criminal charges due to his mental state, he was committed to a psychiatric hospital.

2 October 1973

THE hijacker of a KLM Royal Dutch Airlines DC-9, who commandeered the twin-engine jet during a scheduled service from Duesseldorf, West Germany, to Amsterdam, the Netherlands, was disarmed while talking with the pilot. He was later taken into custody.

10 October 1973

THE lone assailant who tried to hijack a Compania Mexicana de Aviacion SA Boeing 727 jetliner on the ground at Mexico City was captured by a security officer dressed as a crew member.

11 October 1973

THREE hijackers commandeered a Philippine Airlines twin-jet BAC One-Eleven that was on a scheduled domestic service from Davao to Bacolod. They exchanged the passengers for the president of the airline and then flew to Hong Kong. After being granted amnesty by the government of the Philippines they surrendered.

1 December 1973

THE hijacker of a Swissair DC-8 jetliner, which was commandeered during a scheduled domestic service from Geneva to Zurich, demanded money to fight starvation in Africa, a ticket to New York City, and safe conduct. He released all the occupants except for four crew members. He was subsequently arrested by police posing as the newsmen he had requested aboard.

3 January 1974

A lone assailant who claimed to have a hand-grenade wrapped in a handkerchief tried to hijack to Miami an Air Jamaica DC-9 jetliner at the airport serving Kingston, Jamaica, but he was overpowered and captured by security guards.

20 March 1974

A married couple hijacked an East African Airways Fokker F.27 Friendship twin-engine turboprop that was carrying 35 persons on a scheduled internal service from Nairobi to Malindi, Kenya, ordering it to Libya. The airliner landed for refuelling at Entebbe, Uganda, where the hijackers gave themselves up after negotiations.

30 March 1974

AN assailant armed with a shotgun and holding two hostages boarded a National Airlines Boeing 727 jet that was parked at the airport serving Sarasota, Florida, demanding to be flown out of the area. He was disarmed by a maintenance man, the only other occupant of the aircraft, and was later sentenced to 15 years' imprisonment for kidnapping.

15 July 1974

A youth armed with a knife who said he also had a bomb commandeered a Japan Air Lines DC-8 jetliner that was on a scheduled domestic service from Osaka to Tokyo. The hijacker was captured after the aircraft landed at Nagoya, and, in 1977, was sentenced to 10 years' imprisonment.

4 September 1974

AN Eastern Airlines DC-9 jet, operating as Flight 1160 and completing a service from New York City with 100 persons aboard, was commandeered by a lone assailant after it had landed at Boston, Massachusetts. Taking the captain hostage with a razor blade and a nail, he demanded $10,000, but after more than three hours he was persuaded to surrender. He was subsequently committed to a psychiatric facility.

7 October 1974

A Far Eastern Air Transport Viscount 810 turbo-prop airliner on a scheduled domestic flight from T'ainan to Taipei, Taiwan, was hijacked by a single assailant carrying a knife and four bottles of gasoline. He demanded to be flown to mainland China, but was captured by a security guard and a cabin attendant.

23 November 1974

A 16-year-old boy, brandishing what resembled a stick of dynamite, seized a Japan Air Lines DC-8 jet that was on a scheduled domestic service from Tokyo to Sapporo, but he was overpowered by a member of the flight crew.

29 November 1974

A CP Air twin-jet Boeing 737, designated as Flight 71 on a domestic Canadian service from Winnipeg, Manitoba, to Edmonton, Alberta, with 86 persons aboard, got hijacked by a lone assailant who held and slightly wounded a stewardess with a knife. Demanding to be taken to Cyprus, he allowed the aircraft to land at Saskatoon, Saskatchewan, for refuelling, and later surrendered to the pilot. He was sentenced to seven years in prison.

25 December 1974

AN Air-India Boeing 747 wide-bodied jet airliner was commandeered during a scheduled service from Bombay, India, to Rome, Italy, with the lone assailant brandishing a pocket knife and claiming

to have bombs aboard. He demanded passage to a place of his choice, but was subsequently overpowered by the flight crew.

3 January 1975

TRYING to draw attention to himself, a lone assailant armed with a rifle boarded an out-of-service National Airlines Boeing 727 jet at the airport serving Pensacola, Florida. He was subsequently disarmed and overpowered by two aircraft cleaners. The following month he committed suicide in prison.

7 January 1975

THE United Kingdom's first and, to date, only domestic airline hijacking involved a British Airways BAC One-Eleven jet, operating as Flight 4069 from Manchester to London with 52 persons aboard. Carrying a pistol and a hand-grenade (both of which turned out to be fakes), the assailant demanded £100,000 and a trip to Paris. He was tricked, however, the aircraft actually landing at Stansted Airport, Essex, England, and was later arrested while trying to escape with a hostage.

Subsequently convicted of the crime, the hijacker was sentenced to a prison term of seven years. The airline, meanwhile, announced stepped-up security measures to prevent future acts of air piracy.

13 January 1975

A would-be hijacker ordered Eastern Airlines Flight 140 to San Juan, Puerto Rico. However, after the Boeing 727 jet, carrying 60 persons on a domestic service from Atlanta, Georgia, to Philadelphia, Pennsylvania, had landed for refuelling at Dulles International Airport, serving Washington, DC, he locked himself in a lavatory. He was found to be unarmed when apprehended, and was subsequently committed to a psychiatric facility.

25 February 1975

DEMANDING that one of them be pardoned for a previous offence, two men commandeered a Philippine Airlines DC-3 carrying 32 persons on a scheduled domestic service from Pagadian to Zamboanga. After 10 hours of negotiations they both surrendered, but received no pardon, instead being sentenced to death by firing squad.

2 March 1975

A knife-wielding assailant boarded an Air New England Twin Otter turboprop that was on the

Great Britain's only domestic airline hijacking to date, which occurred in January 1975, involved a British Airways BAC One-Eleven like this one. (British Aerospace)

ground at Hyannis, Massachusetts, the pilot being its only other occupant. He demanded to be flown to New Haven, Connecticut, but was later captured by police and convicted on a weapon-possession charge.

9 April 1975

A Japan Air Lines Boeing 747 wide-bodied jet on a scheduled domestic service from Sapporo to Tokyo was commandeered by a lone gunman who demanded 30 million yen, but after it had landed at its intended destination he was overpowered by police while talking with the pilot.

15 May 1975

SAYING that she did not want to land at its intended destination, an unarmed 16-year-old girl attempted to seize a United Airlines Boeing 727 jetliner, operating as Flight 509, bound for San Francisco, California, from Eugene, Oregon, with 80 persons aboard. Captured and held by a crew member until taken into custody by police, she was subsequently returned to the psychiatric facility from which she had escaped.

3 June 1975

DEPENDING on one's viewpoint, RP-C-1184 may be one of the unluckiest or luckiest commercial airliners to have ever carried passengers. Twice the Philippine Airlines BAC One-Eleven Series 500

was targeted in suicide bombings, resulting in death and injury. But both times, despite substantial damage, the twin-engine jet managed a safe landing.

The first case involved Flight 126, which was on a domestic service to Manila from Legaspi. Having just begun its descent, the aircraft was at an approximate height of 20,000ft (6,000m) over Alabat Island when it was jolted by a bomb blast in its right rear lavatory at around 15:30 local time. The alleged saboteur was killed; among the other 63 persons aboard, including a crew of five, 45 were injured, three passengers seriously.

After the pilot had descended to a lower altitude, the One-Eleven continued on toward its intended destination, setting down at Manila's international airport. Subsequently repaired, the same aircraft would experience a remarkably similar incident three years later.

28 June 1975

A Balkan Bulgarian Airlines twin-engine turboprop An-24 was hijacked during a scheduled domestic service from Varna to Sofia, Bulgaria, and forced to land at Thessaloniki, Greece, where the armed assailant asked for political asylum.

15 July 1975

IN a fiery act of suicide, a passenger doused himself with a flammabe liquid and then set himself on fire in a lavatory on a National Airlines

DC-10, which was operating as Flight 1601 on a domestic service from Miami, Florida, to New York City. The wide-bodied jet landed safely at Jacksonville, Florida.

28 July 1975

A youth feigning that he had a knife seized an All Nippon Airways L-1011 wide-bodied jetliner on a scheduled domestic service from Tokyo to Hokkaido, Japan. After the aircraft returned to its point of origin, the passengers and crew disembarked, and the hijacker was then arrested by police.

3 September 1975

THE captain was reportedly shot and killed aboard an Aeroflot Il-62 shortly before the Soviet jetliner was scheduled to land at London, an en-route stop during a service from New York City to Moscow.

27 September 1975

A lone assailant holding a spray bottle that he claimed contained nitric acid tried to take over an Olympic Airways SC-7 twin-engine turboprop during a scheduled domestic Greek service from Athens to the island of Mikonos, but he was overpowered by the crew and turned over to authorities after landing.

5 October 1975

A band of guerrillas commandeered an Aerolineas Argentinas Boeing 737 jet airliner during a scheduled domestic service from Buenos Aires to Corrientes, landing at the city of Formosa, where the passengers were released and more guerrillas boarded. Low on fuel, the 737 landed at Rafaela, in the province of Santa Fe, where the assailants escaped.

22 December 1975

THE hijacker of a Sociedad Aeronautica de Medellin Consolidada SA (SAM) Beechcraft Queen Airliner, who had commandeered the twin-engine aircraft during a domestic Colombian air-taxi service from Barrancabermeja to Medellin, demanded 3 million pesos and safe conduct to an unspecified location, but was shot and wounded by secret police on the ground at its intended destination, and then taken into custody.

5 January 1976

TWO armed men seized a Japan Air Lines stretched DC-8 jetliner with more than 200 persons aboard on the ground at Manila, the Philippines, an en-route stop during a scheduled service to Tokyo from Bangkok, Thailand. They later surrendered to Philippine authorities after Japan refused them entry into the country.

26 January 1976

A lone assailant attempting to flee from the USSR to avoid punishment for a previous crime threatened to blow up an Aeroflot Il-62 jet airliner, designated as Flight 614, which was on a scheduled domestic service, unless he was taken to Tel Aviv, Israel. To make the threat real, he had obtained signal rockets and seven small pyrotechnic devices. However, the aircraft instead landed at Moscow, and he was subsequently sentenced to 10 years' imprisonment.

7–13 April 1976

THREE men commandeered a Philippine Airlines twin-jet BAC One-Eleven jet that was carrying 79 persons on a scheduled domestic service to Cagayan de Oro, on Mactan, demanding a ransom and the release of numerous prisoners. Over a period of six days, the aircraft stopped in Malaysia, then Thailand, where the hijackers switched to a longer-range DC-8 jetliner, then in Pakistan, and finally in Libya, where they requested, but were refused, political asylum.

24 April 1976

TO protest at 'the neglect of the peasants', an armed man commandeered an AVIANCA Boeing 727 jetliner during a scheduled domestic Colombian service to Bogota from Pereira. He surrendered after it had landed at its intended destination.

30 April 1976

A Turkish Airlines DC-10 wide-bodied jet carrying 253 persons was on a scheduled service from Paris to Istanbul, Turkey, when a man threatened a stewardess with a knife and tried to force it to land at either Marseille or Lyon, France. The aircraft instead returned to its point of origin, where the unsuccessful hijacker surrendered without further incident.

10 September 1976

AN Indian Airlines twin-jet Boeing 737, designated as Flight 491 and carrying 83 persons, was commandeered during a domestic service from New Delhi to Bombay, subsequently landing at Lahore, Pakistan. There, the six alleged hijackers were taken into custody, but all were later released on grounds of insufficient evidence.

10 September 1976

FIVE terrorists allegedly carrying plastic explosives (which turned out to be clay) commandeered Trans World Airlines Flight 355, a Boeing 727-231 jetliner en route from New York City to Chicago with 92 persons aboard, with the intention of distributing propaganda regarding Croatian independence. Stopping in Newfoundland and Iceland, the aircraft eventually landed in Paris, France. As another part of their demands, leaflets were dropped over London from another aircraft.

The hijackers were returned to the US to face charges of not only air piracy but also the murder of a police officer, killed by a bomb found at Grand Central Station, New York City. Two were sentenced to life imprisonment, and the other three to 30 years, plus additional time on state charges.

6 October 1976

EMPRESA Consolidada Cubana de Aviacion Flight 455, a Douglas DC-8 Series 43 (CU-T1201), departed from Seawell International Airport, serving Barbados, bound for Kingston, Jamaica, one segment of a service that had originated at Georgetown, Guyana, with an ultimate destination of Havana, Cuba. About 10 minutes after take-off, the crew transmitted a radio distress message, reporting an on-board explosion. Turning back towards its point of departure, the jetliner was observed flying below an overcast, trailing smoke, before it entered a steep climb while banked to the left, then plummeted into the Caribbean Sea some 10 miles (15km) from the coast of Barbados in water more than 1,000ft (300m) deep. All 73 persons aboard perished, including 10 off-duty crew members riding as passengers and a regular crew of 15.

The tragedy was believed to have resulted from the detonation of an explosive device in the rear of the aircraft's cabin. This led to an uncontrollable fire producing toxic fumes that must have eventually incapacitated the flight crew. A decade later, two men were sentenced to 20 years imprisonment by a Venezuelan court for their involvement in the crash.

28 October 1976

A lone assailant armed with a sub-machine-gun and a pistol hijacked a Ceskoslovenske Aerolinie (CSA) Il-18 turboprop that was on a scheduled domestic service from Prague to Bratislava carrying 111 persons. The aircraft landed at Munich, West Germany, the hijacker being later sentenced to eight years' imprisonment in that country.

4 November 1976

USING a dummy bomb, a lone assailant commandeered a Polish Airlines (LOT) Tu-134 jetliner that was on a scheduled service from Copenhagen, Denmark, to Warsaw, Poland. The aircraft landed at Vienna, Austria, where the hijacker surrendered. He was later sentenced to four years' imprisonment.

21 December 1976

A United Airlines employee armed with two revolvers and a knife boarded one of the carrier's empty DC-8 jetliners at San Francisco International Airport. Holding two hostages, he demanded a crew to fly him to the US East Coast. He then surrendered. He was later ruled legally insane and committed to a psychiatric facility.

11 January 1977

A Trans World Airlines Boeing 747 wide-bodied jetliner, operating as Flight 700 on a transatlantic service from New York City to London with 349 persons aboard, was targeted for hijack by a man who claimed to have a hand-grenade and wanted to be taken to Uganda. He was overpowered by other passengers and members of the crew. After being returned to the US, he was sentenced to prison on misdemeanour assault charges and also ordered to receive psychiatric treatment.

13 February 1977

AN attempt to hijack to Yugoslavia a Turkish Airlines DC-9 jet, which was on a scheduled domestic service from Istanbul to Izmir with 62 persons aboard, ended when the 17-year-old assailant surrendered to security forces at a military air base near its intended destination. The pilot and a stewardess were shot and wounded.

14 March 1977

A Boeing 727 jet operated by the Spanish airline Iberia was commandeered by a single assailant during a scheduled domestic service from Barcelona to Palma de Mallorca with 37 persons aboard. The aircraft was flown to Algeria, Ivory Coast, back to Spain, then to Italy, Switzerland, and Poland, and finally back to Switzerland, where the hijacker was arrested. He was sentenced to 10 years' imprisonment, and after failing to return from prison leave and threatening to commandeer another aircraft was apprehended in Italy, and sentenced to another nine years.

17 March 1977

ALL Nippon Airways Flight 724, a Boeing 727 jetliner carrying 43 persons on a domestic Japanese service to Sendai from Chitose Airport, located near Sapporo, got hijacked by a lone assailant who was overpowered by other passengers and turned over to police after the aircraft landed at Hakodate.

31 March 1977

THE pilot of a Swiftair DC-3 that had been on a Philippine non-scheduled domestic service from Zamboanga to the Tawitawi group of islands suddenly went berserk and opened fire with an M-16 rifle. Killed in the attack, which occurred about five minutes before the transport was to have landed, at approximately 11:45 local time, were the stewardess and six of the 34 passengers; 16 other persons aboard were wounded. The pilot was nevertheless subdued, and the co-pilot landed the aircraft safely.

Most of the occupants were military personnel, the weapon used belonging to one of the soldiers. The assailant, who may have been infatuated with the stewardess killed, was later detained at a stockade.

24 April 1977

POLICE overpowered a lone assailant on the ground at the airport serving Krakow, Poland, after he tried to take over a Polish Airlines (LOT) Tu-134 jet that had been on a charter service to Nürnberg, West Germany.

2 May 1977

A Spanish Iberia Boeing 727 jetliner, on a scheduled service from Madrid, was seized by a lone hijacker after landing at Rome, Italy, but he was overpowered and arrested.

8 May 1977

A passenger armed with a razor blade tried to commandeer to the USSR a Northwest Airlines Boeing 747 wide-bodied jet that was operating as Flight 22 on a service from Tokyo, Japan, to Honolulu, Hawaii, with 262 persons aboard. He was overpowered and tied up. Ruled insane, he was committed to a psychiatric facility for two years.

26 May 1977

AN Aeroflot An-24 turboprop on a scheduled domestic service from Riga to Daugavpils, USSR, was successfully commandeered to Sweden, which refused to extradite the lone hijacker and instead sentenced him to a four-year prison term.

17 June 1977

ARMED with a bottle of dark liquid (which turned out to be coloured water), a lone assailant tried to hijack to Sweden an Aeroflot twin-jet Yak-40 that had been on a scheduled domestic Soviet service from Tallin to Kaliningrad. It instead landed at Ventspils, Latvian SSR, where he was arrested.

18 June 1977

A Balkan Bulgarian Airlines An-24 turboprop on a scheduled domestic flight from Vidin to Sofia was hijacked by a lone assailant, who surrendered to Yugoslav authorities after the aircraft had landed at Belgrade.

21 June 1977

A LAN-Chile Boeing 727 jetliner, carrying 78 persons on a scheduled domestic service to Santiago from Antofagasta, was commandeered to Mendoza, Argentina, where the lone hijacker was taken into custody by military personnel.

5 July 1977

A Linea Aerea del Cobre SA (Ladeco) Boeing 727 jet airliner on a scheduled domestic Chilean service from Arica to Santiago with 60 persons aboard was commandeered to Lima, Peru. The four air pirates were subsequently deported to Cuba for asylum.

10–12 July 1977

AN Aeroflot Tu-134 jet airliner on a scheduled domestic service from Petrozavodsk to Leningrad, USSR, was hijacked to Helsinki, Finland. The two assailants held the other passengers and members of the crew hostage, demanding that the aircraft be released to Sweden, but they were returned to the Soviet Union, where they received prison terms of eight years and 15 years respectively.

20 August 1977

WESTERN Air Lines Flight 550, a Boeing 707 jet on a domestic service from San Diego, California, to Denver, Colorado, was hijacked by a lone assailant who claimed to have a bomb and demanded to be taken to Mexico and several other locations. He surrendered to the authorities when the aircraft landed at Salt Lake City, Utah. Criminal charges against him were subsequently dismissed on grounds of mental incompetency.

5 September 1977

A lone assailant held a stewardess at gunpoint aboard a Garuda Indonesian Airways twin-jet DC-9 that was on a scheduled domestic service from Jogjakarta to Surabaja, East Java, but he was overpowered by other members of the crew.

28 September–1 October 1977

A Japan Air Lines DC-8 Super 62 jet with 156 persons aboard was commandeered by five members of the self-proclaimed Japanese 'Red Army', armed with guns and grenades, during a scheduled service from Bombay, India, to Tokyo, Japan. On the ground at Dacca, Bangladesh, the assailants released about 60 passengers in exchange for ransom money and six prisoners held in Japan. They finally surrendered to Algerian authorities when the aircraft reached Algiers.

11 October 1977

A Ceskoslovenske Aerolinie (CSA) twin-jet Yak-40 was hijacked by two employees of the carrier during a scheduled domestic service from Karlovy Vary to Prague, Czechoslovakia, landing at Frankfurt, West Germany. They received prison terms of 3$^{1}/_{2}$ years and 6 years respectively.

17 October 1977

TWO gunmen stormed aboard an Air Djibouti Twin Otter turboprop at the airport serving Tadjoura, Djibouti. Among the 11 persons aboard, the pilot and one passenger were killed in the attack and five others wounded.

18 October 1977

AN attempt to commandeer a Polish Airlines (LOT) An-24 turboprop, carrying 50 persons on a scheduled domestic flight from Katowice to Warsaw, was reportedly foiled by the crew.

20 January 1978

ARMED with a pistol and what he said was a suitcase of explosives, a lone assailant seized a Pakistan International Airlines Fokker F.27 turboprop that was carrying 42 persons on a scheduled domestic service from Sukker to Karachi. He demanded a cash ransom for cancer treatment. The aircraft landed at its intended destination, where the hijacker was overpowered; an airborne security marshal was shot and wounded in the incident. The assailant would lose his life three years later, not to disease but to the hangman's noose.

6 February 1978

FALSELY claiming to have a bomb, a single hijacker commandeered a Ceskoslovenske Aerolinie (CSA) Tu-134 jet that was on a scheduled service to Prague, Czechoslovakia, from East Berlin. The aircraft, with 46 persons aboard, landed at Frankfurt, West Germany, where the assailant

A Japan Air Lines DC-8 Super 62 of the type hijacked and held for three days in the autumn of 1977 by members of the Japanese 'Red Army'. (McDonnell Douglas)

surrendered and asked for political asylum. He was subsequently sentenced to four years' imprisonment.

2 March 1978

A hijacking attempt was made by a single assailant against a Pakistan International Airlines Boeing 747 wide-bodied jetliner that was carrying 357 persons on a scheduled domestic service from Islamabad to Karachi. Three other passengers who overpowered him were injured in a grenade blast. The hijacker lost his hand in the explosion and, convicted of air piracy, he was hanged in 1979.

1 April 1978

ARMED with a rifle, a 15-year-old boy jumped a fence at Byrd International Airport, Richmond, Virginia, and forced his way aboard a Piedmont Airlines Boeing 737 jet, operating as Flight 66 and carrying 66 persons. He demanded a million dollars in ransom and a trip to France, but subsequently surrendered. Convicted of multiple charges, he was remanded to the care of a psychiatrist.

9 April 1978

FIRING shots and spilling gasoline in the cabin and threatening to start a fire, a lone assailant tried to hijack to Sweden an Aeroflot Yak-40 jetliner that was on a scheduled Soviet domestic service originating at Palanga, with an ultimate destination of Tallinn. The aircraft instead landed at Pyarnu, Estonian SSR, where he was captured. Found to be mentally disturbed, he was committed to a psychiatric hospital.

10 May 1978

THREE adults accompanied by two children hijacked a Ceskoslovenske Aerolinie (CSA) Il-18 turboprop that was carrying 39 persons on a scheduled domestic flight from Prague to Brno. All were taken into custody when the aircraft landed at Frankfurt, West Germany.

11 May 1978

TWO men armed with a toy pistol and a homemade nitro-glycerine device commandeered an AVIANCA Boeing 727 jetliner that was on a scheduled domestic Colombian flight from Santa Maria to Bogota with 109 persons aboard. They then took a real revolver from a customs official, which was used to shoot and wound the flight engineer.

After the aircraft had landed at Curacao, Netherlands Antilles, the assailants were disarmed by other passengers and members of the crew. Four persons, including two police officers, suffered injuries.

16 May 1978

TWO men aboard an Aeromexico DC-9 jetliner, carrying 99 persons on a scheduled domestic service from Torreon to Mexico City, handed a stewardess a note on which was written an incoherent message, stating they were carrying explosives and demanding 'justice' for themselves and certain others. Both were taken into custody after the aircraft had landed at its intended destination.

17 May 1978

AN attempt to hijack a Ceskoslovenske Aerolinie (CSA) Yak-40 jet, which was on a scheduled domestic service from Brno to Prague, failed when the lone assailant was overpowered.

29 May 1978

A lone hijacker tried to take over a Ceskoslovenske Aerolinie (CSA) Yak-40 jet that was on a scheduled domestic flight from Brno to Karlovy Vary, demanding to be taken to West Germany, but he was overpowered by members of the crew.

6 August 1978

ARMED with a pistol that turned out to be a toy, a lone assailant seized a KLM Royal Dutch Airlines DC-9 jet that had been carrying 68 persons on a scheduled service from Amsterdam to Madrid, Spain, demanding to be taken to Algeria. He was overpowered by a crew member and three other passengers, and subsequently extradited to Holland for prosecution.

18 August 1978

A Philippine Airlines BAC One-Eleven Series 500 (RP-C-1184), the same aircraft damaged in a 1975 suicide bombing, was targeted in this amazingly similar incident. Designated as Flight 148, on a domestic run to Manila from Cebu, the jetliner was cruising at 24,000ft (c7,300m) in the vicinity of Sibuyan Island when an explosive device detonated in its left rear lavatory. The blast, which took place shortly after 07:00 local time, resulted in the death of the saboteur, who was ejected from the aircraft and lost at sea. Three passengers were injured, while the other 80 persons aboard, including the crew of six, escaped unscathed. Following the explosion, the pilot descended to 12,000ft (c3,700m) in order to equalize pressure, and the One-Eleven proceeded on to Manila, landing safely despite a hole measuring 2ft by 3ft (c0.6 m by 1m) in the rear fuselage area.

The bombing, in August 1978, of a Philippine Airlines BAC One-Eleven Series 500 such as this was the second sabotage attack on the same aircraft. (British Aerospace)

The bomber was found to have purchased a one-way ticket and taken out an insurance policy worth 50,000 pesos the night before.

25 August 1978

A lone assailant claiming to have explosives handed a note to a stewardess aboard Trans World Airlines Flight 830, a Boeing 707 jet on a service from New York City to Geneva, Switzerland, with 88 persons aboard. In the note he demanded the release of a number of individuals imprisoned in the US and elsewhere. After the aircraft had landed at its intended destination, a seven-hour stand-off ensued until he surrendered. He was subsequently sentenced to seven years' imprisonment for interference with an airline crew and making a false bomb threat.

26 August 1978

A Burma Airways Corporation de Havilland Twin Otter Series 300 (XY-AEI) was apparently destroyed by explosives and crashed near Papun, Kayin, Burma, killing all 14 persons aboard (11 passengers and a crew of three). The twin-engine turboprop was on a scheduled domestic service from Moulmein to Pa-an, and crashed seconds after taking off following a blast in its cabin at an approximate height of 400ft (120m) above the ground. It was not known if the explosion was an intentional act of sabotage or an accident.

27 August 1978

A United Airlines DC-8 Super 61 jetliner, desig-

nated as Flight 179, en route from Denver, Colorado, to Seattle, Washington, and carrying 159 persons, was diverted to Vancouver, British Columbia, by a female passenger claiming in a note to have a bomb. She was declared mentally incompetent by a government psychiatrist.

30 August 1978

A lone assailant armed with a starter pistol hijacked a Polish Airlines (LOT) Tu-134 jetliner on a scheduled service from Gdansk, Poland, to East Berlin with 71 persons aboard, ordering it to land in West Berlin. There, he and eight other passengers asked for political asylum. The hijacker was sentenced to nine months' imprisonment.

7 September 1978

THE detonation of an explosive device in the fuselage mid-section of an Air Ceylon Hawker Siddeley 748 Series 2 (4R-ACJ) that was on the ground at Ratmalana Airport, near Colombo, Sri Lanka, resulted in a fire that destroyed the twin-engine turboprop airliner. The blast occurred around 08:40 local time, as the aircraft was being prepared for a ferry flight. The pilot and co-pilot, who had been carrying out their pre-departure checks, were the only occupants and escaped injury.

30 September 1978

A Finnair Super Caravelle jet airliner was seized by a pistol-armed assailant during a scheduled domestic service from Oulu to Helsinki, Finland, with 48 persons aboard. The aircraft proceeded to its intended destination, then returned to its point of origin, with a stop at Amsterdam, the Netherlands. The gunman, who was paid a ransom during the hijacking, was allowed to go home but was arrested the following day. He was subsequently fined and sentenced to seven years' imprisonment.

22 October 1978

THE pilot of a Transportes Aereos Portugueses (TAP) Boeing 727 jetliner on a scheduled service from Lisbon to the Portuguese Island of Madeira, after correctly ascertaining that the two pistols held by the assailant were fakes, overpowered a passenger who had been demanding to be flown to Morocco.

31 October 1978

THREATENING to blow it up, a lone assailant tried to hijack to Norway an Aeroflot twin-jet Tu-134 that had been on a scheduled Soviet domestic flight from Leningrad to Murmansk, but the crew instead landed at Petrozavodsk, Karel'skaya ASSR, where he was arrested. He was subsequently sentenced to six years' imprisonment.

10 November 1978

FALSELY claiming to have an explosive device, a passenger tried to divert to Turkey an Aeroflot An-24 turboprop that had been on a scheduled domestic Soviet service originating at Kharkov, with an ultimate destination of Sukhumi. He was arrested after it instead landed at Batumi, Georgian SSR, and was later sentenced to eight years' imprisonment.

23 November 1978

A would-be hijacker drove his car through a fence at Mitchell Field, serving Madison, Wisconsin, and up to a North Central Airlines twin-jet DC-9, which was operating as Flight 468. He then boarded the aircraft, claiming to have a bomb (which turned out to be a fake) in a trash bag. He was later captured by police on the flight deck of the DC-9, but charges against him were subsequently dropped on grounds of mental incompetency.

20 December 1978

TWO assailants brandishing what appeared to be a pistol and a hand-grenade commandeered Indian Airlines Flight 410, a Boeing 737 jet on a domestic service to New Delhi from Lucknow, forcing it to land at Varanasi, in Pradesh. They were demanding the release of former Indian Prime Minister Indira Gandhi, who at the time was in jail.

After releasing the passengers and crew, the hijackers were flown by light aircraft to Lucknow, where they were taken into custody by police. The gun was a toy and the grenade actually a cricket ball.

21 December 1978

A 17-year-old girl who said she had dynamite strapped to her body commandeered a Trans World Airlines DC-9 jet, designated as Flight 541, on an intrastate service from St Louis to Kansas City, Missouri, with 89 persons aboard. She was demanding the release of a prisoner serving a life sentence for a 1972 hijacking. The aircraft landed at Marion, Illinois, where a nine-hour stand-off ensued until she was arrested by two law enforcement officers.

The hijacker, who actually had three railroad flares, was convicted of air piracy as a juvenile, and placed in a foster home until her 21st birthday, then put on probation.

27 January 1979

A woman claiming to have nitro-glycerine in her possession seized United Airlines Flight 8, a Boeing 747 wide-bodied jet, during a domestic transcontinental service from Los Angeles to New York City with 131 persons aboard. She demanded that certain personalities read on television a message she had written. After six hours of negotiations at John F. Kennedy International Airport, which was the aircraft's intended destination, she was arrested and found not to have any explosives. The assailant was subsequently given five years' probation after being convicted of first degree coercion.

27 February 1979

THREE hijackers, one of whom lit a Molotov cocktail, tried to seize an Aeroflot Tu-154 that was on a scheduled service to Moscow from Oslo, Norway. The assailants were overpowered by other passengers and members of the crew, and the Soviet aircraft landed as planned at Stockholm, Sweden. A Swedish court sentenced two of the hijackers to three years' imprisonment and the third to 18 months.

1 April 1979

TWO assailants tried to divert to Turkey an Aeroflot twin-jet Yak-40, operating as Flight 546, after it had taken off from Simferopol, Ukraine, an en-route stop during a scheduled Soviet domestic service from Odessa to Kutaisi. Both were detained and turned over to the police, being subsequently sentenced to respective prison terms of five and seven years.

26 April 1979

A high-explosive device detonated in the area of the forward lavatory of an Indian Airlines Boeing Advanced 737-2A8 (VT-ECR) after the twin-engine jet, on a scheduled domestic service from Trivandrum, had initiated a descent from 27,000ft (c8,000m) in preparation for landing at the Madras airport. Subsequent to the blast, the aircraft experienced a total electrical and instrument failure, and its cockpit and front cabin area filled with smoke.

A gear-down but flapless landing was accomplished some 2,500ft (750m) beyond the threshold of Runway 25. Due to the high speed of the aircraft when it touched down, and the non-availability of reverse thrust and the anti-skid system due to damage suffered in the blast, it ran off the end of the pavement and ploughed into a field. Among the 61 passengers and six crew members aboard, eight persons were seriously injured. The aircraft was destroyed by both the in-flight explosion and the subsequent crash, which occurred at around noon local time.

8 June 1979

A lone assailant armed with a shotgun seized a Trans-Australia Airlines twin-jet DC-9 that was on a scheduled domestic service from Coolangotta to Brisbane, Queensland. He allowed the aircraft to land at its intended destination and then released the 41 passengers. He was subsequently overpowered by members of the cabin and flight crew and arrested by the police.

20 June 1979

American Airlines Flight 293, a Boeing 727 jetliner on a domestic service from New York City to Chicago with 136 persons aboard, was seized by a lone assailant using two ground-burst simulator projectiles and what he said was a bag of dynamite. He demanded the release of a US federal prisoner and a trip to Peru, which he then changed to South Africa and finally Ireland.

The air pirate, who had been joined by his attorney, switched to a longer-range Boeing 707 in New York for the transatlantic flight. He surrendered in Ireland and was extradited back to the US, where he was sentenced to more than 40 years in prison on multiple charges.

9 July 1979

IT was a bad day all-round for the would-be hijacker of a Condor Aerovias Nacionales twin-engine turboprop Fairchild F-27 that was on a scheduled domestic Ecuadorean service from Tulcan to Quito. Though he had ordered the aircraft to be flown to Costa Rica, it nevertheless set down at Quito, where the passengers escaped through a cabin door. After firing two shots, apparently accidentally, the assailant's gun jammed. He then tried to ignite a stick of dynamite he was holding, but his cigarette lighter failed to operate, after which he was finally overpowered and taken into custody.

25 July 1979

A lone assailant armed with a knife and what later proved to be a toy pistol hijacked a Bangladesh Biman Fokker F.27 turboprop that was carrying 43 persons on a scheduled domestic flight from Jessore to Dacca, diverting it to Calcutta, India. He demanded a ransom and also an escape aircraft, but after 10 hours of negotiations he agreed to surrender. Later in the year he was returned to Bangladesh for prosecution.

5 August 1979

THREE deserters from the Spanish Foreign Legion commandeered an Iberia DC-9 jet that had just landed and was disembarking passengers at Puerto Del Rosario, Fuerteventura, in the Canary Islands. The aircraft flew to Lisbon, Portugal, where all the hostages except the two flight crew members were released, and ultimately to Geneva, Switzerland, where the hijackers surrendered. They were later sentenced to 20 months' imprisonment by a Swiss court.

22 August 1979

A twin-engine turboprop Hawker Siddeley HS 748 Series 2A (FAC-1101), operated by the Colombian carrier Servicio de Aeronavegacion a Territorios Nacionales, crashed in a residential area of Bogota, Colombia, after being stolen by a mechanic and a companion. Both occupants of the aircraft and three persons on the ground were killed.

22 August 1979

A United Airlines Boeing 727 jet, operating as Flight 739 and carrying 120 persons on a domestic service from Portland, Oregon, to Los Angeles, California, was seized by a passenger who claimed to have a bomb. His demand that the aircraft return to Portland having been satisfied, the hijacker subsequently gave himself up. He was sentenced to 60 years in prison for kidnapping.

12 September 1979

ARMED with a very real-looking toy pistol, a lone hijacker took control of a Lufthansa German Airlines Boeing 727 jet that was on a scheduled domestic service from Frankfurt to Cologne with 128 persons aboard. Following seven hours of negotiations, he read a long statement calling for a more humane world; after more negotiations, he surrendered.

30 October 1979

PACIFIC Southwest Airlines Flight 784, a Boeing 727-214 jetliner on a short-haul service from Los Angeles to San Diego with 108 persons aboard, got hijacked over Southern California by a passenger who claimed to have a bomb and wanted to be taken to Mexico City. He was apprehended during a refuelling stop at Tijuana, Mexico, and sent back to the US, where he was sentenced to prison for 16 months on the charge of interfering with an airline crew.

13 November 1979

THE pilot of a Japan Air Lines DC-10, which had been seized during a scheduled domestic service from Osaka to Tokyo with 356 persons aboard, overpowered the hijacker of the wide-bodied jet after he had threatened a stewardess with a can-opener and demanded to be flown to Moscow, USSR.

15 November 1979

AN American Airlines Boeing 727 jet, on a scheduled domestic US service from Chicago to Washington, DC, landed safely after the pilot had reported smoke, later determined to have resulted from the detonation of an explosive device in the baggage compartment. There were no injuries among the 78 persons aboard.

24 November 1979

AN 18-year-old man armed with a hunting knife tried to hijack to Iran an American Airlines Boeing 727 jet, operating as Flight 395 and carrying 74 persons on an intrastate service from San Antonio to El Paso, Texas. On the ground in El Paso he was overpowered by FBI agents and later given a 10-year prison sentence.

30 January 1980

TWO men were overpowered by other passengers and members of the crew after trying to hijack an Interflug Il-18 turboprop that had been on a scheduled domestic East German service from Erfurt to East Berlin.

29 February 1980

ARMED with an arsenal of weapons, including a rifle and two sticks of dynamite, a lone assailant took four hostages and tried to board a Compania Ecuatoriana de Aviacion SA Boeing 707 jetliner on the ground at Guayaquil, Ecuador, but was unable to gain entry. He subsequently surrendered to the authorities.

20 March 1980

DEMANDING to be flown to Turkey, a knife-wielding hijacker was overpowered by other passengers and crew members aboard an Aeroflot Tu-134 jetliner, designated as Flight 6647, on a domestic Soviet service from Baku to Yerevan. He was later sentenced to eight years' imprisonment.

14 April 1980

AT Denver, Colorado, a knife-wielding assailant boarded Continental Airlines Flight 11, a Boeing 727 jet bound for California, demanding that it take off, but he gave himself up on hearing of a possible mechanical problem with the aircraft. He was sentenced to 20 years' imprisonment for air piracy.

1 May 1980

PACIFIC Southwest Airlines Flight 818, a Boeing 727 jet that was preparing to take off from Stockton, California, was targeted for hijack by a pistol-armed assailant. He was disarmed by the flight engineer and then surrendered, being later sentenced to 15 years' imprisonment.

6 May 1980

AIR Portugal Flight 131, a Boeing 727 jetliner carrying 90 persons on a domestic service from Lisbon to Faro, was seized by a 16-year-old boy who demanded a ransom and wanted to be taken to Switzerland. On the ground at Madrid, Spain, he dropped his demands, and was taken into custody after returning to Lisbon.

6 June 1980

AN explosive device that apparently failed to detonate was found in the luggage compartment of a Dutch Transavia twin-jet Boeing 737 that had landed on the Greek island of Rhodes at the end of a non-scheduled service from Amsterdam carrying 96 persons.

27 June 1980

EARLY suspicions of sabotage would, many years later, be confirmed in this disastrous airliner crash.

Aerolinee Italia SpA Flight 870, a twin-jet Douglas DC-9 Series 15 (I-TIGI), had departed from Bologna, Italy, on a domestic service to

Palermo, Sicily. It had been cruising on an almost due southerly heading in darkness at an approximate height of 25,000ft (7,500m) over the Tyrrhenian Sea when, shortly before 20:00 local time, something happened to the aircraft of a sudden and catastrophic nature. The bodies of more than 40 victims were subsequently found; there was no hope of survival among the 81 persons aboard (77 passengers and a crew of four). The scene of the crash was some 15 miles (25km) north-east of the Italian island of Ustica, in water about 12,000ft (3,700m) deep.

Tests performed on recovered debris and pathological examinations of the deceased seemed to indicate that the airliner had either collided with, or suffered damage from the nearby explosion of, a missile. In 1990, an investigative commission was unable to agree on whether the loss of the DC-9 resulted from a missile strike or an internal explosion. Later, an international commission was formed to probe the mystery of Flight 870, and its findings were released in 1994.

A considerable amount of additional wreckage was raised from the seabed as part of the second investigation, which led to a determination of the probable cause of the tragedy. Particularly revealing was the damage and distortion around the right rear lavatory, which the commission found had preceded the more general in-flight disintegration of the aircraft. It was concluded that only the detonation of an explosive device could have caused such internal damage. Structural failure due to fatigue, corrosion or overload was discarded. Also ruled out was the original missile theory, which seemed tenable when little wreckage was available for examination but would not have explained the interior damage.

The commission determined that the blast produced a shock wave that tore off a considerable amount of aircraft skin atop the rear fuselage area, with internal parts and passengers being flung out of the cabin. Both engines then broke away, followed by the separation of the empennage. The resulting pitch-down of the rest of the aircraft caused a down-load that snapped off the left outer wing. The break-up sequence occurred in a matter of only a few seconds, after which the jet plummeted almost vertically into the water.

The bomb used to destroy I-TIGI must have been a relatively small amount of explosive, probably wrapped only in plastic; the absence of penetration marks or pitting in recovered structures indicated that it was not in a hard container. Most likely, the device had been placed between the outer wall of the lavatory and the skin of the aircraft, access to which would have been available several ways, and where it would have been difficult to detect.

No claim of responsibility was ever made in connection with the Itavia disaster, though it may

have been related to a wave of terrorism blamed largely on right-wing extremists that plagued Italy from the late 1960s into the 1980s. The most serious such case was the bombing of the Bologna railway station some five weeks after the destruction of Flight 870, which claimed 85 lives.

30 June 1980

ARMED with a pistol and a hand-grenade, a lone assailant commandeered an Aerolineas Argentinas twin-jet Boeing 737 that was on a scheduled domestic service from Mar del Plata to Buenos Aires, demanding a ransom and a trip to Mexico. After the aircraft had landed at its intended destination, he was convinced by the pilot to give himself up.

12 July 1980

A hijacking extortionist used a bomb threat against a Philippine Airlines Boeing 727 jet that was on a scheduled domestic flight from Manila to Cebu, demanding $6 million. However, he was duped by the crew, who locked the cockpit door and returned to the capital, where he was arrested by security personnel.

29 August 1980

A mob of Cuban refugees forced their way aboard Braniff International Airways Flight 920 when the DC-8 jetliner was on the ground at Lima, Peru. Three persons were injured after the police fired shots and pulled the ramp away from the US aircraft. After a siege lasting 23 hours, and after being convinced that they would be prosecuted if flown to the US, the 168 refugees surrendered.

9 September 1980

ABOUT two minutes after a United Airlines Boeing 727 jet had landed at Sacramento, California, following a scheduled domestic service from Portland, Oregon, a bomb in a cardboard box exploded aboard as the passengers were disembarking. Two cargo handlers were injured in the blast.

17 September 1980

A French Army ordnance specialist trying to deactivate a bomb placed on the outside of an Air France Boeing 737 on the ground at Le Raizet Airport, serving Pointe-a-Pitre, Guadeloupe, was killed when the device detonated, badly damaging the jet airliner.

4 December 1980

A lone assailant commandeered a Polish Airlines

(LOT) An-24 turboprop, operating as Flight 770 on a domestic service from Zielena Gora to Warsaw with 25 persons aboard, diverting it to West Berlin. He asked for asylum there but instead received a four-year prison sentence.

5 December 1980

REPORTEDLY to protest the acquittal in Venezuela of persons suspected of blowing up a Cuban airliner in 1976, four hijackers commandeered a Linea Aeropostal Venezolana DC-9 jet that was carrying 120 persons on a scheduled domestic service from Porlamar to Caracas. After it had landed at Higuerote, Venezuela, they stole from it two chests containing 7.5 million Bolivars. The money was subsequently located and 35 persons were arrested in connection with the crime.

21 December 1980

AN Aerovias del Cesar (Aerocesar Colombia) Sud-Aviation Caravelle VI-R (HK-1810) crashed some 15 miles (25km) south of the airport at Riohacha, Guajira, from where it had taken off about five minutes earlier, on a scheduled domestic service to Medellin. All 70 persons aboard (63 passengers and seven crew members) perished.

There appeared to have been a fire in its right-hand aft section before the twin-jet airliner plunged into the Guajira Desert at around 14:25 local time, scattering wreckage about half-a-mile (0.8km) in length. The weather at the time was good. All Caravelles registered in Colombia were subsequently grounded for the purpose of an airworthiness check. But the crash did not result from a technical fault. It was subsequently determined that an explosive substance, apparently nitro-glycerine, had detonated in a rear lavatory and damaged the aircraft, primarily its hydraulic system, apparently leading to a loss of control.

10 January 1981

FOUR men tried unsuccessfully to hijack to the West a Polish Airlines (LOT) An-24 turboprop that was on a scheduled domestic service from Katowice to Warsaw. After it had landed at its intended destination, supposedly for refuelling, the assailants were captured as they tried to switch to another aircraft.

6 February 1981

PROTESTING against the Colombian political system, two men hijacked an AVIANCA Boeing 727 jet airliner that was on a scheduled domestic service from Bucaramanga to Cucuta with 77 persons aboard, but after a siege lasting 10 hours they surrendered on the ground at the intended destination.

5 March 1981

A lone assailant took seven hostages aboard a Continental Air Lines Boeing 727 jet, designated as Flight 72, at Los Angeles International Airport. He demanded $3 million, but after hours of negotiations he released them and then surrendered.

27 March 1981

CLAIMING to be terrorists opposed to the Honduran Government, three men and a woman commandeered a Servicio Aereo de Honduras SA Boeing 727 jet, designated as Flight 414, on a domestic service from Tegucigalpa to San Pedro Sula with 87 persons aboard. Landing first at Managua, Nicaragua, the aircraft proceeded on the following day to Panama City, where the hijackers surrendered.

2 May 1981

WITH the intention of getting newspapers to publish a lengthy religious statement, a lone assailant carrying bottles of gasoline commandeered an Aer Lingus-Irish International Airlines Boeing 737 jet, designated as Flight 164, on a service from Dublin with 118 persons aboard, just before it was to have landed at London. The aircraft landed at Le Touquet, France, where a police unit boarded it secretly and arrested the hijacker.

24 May 1981

FOUR men commandeered Turkish Airlines Flight 104, a twin-jet DC-9 that was on a domestic service from Istanbul to Ankara with 84 persons aboard, forcing it to land at Burgas, Bulgaria, and demanding a ransom and the release by Turkey of 47 fellow terrorists being held in prison. The following day, two of the hijackers were arrested after getting off to give a press conference, and the remaining two were overpowered by passengers, with both of them and four other persons being injured in the process. Bulgaria sentenced the hijackers to three years' imprisonment.

21 July 1981

USING a dummy hand-grenade, a lone assailant hijacked a Polish Airlines (LOT) An-24 turboprop to West Berlin. It had been on a scheduled domestic service from Katowice to Gdansk with 55 persons aboard. He was later sentenced to three years' imprisonment by German authorities.

5 August 1981

A lone assailant attempting to hijack a Polish Airlines (LOT) An-24 turboprop, which was on a scheduled domestic service from Katowice to Gdansk with 49 persons aboard, was arrested after it landed at its intended destination.

11 August 1981

THE hijacker of a Polish Airlines (LOT) An-24 turboprop was tricked by the pilot into believing that it had landed in West Berlin, when in fact it had set down at Warsaw, Poland. The assailant was arrested.

22 August 1981

THIS successful hijacking of a Polish Airlines (LOT) An-24 turboprop, which had been on a scheduled domestic flight from Wroclaw to Warsaw, ended with the sole assailant surrendering in West Berlin. German authorities subsequently sentenced him to $5^{1}/_{2}$ years' imprisonment.

18 September 1981

A dozen youths aged 17 to 22 commandeered a Polish Airlines (LOT) An-24 turboprop on a scheduled domestic service from Katowice to Warsaw with 49 persons aboard. After the aircraft had landed in West Berlin they surrendered to the American authorities. Eight of the hijackers were sentenced to between one and four years' imprisonment by a German court.

22 September 1981

THREE men and a woman tried to hijack a Polish Airlines (LOT) An-24 turboprop to West Berlin, but they were captured after the pilot landed at Warsaw, from where the flight had taken off earlier on a scheduled domestic service to Koszalin.

26 September 1981

A Jugoslovenski Aerotransport (JAT) Boeing 727 jet carrying 101 persons on a scheduled domestic Yugoslavian service from Titograd to Belgrade was commandeered by three assailants who wanted to go to Italy and then Israel. Both countries refused them entry and the airliner landed at Larnaca, Cyprus, where the hijackers surrendered. They were given prison terms ranging from $3^{1}/_{2}$ to $8^{1}/_{2}$ years.

29–30 September 1981

USING daggers that they had been allowed to carry for religious reasons, six assailants took over Indian Airlines Flight 425, a Boeing 737 jet carrying 117 persons on a domestic service from New Delhi to Srinagar, forcing it to Lahore, Pakistan. Their demands included a ransom of half-a-million dollars and the release of other Sikh separatists by India. Shortly before 08:00 local time on the second day, as the hijackers were negotiating, disguised Pakistani Army personnel boarded the aircraft and captured them.

29 September 1981

A lone assailant armed with a razor blade tried to commandeer a Polish Airlines (LOT) An-24 turboprop on the ground at Warsaw, Poland, but he was threatened by other passengers and then arrested by police.

5 October 1981

A passenger who claimed to have a bomb tried to hijack to the USSR a US Air BAC One-Eleven jet, which was operating as Flight 455 on a domestic intrastate service from Albany to Buffalo, New York, with 66 persons aboard. He surrendered, and charges against him were dismissed on grounds of mental illness.

21 October 1981

TWO men and two women who had chartered an Aeropesca Colombia C-46 hijacked the airliner, which was loaded with weapons, and forced it down on the Guajira Peninsula, in Colombia. Taken hostage, five employees of the company were released the following month.

23 October 1981

WHILE en route to New York City from San Juan, Puerto Rico, American Airlines Flight 676, a DC-10 wide-bodied jet carrying 109 persons, was targeted for hijack by a lone assailant who claimed to have a bomb and wanted to be taken to Quebec, Canada. He surrendered when the aircraft landed at its intended destination to refuel. Air piracy charges against him were later dismissed.

29–30 October 1981

A Servicios Aereos Nacionales (SAN) CASA-212 twin-engine turboprop airliner was commandeered by five assailants just after landing at San Jose, Costa Rica, on a scheduled domestic service from Quepos. They demanded the release of seven prisoners, six of whom joined the hijackers on the second day (the seventh prisoner choosing to remain in Costa Rica). They then flew to El Salvador, where they were taken into custody.

25 November 1981

FORTY-FOUR men, part of a group that had tried

to take over the Seychelles airport, located on Mahe Island, boarded an Air-India Boeing 707 jetliner, designated as Flight 224, which had just landed during a service to Bombay from Salisbury, Zimbabwe, with 79 persons aboard. It was ordered to be flown to Durban, South Africa. After about six hours of negotiations there, the hostages were released and the hijackers surrendered. The leader was sentenced to 20 years' imprisonment for air piracy, seven others were given terms of from one to five years, and 34 others were sentenced to six months.

12 December 1981

WHILE it was on the ground at Mexico City international airport, an explosive device rocked an Aerolineas Nicaraguenses (Aeronica) Boeing 727-25 jet airliner, operating as Flight 527 and carrying 117 persons. Three crew members aboard the aircraft, and three baggage handlers outside, suffered injuries in the blast, which occurred around 12:40 local time as it was preparing to take off, bound for San Salvador, El Salvador, one segment of a service originating at Managua, Nicaragua. The bomb had detonated between the rearmost seat on the left side and the cabin wall, and blew a hole in the fuselage of the 727.

7 January 1982

IN an attempt to release his brother, imprisoned for a failed hijacking four years earlier, a lone assailant carrying a bottle of gasoline and a stick of dynamite tried to hijack an Aerotal Colombia Boeing 727 jetliner on a scheduled domestic flight from Santa Marta to Barranquilla. This hijacker had no greater success, being overpowered by other passengers and later arrested.

13 February 1982

DEMANDING a pilot, an unarmed assailant boarded an out-of-service Braniff International Airways Boeing 727 jetliner that was parked at Amarillo airport, Texas. He later surrendered, and charges against him were subsequently dismissed on grounds of mental incompetency.

20 February 1982

THREE baggage handlers were killed and four other persons suffered injuries when an explosive device hidden in a suitcase detonated on a conveyor belt at the international airport serving Managua, Nicaragua. The suitcase containing the bomb had just been unloaded from a Servicio Aereo de Honduras SA (SAHSA) Boeing 737 jetliner, which had landed some 15 minutes earlier on a scheduled service from Tegucigalpa, Honduras.

26 February–1 March 1982

FIVE hijackers who claimed to be members of the Tanzanian Revolutionary Youth Movement took over Air Tanzania Flight 206, a Boeing 737 jet on a domestic service from Mwanza to Dar-es-Salaam with 99 persons aboard. They demanded the resignation of the President of Tanzania. During the hijacking the co-pilot was shot and wounded, the aircraft finally landing at Stansted Airport, Essex, England. The assailants were subsequently sentenced to prison terms ranging from three to eight years by a British court.

30 April 1982

EIGHT men disarmed the six security guards aboard a Polish Airlines (LOT) An-24, injuring two of them in the process, and then hijacked the twin-engine turboprop to West Berlin; it had been on a scheduled domestic flight from Wroclaw to Warsaw at the time, with 52 persons aboard. More than half of the other passengers, who were related to the hijackers, got off with them in Berlin, where the air pirates were sentenced to prison terms of from 2½ to 4 years for 'endangering air traffic'.

10 May 1982

DURING an internal flight, a twin-engine C-46 of the Nicaraguan airline Aerolineas Nicaraguenses (Aeronica) was hijacked to Limon, Costa Rica, where the two air pirates responsible requested political asylum.

21 May 1982

ARMED with a hand-grenade, a lone hijacker commandeered a Philippine Airlines twin-jet BAC One-Eleven that was carrying 114 persons on a scheduled domestic service from Bacolod to Cebu. Besides 60,000 pesos, he demanded various government reforms, but was overpowered and captured.

9 June 1982

TWO men who tried to hijack a Polish Airlines (LOT) An-24 turboprop to West Berlin during a scheduled domestic service from Katowice to Warsaw were captured by police.

23 June 1982

A woman who claimed to be armed confronted the co-pilot of Henson Airlines Flight 611, a four-engine turboprop Dash-7, at the Staunton airport, Virginia. She first demanded to be flown out, but when the crew member escaped, she went back into the terminal building and was subsequently apprehended by police. Charges against her were later dismissed.

30 June 1982

AN Italian Alitalia Boeing 747 wide-bodied jet airliner with 261 persons aboard was commandeered during a scheduled service from New Delhi, India, to Bangkok, Thailand. The lone assailant demanded a ransom and wanted to be reunited with his wife and child in Italy. They arrived the following day in Bangkok, and the three were then flown to Sri Lanka, where he was later arrested and sentenced to a prison term of 20 years to life.

3 July 1982

IN a note to the crew, a passenger of Aeroflot Flight 8690, a Tu-154 jetliner on a Soviet domestic service from Murmansk to Leningrad, asked for 250,000 roubles and for the aircraft to fly 'in a direction we'll give'. He was instead arrested and later sentenced to five years imprisonment.

25 July 1982

FIVE hijackers experienced the harshness of Chinese law when they tried to commandeer to Taiwan a Civil Aviation Administration of China (CAAC) Il-18, which, operating as Flight 2502, was on a domestic service from Xian to Shanghai. They wounded two flight crew members, and about a dozen others were also injured, mostly when an explosive device detonated, but the assailants were nevertheless overpowered and the four-engine turboprop landed safely at its intended destination. The five hijackers were executed the following month.

4 August 1982

INDIAN Airlines Flight 423, a twin-jet Boeing 737 carrying 135 persons on a domestic service from New Delhi to Srinagar, with an en-route stop at Amritsar, was hijacked by a lone assailant holding what he said was a bomb. Denied permission to land at Lahore, Pakistan, the aircraft set down at Amritsar, where the hijacker was subsequently overpowered. His bomb turned out to be a rubber ball.

25 August 1982

A Polish Airlines (LOT) Il-18 turboprop that had been on a scheduled service to Warsaw from Budapest, Hungary, was successfully diverted to West Germany by two men; there they were each sentenced to 4^1/$_2$ years in prison.

25 September 1982

AN Italian Alitalia Boeing 727 jetliner, designated as Flight 871 and en route to Rome from Algiers, Algeria, with 109 persons aboard, was hijacked by a lone assailant armed with a knife. The aircraft was denied entry by both Libya and Malta, and finally landed at Catania, Sicily. The hijacker was subsequently overpowered and injured; a police officer was also hurt.

14 October 1982

A married couple commandeered a Balkan Bulgarian Airlines twin-jet Tu-134 that was on a scheduled service from Burgas, Bulgaria, to Warsaw, Poland, demanding to be flown to West Germany. Because it was low on fuel, the aircraft landed at Vienna, Austria. There the man was sentenced to two years' imprisonment for air piracy and the woman was given a one year suspended sentence.

27 October 1982

AT Los Angeles International Airport a man forced his way aboard Trans World Airlines Flight 72, an L-1011 wide-bodied jet carrying 109 persons, in an apparent hijacking attempt. However, he was shoved out of the door by a passenger and was injured in the fall. Convicted of air piracy, he was sentenced to 12 years' imprisonment.

7 November 1982

INJURING the flight engineer and one passenger in the process, three men commandeered an Aeroflot An-24 as the Soviet twin-engine turboprop airliner was on a scheduled domestic service from Novosibirsk to Odessa. They surrendered when it landed at a NATO air base in Turkey and were later sentenced to prison terms of from eight to nine years.

22 November 1982

ONE of three security guards assigned to a Polish Airlines (LOT) An-24 turboprop, which was on a scheduled domestic service from Wroclaw to Warsaw with 38 persons aboard, ended up hijacking the aircraft to West Berlin. Though he was shot and wounded, and suffered further injury when he jumped out after the aircraft had landed, he survived to be taken into custody by US authorities.

27 November 1982

A uniformed man who appeared to be a security guard tried to hijack to West Berlin a Tu-154 jetliner operated by the Hungarian airline MALEV, which was on a scheduled service from Warsaw, Poland, to Budapest, Hungary, but he was overpowered.

30 December 1982

A passenger who claimed to have a bomb aboard United Airlines Flight 702, a Boeing 727 jet on a domestic service from Chicago, Illinois, to Pittsburgh, Pennsylvania, demanded to be taken to Washington, DC. Convinced by the flight engineer that it did not have enough fuel, he allowed it to land at its intended destination, where he subsequently surrendered. Prosecution was deferred and he was enrolled in a mental health programme.

7 January 1983

AN emotionally disturbed passenger aboard Delta Air Lines Flight 177, a Boeing 727 jet carrying 30 persons on a domestic service from Portland, Maine, to Boston, Massachusetts, asked to be taken to Las Vegas, Nevada. A bag that he said contained explosives was taken away from him and he was taken into custody. Charges against him were later dismissed on grounds of mental incompetency.

13 February 1983

A Trans-Australia Airlines A300 wide-bodied jet, operating as Flight 5 on a domestic service from Perth, Western Australia, to Melbourne, Victoria, with 204 persons aboard, was targeted for hijack by a lone assailant who claimed to have a bomb and wanted to be taken to Adelaide, South Australia. He allowed it to land at its intended destination, and while on the ground at Tullamarine Airport he surrendered. His 'bomb' was not real.

15 April 1983

A lone assailant armed with a knife and what he said was a bottle of liquid explosive commandeered a Turkish Airlines Boeing 727 jet carrying 115 persons on a scheduled domestic service from Istanbul to Izmir, demanding to be taken to Australia. After it landed for refuelling at Athens, Greece, he was captured by police. He was sentenced to a prison term of $13^{1}/_{2}$ years by a Greek court.

5 May 1983

FIVE hijackers commandeered a Civil Aviation Administration of China (CAAC) Trident 2E jet airliner that was on a scheduled domestic service from Shenyang to Shanghai with 102 persons aboard. Shooting their way into the cockpit, and in the process injuring two crew members, the assailants forced the aircraft to land at a military airbase in South Korea. Sentenced to jail terms, they were expelled by South Korea and taken to Taiwan the following year.

1 September 1983

THE hijacker of a Compania Mexicana de Aviacion SA Boeing 727 jetliner, which had been on a scheduled service from Mexico City to Miami carrying 144 persons, was arrested by disguised security

A Civil Aviation Administration of China Trident, similar to the aircraft hijacked to South Korea in May 1983. (British Aerospace)

personnel when he allowed the aircraft to land for refuelling at Merida, Yucatan.

15 October 1983

A lone assailant, allegedly carrying a gun but in fact unarmed, hijacked a People Express Airlines Boeing 737 jetliner, designated as Flight 104, carrying 107 persons on a domestic service from Buffalo, New York, to Newark, New Jersey. He ordered it to land at Atlantic City, New Jersey, and was arrested in the airport terminal there after demanding a taxi. The following year he was committed to a psychiatric facility.

28 October 1983

A passenger opened an emergency door and jumped to his death from a Pennsylvania Airlines Shorts 330 twin-engine turboprop that was flying at a height of 3,500ft (c1,050m) near Harrisburg, Pennsylvania, on a scheduled domestic US service to Washington, DC.

21 November 1983

A single assailant 'disrupted' Republic Airlines Flight 277, a twin-jet DC-9 that had been on a US domestic intrastate service from Detroit to Kalamazoo, Michigan, with 41 persons aboard. He shouted incoherently and threatened to blow up the aircraft, and after it had set down at its intended destination he ordered it to Chicago, Illinois.

During the trip there he struck a number of passengers until one hit him back, whereupon he was overpowered. Charged with air piracy, he was convicted on the lesser crimes of assault and intimidation and sentenced to eight years' imprisonment.

20 January 1984

ONE person was killed when a Douglas DC-6B (YS-37C) operated by the Salvadoran carrier ALAS struck a mine on landing at San Miguel, El Salvador.

9 February 1984

SHORTLY after it had taken off from the Angolan province of Huambo on a scheduled domestic service to Luanda, an explosive device detonated in the forward cargo hold of a Lineas Aereas de Angola (TAAG-Angola Airlines) twin-jet Boeing Advanced 737-2M2 (D2-TBV), necessitating an off-airport forced landing. The aircraft was destroyed, but there were no serious injuries among its 142 passengers and crew members.

11 February 1984

AT Port-au-Prince, Haiti, a corporal in the Haitian Army boarded an American Airlines Boeing 727 jet, designated as Flight 658 and carrying 152 persons. Armed with an automatic weapon, he asked to be taken to New York City, which was the intended destination of the aircraft. During the trip there he surrendered his weapon to the crew and later asked for political asylum, but he was convicted in the US of air piracy and sentenced to 10 years' imprisonment.

10 March 1984

AN explosive device detonated in the aft cargo compartment of a Union de Transports Aeriens (UTA) DC-8 Super 63PF jet airliner (F-BOLL), which, operating as Flight 772, was preparing to take off from Ndjamena, Chad, on a service with an ultimate destination of Paris. All 23 persons aboard at the time (18 passengers and five crew members) were evacuated safely before the French-registered aircraft was destroyed in the resulting fire.

22 March 1984

BRITISH Airways Flight 003, a Boeing 747 wide-bodied jet carrying 354 persons on a service from Hong Kong to Beijing, China, was commandeered by a lone assailant who claimed to have explosives and wanted to be taken to Taiwan. Upon landing at T'aipei, he was arrested and subsequently sentenced to 1½ years in prison for 'endangering aviation safety'.

25 June 1984

AN attempt to commandeer a Civil Aviation Administration of China (CAAC) An-24 turboprop airliner during a scheduled domestic service from Nanch'ang, Chianghsi, to Fuchou, Funchien, ended in failure when the lone hijacker was overpowered.

5–6 July 1984

AN Indian Airlines A300 wide-bodied jet, designated as Flight 405, carrying 264 persons on a domestic service from Srinagar to New Delhi, was commandeered by eight assailants demanding the release of Sikhs arrested during a siege the previous month and also restitution for damage done to their temple. Their demands were not met and the hijackers surrendered the second day at Lahore, Pakistan. Two of them were later sentenced to death and three to life prison sentences.

10 August 1984

A lone assailant, armed with what turned out to be a toy gun and unclear about his intended destination, commandeered an Indian Airlines Boeing 737 jet that was on a scheduled domestic flight from

An Indian Airlines Boeing 737, two of which were hijacked on scheduled domestic flights in August 1984. (Photo by Douglas Green)

Mangalore to Bangalore. He gave up when it landed at its intended destination.

24 August 1984

SEVEN Sikh terrorists hijacked Indian Airlines Flight 421, a Boeing 737 jet with 88 persons aboard on a domestic service originating at New Delhi with an ultimate destination of Srinagar, demanding the release of cohorts from Indian prisons. The aircraft was first diverted to Lahore, Pakistan, and ultimately reached Dubai, where the hijackers surrendered. All received life prison terms.

24–27 November 1984

THREE Somali soldiers armed with sub-machine-guns and grenades took over a Somali Airlines Boeing 707 jet, operating as Flight 414, on a service from Mogadiscio, Somalia, to Jiddah, Saudi Arabia, with 111 persons aboard, diverting it to Addis Ababa, Ethiopia. Their demands were for the release of political prisoners held in Somalia and stays of execution for seven condemned men. The latter demand having been met, the hijacking ended after 75 hours of negotiations, with the air pirates being granted political asylum.

29 November 1984

A lone assailant who claimed to be carrying dyna-mite seized Eastern Metro Flight 1962, a twin-engine turboprop Jetstream on an intrastate commuter service from Augusta to Atlanta, Georgia, with 13 persons aboard. He demanded to speak with designated friends and relatives, but after a radio conversation with one of these he surrendered. He was sentenced to six years' impris-onment for interference with an airline crew.

4 January 1985

A ticket-less woman who wanted to go to South America forced her way aboard a Pan American World Airways Boeing 727 jetliner, operating as Flight 558, which was on the ground at Cleveland, Ohio, preparing for a domestic service to New York City. Having shot and wounded a ticket agent in the process, she was herself subsequently wounded by police and captured. She was later found not guilty by reason of insanity.

23 January 1985

IN an ironic twist of fate, the saboteur who tried to destroy a jet airliner in an apparent suicide-for-insurance plot may have inadvertently saved it. The incident involved a Lloyd Aereo Boliviano SA Boeing Advanced 727-2K3 in the air near Santa Cruz, Bolivia. Operating as Flight 900, the aircraft was at an approximate height of 10,000ft (3,000m) and descending for a landing at Viru-Viru

International Airport, serving Santa Cruz, when the passenger set off a stick of dynamite in the forward lavatory at 22:15 local time. He was the only fatality among the 127 persons aboard, including a crew of seven, his body having apparently absorbed much of the blast and prevented what could have been catastrophic damage to the 727. Three other passengers suffered injuries.

The aircraft had been en route from La Paz, Bolivia, with an ultimate destination of Asuncion, Paraguay, and after this incident new security measures were recommended for the boarding of local (transit) passengers on such international flights.

27 February 1985

WIELDING knives and broken bottles, two men being deported from Germany commandeered a Lufthansa German Airlines Boeing 727 jet after it had taken off from Frankfurt with 43 persons aboard. The aircraft was diverted to Vienna, Austria, where both gave themselves up. They were sentenced to prison.

29 March 1985

A mentally disturbed assailant who claimed to have a gun commandeered a Lufthansa German Airlines Boeing 727 jetliner that had been on a scheduled service to London from Hamburg, West Germany, carrying 114 persons. He demanded to be taken to Hawaii, but after about an hour at Heathrow Airport he surrendered.

26 April 1985

A disgruntled Taiwanese Air Force sergeant who said he was carrying a bottle of sulphuric acid tried to hijack to Hong Kong a China Airlines Boeing 737 jet that was carrying 80 persons on a scheduled domestic flight from T'aipei to Kaohsiung. The pilot ignored his order and proceeded on to his intended destination, where the assailant surrendered; the bottle was found to contain water.

18 May 1985

A lone assailant tried to hijack to North Korea a South Korean Air Lines Boeing 727 jet on a scheduled domestic service from Seoul to Cheju with 118 persons aboard, announcing that he had planted a bomb in the aircraft. He was overpowered by security guards and other passengers, and a search revealed no explosive device.

21 June 1985

NORWAY'S first case of aerial hijacking involved a Braathens SAFE Boeing 737 jetliner, operating as Flight 139 on a domestic service from Trondheim to Oslo with 121 persons aboard. Armed with a handgun, the assailant spoke about his personal problems and dissatisfaction with society in general before releasing his hostages and giving himself up at the aircraft's intended destination.

23 June 1985

TWO ground workers were killed and four injured when a bomb contained within a suitcase exploded in the tourist area at Narita Airport, serving Tokyo, Japan. The suitcase had just been unloaded from CP Air Flight 003, arriving from Vancouver, British Columbia, and was to have been placed aboard Air-India Flight 301, which was bound for Bangkok, Thailand.

Investigation revealed that four days earlier a man with an Indian accent had made bookings for two men with the same surname as his own on two CP Air flights, one of which was 003. The other was Flight 60, which interconnected with Air-India 181/182, a Boeing 747 that would crash in the Atlantic Ocean only about an hour after the blast at Narita.

The bomb targeted against Air-India 301 was apparently in retaliation for the Indian Army's attack the previous year on the Golden Temple, a shrine of the Sikh religious sect located in Amritsar, Punjab. Its premature detonation probably resulted from an incorrectly-set timer. One man would later be sentenced to 10 years' imprisonment in Canada for involvement in the Narita Airport explosion.

23 June 1985

THE worst single case of aerial sabotage, which would also result in the worst aviation disaster occurring over water, involved Air-India Flight 182, a Boeing 747-237B (VT-EFO) making a transatlantic trip from Montreal, Canada, to London, one segment of a service with an ultimate destination of Bombay, India. The wide-bodied jet airliner crashed about 110 miles (175km) east of Cork, Ireland, and all 329 persons aboard (307 passengers and 22 crew members) were killed.

As Flight 181, the doomed aircraft had originated at Toronto, Canada. At Montreal it was re-designated Flight 182. It was last observed on radar as it cruised above a solid overcast at flight level 310 before suffering catastrophic structural failure at around 07:15 local time, falling in an area where the depth of the ocean was about 7,000ft (2,000m). Searchers eventually recovered the bodies of 132 victims and between three and five per cent of the aircraft's structure. A photographic and video-graphic map made of the wreckage on the seabed confirmed that the 747 had broken up in the air. Further investigation, including examination of recovered debris and the flight data and cockpit

A piece of wreckage from the downed Air-India Boeing 747, floating in the Atlantic Ocean off the Irish coast in June 1985. (Wide World Photos)

voice recorders, pointed to an explosion in its forward cargo hold, leading to the conclusion by the Indian investigative commission that the aircraft had been sabotaged.

The blast which had earlier taken place at Tokyo's Narita Airport further substantiated the sabotage theory, as did the story of the simultaneous bookings of a man with the same surname on two CP Air flights that interconnected with Air-India Flights 181/182 and 301, the apparent target of the bomb that exploded in Japan. The suspected device that destroyed VT-EFO may also have originated at Vancouver, British Columbia, where, the day before, a passenger booked on Toronto-bound CP Air Flight 60 had requested that his suitcase be interlined through to the doomed Air-India 747.

Since his seat on the latter was only stand-by and not reserved, the ticket agent explained that this was not possible. The man persisted, and the agent gave in to his demands. Due to equipment and personnel shortcomings at Air-India, luggage was not properly inspected, and the explosive device may have been loaded aboard Flight 182 in an unaccompanied suitcase, which was contrary to company policy.

Seven years later, a 30-year-old suspected Sikh terrorist believed responsible for the bombing was arrested in Bombay, India.

28 June 1985

A lone assailant rushed into the cockpit of a Turkish Airlines Boeing 727 jet on a scheduled service to Istanbul from Frankfurt, West Germany, shouting that he wanted to blow up the aircraft and spraying its instruments and the flight crew with foam. Several of the 81 passengers subdued him, and he was arrested after a safe landing at the intended destination.

27 October 1985

FOUR armed assailants assaulted and robbed passengers aboard an Aerolineas Centrales de Colombia SA (ACES) Twin Otter turboprop that was on a scheduled domestic service from El Bagre to Medellin with 20 persons aboard. They then forced the aircraft to land at Amalfi, where they fled.

10 November 1985

TWO men commandeered an Uganda Airlines Fokker F.27 Friendship turboprop carrying 49 persons on a scheduled domestic service from Entebbe to Arua, the aircraft landing in rebel-held Kasese. It and the hostages were released over a period of approximately one month.

19 November 1985

A lone assailant wielding a lighter and an electrical switch threatened to hijack America West Airlines Flight 261, a twin-jet Boeing 737 with 63 persons aboard, which was preparing to take off at Phoenix Sky Harbor International Airport, Arizona, on a domestic service to Ontario, California. He was removed from the aircraft, charges against him subsequently being dismissed on grounds of mental incompetency.

19 December 1985

AN Aeroflot An-24 turboprop, carrying 44 persons on a scheduled Soviet domestic service originating at Yakutsk, with an ultimate destination of Irkutsk, got commandeered by its first officer. Low on fuel, the aircraft force-landed in a pasture near Gannon, Heilongjiang, China. Chinese authorities sentenced the hijacker to eight years' imprisonment.

8 January 1986

IN a harrowing incident that may have been an attempted suicide, a passenger went berserk aboard an Allegheny Commuter Twin Otter turboprop on a scheduled service from Atlantic City, New Jersey, to Islip, New York. His interference with the flight crew sent the aircraft plunging from 5,000 to 1,500ft (1,500–500m) before he was knocked out by two other passengers and later taken into custody.

5 February 1986

A knife-wielding assailant took a stewardess hostage aboard Delta Air Lines Flight 139, an L-1011 wide-bodied jetliner with 232 persons aboard that had just landed at Dallas/Ft Worth International Airport, located between those cities near Irving, Texas, an en-route stop during a domestic service from Ft Lauderdale, Florida, to Los Angeles, California. He gave himself up and was later found not guilty by reason of insanity.

25 February 1986

A group of soldiers commandeered a Philippine Airlines twin-jet BAC One-Eleven after landing at Cotabato, the Philippines, and were flown to Manila to join other rebel forces. All were captured after it had landed.

14 March 1986

A lone gunman boarded a Delta Air Lines DC-9 jet at the airport serving Daytona Beach, Florida, where it had just landed and unloaded its passengers, and ordered the co-pilot to take off. After

police had shot out the aircraft's tyres the hijacker gave himself up.

2 May 1986

A Horizon Air Metroliner turboprop, on a scheduled intrastate commuter service from Medford to Portland with 14 persons aboard, was hijacked by a man who said he had a gun and forced to land at Hillsboro, Oregon. He released his hostages and gave himself up after a siege lasting about three hours. He would later kill himself while in custody.

3 May 1986

A Taiwanese-registered China Airlines Boeing 747 wide-bodied cargo jet on a scheduled service to Hong Kong from Bangkok, Thailand, was flown to Guangzhou, on mainland China, by the pilot, who subdued his two fellow flight crewmen. He took the action because he wanted to see his 82-year-old father.

3 May 1986

TAMIL separatist activity was suspected in the bombing of an Air Lanka Lockheed L-1011–100 TriStar (4R-ULD) on the ground at Bandaranaike International Airport, located at Katunayake, Sri Lanka, and serving Colombo. Operating as Flight 101, the wide-bodied jet airliner was preparing for its departure on a service to Male, in the Maldive Islands, when the blast occurred in a rear cargo hold shortly after 09:00 local time. Killed in the explosion were 16 of the 128 persons aboard, including one member of the crew of 16. More than 40 others suffered injuries and the L-1011 itself was destroyed, its fuselage being broken in two.

The single suspect later arrested was a customs employee; he allegedly placed the explosive device aboard in a consignment of tea.

23 May 1986

A Swissair DC-10, operating as Flight 125 and preparing for a service to Zurich, Switzerland, was boarded by a man at O'Hare International Airport, Chicago, who held a knife at a woman's throat for half-an-hour before he surrendered. The victim was slightly injured.

6 June 1986

A lone assailant commandeered an Aerolineas Nicaraguenses (Aeronica) Boeing 727 on the ground at Managua, Nicaragua, as the jetliner, designated as Flight 726, was preparing to take off on a service to El Salvador. He held the passengers and crew hostage until arrested by police.

28 August 1986

IN the attempted hijacking of a Polish Airlines (LOT) Tu-134 jet, which had been on a scheduled domestic service from Wroclaw to Warsaw, a passenger held a razor blade to the throat of a stewardess. He was seized by security guards and later sentenced to five years' imprisonment.

26 October 1986

A Thai Airways International Airbus A300B-600 wide-bodied jetliner, operating as Flight 620 and carrying 249 persons, was cruising at an altitude of 33,000ft (c10,050m) in the vicinity of Kochi, Shikoku, Japan, when an explosion occurred in a rear lavatory. The blast was followed by a rapid decompression of the cabin. The aircraft, which was bound for Osaka during a service originating at Bangkok, Thailand, landed safely at its intended destination despite the loss of two hydraulic systems, which made it difficult for the crew to maintain control. Injured either in the explosion, the uncontrolled flight deviations, or the high loads imposed during an emergency descent, were a total of 62 persons, eight of them (five passengers and three crew members) seriously. Among the former was the saboteur, who was attempting to smuggle a hand-grenade into Japan and dropped it in a waste basket when the pin accidentally fell out.

10 January 1987

SHORTLY after it had taken off from Newark, New Jersey, bound for Washington, DC, a New York Air DC-9 jet, designated as Flight 681 and carrying 50 persons, was taken over by a man who threatened to set it on fire. He surrendered after it had landed at Dulles International Airport, which was its intended destination.

19 May 1987

AN Air New Zealand Boeing 747 wide-bodied jetliner, carrying 129 persons on a scheduled service to Auckland, New Zealand, from Tokyo, Japan, was commandeered on the ground after it had landed at Nadi International Airport, Suva, Viti Levu, Fiji. Claiming to have dynamite strapped to his body, the air pirate demanded the release of the 11-member government of Timoci Bavadra, which had been overthrown and placed under house arrest. He was overpowered by the flight crew and taken into custody.

6 September 1987

A lone assailant was thwarted by other passengers in an attempt to hijack to West Germany a Polish Airlines (LOT) An-24 turboprop, which had been on a scheduled domestic service from Warsaw to Krakow.

13 September 1987

AN attempt was made by a lone assailant to hijack to Paris an Aeroflot twin-jet Tu-134 that was on a scheduled Soviet domestic service from Minsk to Rostov. The pilot agreed to his demands, but instead landed at Rostov, where the hijacker was arrested. Found to be mentally unstable, the assailant was subsequently committed to a psychiatric hospital.

6 November 1987

AN Air Canada Boeing 767 wide-bodied jet that had just landed on a scheduled service from Toronto and disembarked its passengers, was commandeered at San Francisco International Airport, California, by a lone assailant who threatened the pilot with an axe. He first demanded to be taken to either England or Ireland, but after about three hours surrendered. He was subsequently ruled not mentally competent to stand trial.

29 November 1987

KOREAN Air, which had found itself thrust into the world political arena four years earlier when its Flight 007 was shot down by Soviet jet fighters, was the target in this terrorist attack that also had international ramifications.

Flight 858, a Boeing 707-358C (HL-7406), had originated at Baghdad, Iraq, with an ultimate destination of Seoul, South Korea, and en-route stops at Abu Dhabi, United Arab Emirates, and Bangkok, Thailand. During the second leg of the service, the jet airliner, with 104 passengers and crew of 11 aboard, vanished over the Andaman Sea off the western coast of Burma (Myanmar).

No survivors or bodies were ever found, though a partially-inflated life-raft identified as belonging to HL-7406, and part of a folding meal-table from the back of a passenger seat, were recovered some 30 miles (50km) south-west of the mouth of the Ye River. Eye-witnesses who had been fishing in the area later reported seeing a bright flash in the sky followed by a trail of smoke descending into the sea, then black smoke rising from the site of impact, which was fixed as being about 70 miles (110km) north-west of the city of Tavoy.

The sudden and catastrophic nature of the crash seemed to indicate foul play, stirring airline personnel into almost immediate action, starting with a review of the passenger manifest. Two of the passengers who had disembarked at Abu Dhabi were an elderly man and a woman in her 20s who said they were Japanese, ostensibly travelling as father and daughter. But an inquiry showed that the woman's passport had been forged. As they were being detained by immigration authorities in Bahrain, to where they had flown two days after the disappearance of Flight 858, the couple swallowed cyanide ampoules concealed in cigarette filters. The man, later identified as 70-year-old Kim Sung-il, died, but his accomplice, Kim Hyon Hui, 24, survived the suicide attempt. She later confessed to sabotaging the aircraft, and said they were acting under orders from North Korean officials in what may have been an attempt to frighten other countries away from attending the 1988 Olympic Games in Seoul. The terrorist attack was carried out with a time bomb, using the composition C-4, which was hidden within a portable radio; and a bottle of PLX liquid explosive, which had been left in an overhead rack above seat row No 7 within the passenger cabin. It was possible that the blast, the explosive decompression of the cabin at the cruising altitude of 37,000ft (c11,300m), and the accompanying flash fire could have caused instant death to the occupants of the 707.

The surviving saboteur, who at her trial exclaimed, 'It is natural that I be punished and killed a hundred times for my sin', was sentenced to death but was later pardoned by the President of South Korea.

7 December 1987

IN a disaster reminiscent of the 1964 Pacific Air Lines crash (see page 98), which also took place in California, this case of suicide and mass murder stemmed from an employer–employee dispute.

The genesis of this tragic tale dated back some three weeks, to 19 November, when David Burke, a 35-year-old customer service agent for US Air, the parent company of Pacific Southwest Airlines (PSA), was fired for allegedly pilfering petty cash from in-flight cocktail sales. Directly responsible for his dismissal was his supervisor, 48-year-old Ray Thomson, who was stationed at Los Angeles but lived in the San Francisco Bay area, commuting by air to and from work every weekday. He was on his way home when, on this Monday afternoon, he boarded PSA Flight 1771 at Los Angeles International Airport.

At around 16:15 local time, the British Aerospace BAe 146 Series 200 (N350PS) was cruising in clear weather conditions at 22,000ft (c6,700m), about half-way to San Francisco. It was then that the Oakland air-traffic control centre received an ominous 'squawk' from the aircraft's transponder, indicating an on-board emergency. The pilot also reported by radio that gunshots had been fired in the cabin. Less than 30 seconds later, eye-witnesses observed the four-engine jetliner descending in a steep nose-down attitude. It crashed on the sloping terrain of a cattle ranch near Paso Robles.

All 43 persons aboard perished, including the crew of five. Much of the evidence of what had

A Pacific Southwest Airlines British Aerospace BAe 146 Series 200, identical to the aircraft brought down on 7 December 1987 by the shooting of its flight crew. (Photo by Douglas Green)

Hundreds of fragments of wreckage litter the countryside where Pacific Southwest Airlines Flight 1771 plummeted to earth near Paso Robles, California. (Wide World Photos)

transpired aboard Flight 1771 was destroyed in the crash, but amid the shattered, burned wreckage and pitiful human remnants lay some of the answers.

Written on an air-sickness bag was an unsigned note that read, 'Hi Ray. I think it's sort of ironical that we end up like this.' It went on, 'I asked for some leniency for my family, remember. Well I got none and you'll get none.' Also found in pieces was a .44 calibre Smith & Wesson revolver, with all six rounds expended. A portion of a human finger was found in the trigger of the weapon; prints identified it as belonging to David Burke. He had also left a prophetic message on his girlfriend's telephone answering machine stating that he was on his way to San Francisco on Flight 1771 and ended with, 'I really wish I could say more but I do love you'.

The rest of the story was told by the aircraft's cockpit voice recorder (CVR), which survived the crash. Two shots were heard, apparently in the passenger cabin, and a stewardess then entered the flight deck and announced, 'Captain, we have a problem'. A male voice then interjected, 'I'm the problem'. The sounds of a scuffle ensued, and three more shots were fired in or near the cockpit, presumably at the two pilots and, possibly, a flight attendant. A final shot was believed to have been the suicide of the gunman.

The US Federal Aviation Administration (FAA) rules then in effect permitted employees to bypass security check-points, which could account for how the pistol was smuggled aboard the aircraft. Two weeks after the tragedy, procedures were changed so that even crew members had to be screened prior to boarding.

23 December 1987

A teen-age boy who said he had a bomb hijacked KLM Royal Dutch Airlines Flight 343, a twin-jet Boeing 737 with 97 persons aboard, which was en route from Amsterdam to Milan, Italy. He forced it to land at Rome and demanded a million dollars, but after releasing about half of the passengers was overpowered by police.

4 January 1988

An Aeromexico DC-9 Series 32 jetliner, operating

as Flight 179 on a domestic service from Tijuana to Mexico City with 119 persons aboard, was hijacked by a man who claimed to have an explosive device and wanted to be taken across the US border to Brownsville, Texas. He surrendered after the aircraft landed for refuelling at Monterrey, Mexico, and subsequently committed suicide while in custody.

13 February 1988

FOUR young men armed with knives commandeered an Air Tanzania Boeing 737 jetliner that had been on a scheduled domestic service from Dar-es-Salaam to Mount Kilimanjaro with 76 persons aboard, demanding to be flown to London. Tricking the hijackers, the pilot landed the aircraft at a darkened Dar-es-Salaam airport; he and the co-pilot were then attacked and injured when the act of deception was realised. However, the assailants were overpowered and captured, and were each subsequently sentenced to 15 years' imprisonment.

22 February 1988

AN attempt to hijack to the mainland a China Airlines A300 wide-bodied jet, which had been on a scheduled domestic Taiwanese service, ended in failure, with the lone assailant being overpowered.

1 March 1988

ALTHOUGH this may not have been an intentional act of sabotage, the detonation of a commercial explosive was firmly established as the reason for the destruction of a Commercial Airways (Comair) Ltd EMBRAER EMB-110P1 Bandeirante (ZS-LGP). Designated as Flight 206, the Brazilian-built twin-engine turboprop, which had been leased from Bophuthatswana Air and was on an internal South African service from Phalaborwa to Johannesburg, crashed and burned about eight miles (13km) south-west of Jan Smuts Airport, where it was scheduled to land. All 17 persons aboard perished, including a two-member flight crew.

The commuter airliner was last reported on the instrument landing system (ILS) localiser on an approach course to Runway 03-Left, in conditions of reduced visibility, with scattered clouds, when it was shattered by an explosion at an approximate height of 7,500ft (2,300m), or about 2,500ft (750m) above the terrain elevation. Its cockpit section, containing the two pilots, was torn away from the rest of the fuselage by the force of the blast; the aircraft then fell in pieces into the grounds of a factory.

The local time of the crash was fixed at 17:28. Tests confirmed the presence of an explosive consisting of nitro-glycerine and ammonium nitrate. An investigation by South African police failed to identify the person responsible for taking the material aboard the flight or the manner by which it had been set off. As noted in the investigative report, nitro-glycerine can become extremely unstable with age. It was perhaps significant that a briefcase known to have been placed aboard at Phalaborwa could not be located, despite an extensive search.

At the time there were no requirements to screen carry-on baggage at the point of departure. In the wake of this tragedy the urgent implementation of measures designed to prevent dangerous goods from being placed aboard commercial aircraft at airports lacking sufficient security services was recommended.

12 March 1988

A lone assailant who wanted to be taken to either India or Afghanistan commandeered Pakistan International Airlines Flight 320, an A300 wide-bodied jet carrying 156 persons on a domestic service from Karachi to Quetta. He shot and wounded a guard before being subdued and captured.

29 March 1988

A gunman demanding to be taken to either India or Afghanistan commandeered a Pakistan International Airlines Boeing 707 jet that was on a scheduled domestic service from Karachi to Quetta with 143 persons aboard. He was subdued and captured.

30 March 1988

IT was no laughing matter aboard Aeroflot Flight 38422, a Tu-134 jetliner on a domestic Soviet service from Frunze to Moscow, when a passenger handed a note to a stewardess that read 'Divert to Istanbul'. The passenger who wrote it later explained that he had been kidding; he was nevertheless arrested when the aircraft landed at Moscow.

13 April 1988

A man armed with scissors who said he was terminally ill attempted to hijack a Korean Air Boeing 747 wide-bodied jetliner that had been on a scheduled service to New York City from Seoul, South Korea. He and a few others suffered injuries during a struggle, but the aircraft landed safely at Anchorage, Alaska.

12 May 1988

A Xiamen Airlines Boeing 737 jet, on a scheduled domestic Chinese flight from Xiamen to Canton with 118 persons aboard, was commandeered by two defectors who forced it to land in Taiwan, where they were granted asylum.

5 August 1988

A mentally-disturbed passenger tried to force his way into the cockpit of a Delta Air Lines DC-9 jetliner carrying 47 persons, which was approaching to land at Greenville-Spartanburg airport, South Carolina. Throwing a cabin attendant to the floor before he was subdued, he was subsequently found not guilty by reason of insanity.

1 October 1988

THREE Haitian soldiers boarded and temporarily commandeered American Airlines Flight 658, an A300, on the ground at Port-au-Prince, Haiti. They surrendered their weapons after the wide-bodied jet had taken off, bound for New York City with 233 persons aboard, and requested asylum on arrival at its intended destination.

1–2 December 1988

FOUR heavily armed men who first seized a school bus in Ordzhonikidze, RSFSR, USSR, then asked for $2 million US and transportation to any capitalist country that had no diplomatic relations with the Soviet Union, were provided with an Aeroflot Il-76 wide-bodied jet, which flew them to Israel. They were returned to the USSR by Israeli authorities and subsequently sentenced to prison terms of 14 to 15 years.

20 January 1989

THREATENING that, unless he was flown to Bucharest, Romania, he would blow the aircraft up, a lone assailant commandeered an Aeroflot Tu-134 jetliner that was on a scheduled Soviet domestic service originating at Arkhangel'sk, with an ultimate destination of Odessa. He was arrested when it nevertheless landed at Odessa.

21 January 1989

IN what may have been an attempted hijacking, a passenger aboard an Aeroflot An-24 got up holding a bottle of gasoline and a lit cigarette-lighter while the twin-engine turboprop was still on the ground at the airport serving Ivano-Frankovsk, Ukraine, USSR, about to take off on a scheduled domestic flight to Kiev. He was detained and subsequently found to have been schizophrenic for nearly a decade.

31 January 1989

AN Aerolineas Centrales de Colombia SA (ACES)

Boeing 727 jet airliner, carrying 123 persons on a scheduled domestic service to Medellin from San Andres Island, was commandeered by an assailant who doused another passenger with gasoline and threatened to start a fire. The aircraft landed at San Jose, Costa Rica, where the principal hijacker and three accomplices were arrested.

29 March 1989

TWO teen-age boys commandeered a Tu-154 jetliner of the Hungarian airline MALEV at Prague, Czechoslovakia, where it had stopped during a scheduled service from Budapest, Hungary, to Amsterdam, the Netherlands, forcing it to Frankfurt, West Germany.

30 March 1989

A lone assailant claiming to have an explosive device tried to hijack to Pakistan or Nepal an Aeroflot Tu-154 jetliner that had been on a scheduled domestic Soviet service originating at Astrakhan. He also demanded $500,000 US. He was arrested when the aircraft landed at Baku, Azerbaydzhan, which was its intended destination. No bomb was found.

24 May 1989

CARRYING 13 persons, a Bell 212 turbine-engine helicopter operated by the Colombian firm Helico was hijacked after leaving Medellin on a domestic service to the town of Antioquia. The six assailants, who may have been cocaine traffickers, robbed the other passengers and then escaped after ordering the aircraft to land at a site where a number of accomplices were waiting.

31 May 1989

TWO men who said they had a bomb and that they wanted to be taken to Israel commandeered an ALM Antillean Airlines twin-jet MD-82 that had been on a scheduled service originating at Miami, Florida, with an ultimate destination of Curacao, Dutch Antilles. The aircraft landed at New York City, where both hijackers were taken into custody.

19 September 1989

A Royal Air Maroc ATR-42 turboprop airliner carrying 10 persons was hijacked during a scheduled domestic service and forced to Gran Canaria, in the Spanish Canary Islands, where the lone assailant surrendered.

6 October 1989

TWO students commandeered a Myanma Airways

Fokker F. 28 Fellowship jetliner that had been on a scheduled domestic service from Mergui to Yangoon (Rangoon) with 85 persons aboard. They surrendered after it landed at a military air base in Thailand.

27 November 1989

FIVE police informants flying as passengers were marked for death by a drug cartel and would perish along with everyone else aboard Aerovias Nacionales de Colombia SA (AVIANCA) Flight 203.

The Boeing 727-21 jetliner (HK-1803) took off from El Dorado Airport, serving Bogota, Colombia, on a domestic service to Cali, Tolima. Some five minutes later it plunged to earth in flames into hilly terrain. The death toll of 110 included six crew members and three unidentified victims who were either passengers not on the manifest or persons killed on the ground.

The detonation of an explosive device apparently placed in a seat on the right-hand side of the aircraft's passenger cabin had ruptured its fuel tanks and caused other serious damage. A passenger who may have brought the bomb aboard the 727 probably disembarked before its departure. The terrorist leader who was believed responsible for arranging this act of sabotage was himself killed in a police raid in 1992.

16 December 1989

AN Air China Boeing 747 wide-bodied jetliner, operating as Flight 981 and carrying 233 persons, was hijacked during a domestic service from Beijing to Shanghai, landing at Fukuoka, Japan. The lone assailant was returned to China by the Japanese authorities the following April.

14 January 1990

IN an apparent act of suicide, an American tourist threw himself into an engine of a British Airways Boeing 747 wide-bodied jetliner that was preparing to take off at Port-of-Spain, Trinidad. He had first stolen a jeep and rammed it into the aircraft, subsequently smearing grease on his bleeding shoulder before killing himself.

26 April 1990

A candidate for Colombia's presidency was assassinated by a member of the rebel group M-19 aboard

The charred remains of an AVIANCA Boeing 727 destroyed in an apparently drug-related act of sabotage in November 1989. (Reuters/Corbis-Bettmann)

an AVIANCA Boeing 727 jetliner shortly after it had taken off from Bogota on a scheduled domestic service to Barranquilla. The gunman was then himself killed.

6 June 1990

USING a grenade that turned out to be only a training device, a teenager commandeered to Stockholm, Sweden, an Aeroflot Tu-154 jet that had been on a scheduled Soviet domestic service from Minsk to Murmansk. He was subsequently returned to the USSR and sentenced to a four-year prison term.

19 June 1990

CLAIMING to have an explosive device, a lone assailant hijacked an Aeroflot Tu-134 jetliner during a scheduled Soviet domestic service from Tallinn, Estonia, to L'vov, Ukraine. The aircraft landed at Helsinki, Finland, and the air pirate was returned to the USSR for prosecution. He was later sentenced to four years' imprisonment.

30 June 1990

AN Aeroflot Tu-154 jetliner on a scheduled Soviet domestic service from L'vov to Leningrad was commandeered to Stockholm, Sweden, by a passenger carrying a grenade that turned out to be a harmless imitation. He was returned by Swedish authorities and later sentenced to three years' imprisonment in the USSR.

5 July 1990

DURING a scheduled Soviet domestic flight from Leningrad to L'vov, yet another Aeroflot Tu-154 jet was hijacked to Sweden by a lone assailant, whose motive was to avoid military service. He was sentenced to four years' imprisonment in Sweden.

10 July 1990

A lone assailant attempted to hijack to Paris an Aeroflot Tu-154 jetliner after it took off from Leningrad, an en-route stop during a scheduled Soviet domestic service from Nikolaev to Murmansk. An explosive device he was purported to have was deemed harmless by the crew, who returned to Leningrad. The hijacker was later sentenced to a prison term of eight years.

28 July 1990

THREATENING to release poisonous gas, a teenage boy tried to hijack to Turkey an Aeroflot Tu-154 jet that had been on a scheduled Soviet domestic service from Krasnodar to Krasnoyarsk.

He was convinced by the crew that the aircraft had to land at Orenburg, RSFSR, its intended en-route stop, where he was arrested.

19 August 1990

A group of convicts who were supposedly being guarded by three police officers seized an Aeroflot Tu-154 jetliner after it had taken off from Neryungri, USSR, on a scheduled domestic service to Yakutsk. Eventually, the aircraft landed at Karachi, Pakistan, were they all gave up.

13 September 1990

AN attempt to hijack Indian Airlines Flight 534, as the Boeing 737 jet was on a domestic service from Coimbatore to Bangalore, was made by a young man who wanted to go to Australia. The pilot was able to convince him that the aircraft needed to land for refuelling at its intended destination, and there the assailant surrendered.

10 November 1990

THAI Airways International Flight 305, an A300 wide-bodied jetliner carrying 221 persons, was hijacked during a service from Bangkok, Thailand, to Rangoon, Myanmar, landing at Calcutta, India. The two assailants demanded the release of a pro-democratic leader under house arrest in Myanmar, and of two others jailed in Thailand for a hijacking the previous year. A few hours later they surrendered.

23 November 1990

ON a service to Tahiti from Santiago, Chile, a LAN-Chile Boeing 707 jet airliner, designated as Flight 33, was seized after it had landed on Easter Island, an en-route stop, with a number of passengers demanding a reduction in air fares by the Chilean government. The bizarre protest ended when their hostages were released.

15 December 1990

AN Aires Colombia EMB-110P Bandeirante (HK-3195X) was seized by guerrillas after landing at Villa Garzon, Colombia. After its eight occupants had been forced off, the twin-engine turboprop was doused with gasoline, set on fire, and destroyed.

28–30 December 1990

AN Air Algerie twin-jet Boeing 737, on a scheduled domestic service from Ghardaria to Algiers with 88 persons aboard, was hijacked by two young men who were apparently protesting against a crackdown on Muslim fundamentalists in Tunisia. That nation and also Egypt refused the aircraft entry, and it ultimately landed at Annaba, Algeria. Two days later the stand-off there ended, and the hijackers were taken into custody.

21 January 1991

AN Aeroflot Tu-154 jetliner on a scheduled domestic service within the USSR was commandeered by a lone assailant and landed in Bulgaria, after being refused entry into Turkey.

28 March 1991

FOLLOWING an attempt to hijack to Sweden an Aeroflot twin-jet Tu-134 that had been on a scheduled domestic Soviet flight, the pilots tied up the unarmed assailant and kept him in the luggage compartment until the aircraft landed, as planned, at Kaliningrad, RSFSR.

31 March 1991

IN an apparent protest over an election in Algeria, an Air Algerie Boeing 737 jet was hijacked during a scheduled domestic service from Bechar, but the lone assailant later gave up after the aircraft had landed at Algiers, its intended destination.

29 April 1991

AN Aeroflot jet transport, possibly a Tu-154, was commandeered during a scheduled domestic service at Barnaul, RSFSR, USSR. The three hijackers were subsequently arrested at Domodedovo Airport, serving Moscow.

19 September 1991

AN attempt to hijack to Algeria an Italian Alitalia jetliner, which was carrying 117 persons on a scheduled service from Rome to Tunis, Tunisia, ended with the aircraft, possibly an Airbus, landing at its intended destination and the lone assailant being captured by security forces.

9 November 1991

IN the waning days of the USSR, an Aeroflot Tu-154 jetliner with 178 persons aboard was commandeered by four men during a scheduled domestic Soviet service and flown to Ankara, Turkey, where the hijackers surrendered.

15 June 1992

A RUTACA twin-engine turboprop EMB-110P1 Bandeirante with 14 persons aboard was hijacked during a scheduled domestic Venezuelan service.

29 August 1992

AN Ethiopian Airlines Boeing 727 jet with 94 persons aboard was commandeered by five men during a scheduled service from Addis Ababa, Ethiopia, to Djibouti. The hijackers surrendered when the aircraft landed at Rome, Italy.

29 December 1992

AN Aero Caribbean An-26 turboprop airliner on a scheduled domestic Cuban service from Havana to Varadero was flown to Miami, Florida, by its pilot, who immobilised his two fellow crew members. All but five of the 53 persons aboard requested asylum in the US.

11 February 1993

A Lufthansa German Airlines A310 wide-bodied jet, operating as Flight 592 en route from Frankfurt, Germany, to Cairo, Egypt, was hijacked by a sole assailant armed with a starter's pistol. The aircraft completed a transatlantic journey and ultimately landed at Kennedy Airport, New York City, where the hijacker surrendered. He was later given a prison sentence of 20 years by a US Federal Court judge.

20 February 1993

AN armed man who had seized an Aeroflot Tu-134 that was on a scheduled domestic Russian service surrendered when the twin-engine jet landed at Stockholm, Sweden.

6 April 1993

A China Southern Airlines Boeing 757 jetliner was hijacked during a scheduled domestic service from Peking to Shenzhen with 204 persons aboard. It landed on Taiwan, where the two assailants asked for political asylum.

4 July 1993

IN an attempt to hijack to Australia a Royal Swazi National Airways twin-jet Fokker F.28, the lone assailant was shot and wounded at Jan Smuts Airport, serving Johannesburg, South Africa.

10 August 1993

AN Air China Boeing 767 wide-bodied jet airliner on a scheduled flight to Beijing, China, from Jakarta, Indonesia, was hijacked to Taiwan by a lone assailant.

15 September 1993

AN Aeroflot Tu-134 jet airliner carrying 50 persons

on a scheduled domestic service from Baku to Perm, CIS, was diverted to Norway, where the three hijackers surrendered.

30 September 1993

TRAVELLING with his wife and 6-year old son, a man seized a Sichuan Airlines Tupolev Tu-154 jetliner during a scheduled domestic Chinese service from Jinan to Guangzhou, and he asked for political asylum when it landed on Taiwan.

6 November 1993

A Boeing 737 jetliner of China's Xiamen Airlines, carrying 140 persons on a scheduled domestic flight from Guangzhou to Xiamen, was hijacked to Taiwan by a lone assailant.

12 November 1993

TWO men, one of them a doctor, commandeered a China Northern Airlines twin-jet MD-82 that was on a scheduled domestic Chinese service from Changchun to Fujian with 81 persons aboard, diverting it to Taiwan.

10 December 1993

AN Air France Airbus A320 jet airliner with 129 persons aboard was seized at Cote D'Azur Airport, serving Nice, France, by a previously convicted robber who claimed to have explosives and wanted to be taken to Libya. He released the other passengers before being captured by police.

28 December 1993

ANOTHER hijacking of a Chinese domestic flight involved a Fujian Airlines twin-engine turboprop Yun-7, which was commandeered by a couple accompanied by their 11-year old son, and diverted to Taiwan.

28 February 1994

THREE police officers hijacked an Air Algerie jetliner that had been on a scheduled domestic service with 131 persons aboard. They surrendered after it landed in southern Spain.

21 March 1994

AN Alitalia airliner, probably a twin-jet DC-9, was commandeered during a scheduled Italian domestic service from Palermo, Sicily, landing at Rome, its intended destination. There, the lone hijacker was overpowered by police.

7 April 1994

AN off-duty pilot riding as a passenger, who had been facing a disciplinary hearing for falsifying his employment application, attacked the three regular flight crew members of a Federal Express DC-10 wide-bodied cargo jet shortly after it had taken off from Memphis, Tennessee, on a scheduled service to Los Angeles, California. All four men were injured, but the aircraft returned safely to its point of departure. The assailant, who had wielded a hammer and a spear-gun in the assault, was later convicted of air piracy.

7 August 1994

A lone assailant commandeered a Panamanian Compania Panamena de Aviacion SA (COPA) Boeing 737 jet airliner, which was on a scheduled service from Guatemala to El Salvador with 78 persons aboard. He was captured after the aircraft had landed at Managua, Nicaragua.

21 August 1994

IN the only known case of its kind, the captain of a Royal Air Maroc ATR-42-300 (CN-CDT) apparently committed suicide by crashing the twin-engine turboprop airliner near Tzuonine, Morocco, some 20 miles (35km) north of Agadir, from where it had taken off about 10 minutes earlier. Operating as Flight 630 and on a domestic service to Casablanca, the aircraft entered a steep dive from a height of about 15,000ft (5,000m) and plunged to earth. All 44 persons aboard (40 passengers and a crew of four) perished in the disaster, which occurred around 18:50 local time. The actions of the captain may have been motivated by a failed romance, but the Moroccan Pilot's Union found it 'difficult to accept' the conclusions of the crash investigation.

22 October 1994

A scheduled intrastate flight of the Brazilian regional carrier Transportes Aereos Regionais da Bacia Amazonica SA (TABA) was targeted for hijack by five armed men, whose interest was in the cargo being carried aboard the twin-engine turboprop DHC-8-300, a shipment of gold valued at about $1 million.

The Belem-bound airliner was commandeered shortly after taking off from Itaituba, Para, and forced to return to its point of departure; the hijackers told the pilot to report that he was experiencing mechanical trouble. After it landed at the Itaituba airport, the assailants removed the gold from the cargo compartment and disappeared with the booty into dense forest under the cover of darkness.

3 November 1994

SCANDINAVIAN Airlines System (SAS) Flight 347, an MD-82 jetliner with 128 persons aboard, was hijacked during an internal Norwegian service from Bardufoss to Oslo. After an eight hour siege at Gardermoen airport, near the capital, the lone assailant surrendered.

8 November 1994

AN Olympic Airways twin-jet Boeing 737 carrying 77 persons was hijacked during a scheduled service from Germany to Greece, landing at the Greek city of Salonika, where the lone assailant surrendered.

13 November 1994

AN Air Algerie Fokker F.27 Friendship turboprop was hijacked during a scheduled domestic service from Algiers to Ouargla, and diverted to Majorca, Spain, where the three assailants surrendered.

15 December 1994

A Transportes Aereos da Bacia Amazonica SA (TABA) EMB-110 Bandeirante turboprop with nine persons aboard was hijacked during a scheduled domestic Brazilian service from Caryari to Teti.

21–22 June 1995

AN All Nippon Airways Boeing 747 wide-bodied jetliner with 365 persons aboard was commandeered during a scheduled domestic Japanese service from Tokyo to Hakodate, where it landed. The lone hijacker was demanding the release of the religious leader held in connection with a gas attack on a Tokyo subway that had taken 12 lives. At dawn on the second day of the hijacking, police rushed the aircraft and arrested the assailant, who was injured along with another passenger.

3 September 1995

OPERATING on a scheduled service to Paris from Palma de Mallorca in the Spanish Balearic Islands, an Air Inter Airbus A300 wide-bodied jet with 298 persons aboard was commandeered by a man protesting against France's resumption of nuclear tests in the South Pacific. The aircraft landed at Geneva, Switzerland, where the hijacker, who claimed to have a remote-controlled bomb that was actually a mobile telephone with batteries strapped to it, surrendered.

9 November 1995

AN Olympic Airways Boeing 747 was seized by an Ethiopian man who, saying he did not want to return to his country, held a knife to the throat of a stewardess about 30 minutes before the Greek-registered wide-bodied jetliner was to have landed at Athens during a scheduled service from Sydney, Australia. After landing at the flight's intended destination, the hijacker was overpowered and arrested.

6 January 1996

AN unsuccessful attempt was made to hijack a Transavia Airways aircraft, believed to have been a twin-engine turboprop ATR 72 on a scheduled domestic Taiwanese flight.

8–9 March 1996

AFTER it had taken off from Ercan, Cyprus, on a scheduled flight to Istanbul, Turkey, a Turkish Airlines (THY) Boeing 727 jet carrying 110 persons was hijacked by a man using a fake pistol. The aircraft was diverted to Munich, Germany, where the following day the hijacker was arrested after releasing all his hostages.

10 March 1996

AT least one knife and dynamite-wielding assailant attempted to divert a Hainan Airlines Boeing 737 jetliner to Taiwan during a scheduled Chinese domestic service from Yiwu to Guangzhou. The hijacking was thwarted when the aircraft landed at Zhuhai on the mainland, instead of at Taipei.

24 March 1996

A Sudan Airways aircraft, believed to have been a twin-jet Airbus on a scheduled domestic flight, was hijacked to Ethiopia.

4 April 1996

NO details are available regarding the attempted hijacking of a Biman Bangladesh Airlines aircraft, which had been on a scheduled domestic service.

7 July 1996

AN Empresa Consolidada Cubana de Aviacion airliner, probably a twin-engine turboprop An-24, was hijacked by an armed assailant during a scheduled domestic service, and forced to land at the US Naval base at Guantanamo Bay.

9 August 1996

THE unsuccessful attempt was made to hijack an Air Mauritanie F.28 jetliner on a scheduled domestic Mauritanian service.

16 August 1996

FOR the second straight month, an Empresa Consolidada Cubana de Aviacion aircraft was commandeered to the US. This time a small, single-engine Wilga, on a domestic tourist run from Havana to Varadero, was reportedly hijacked 'at knifepoint' by three men, who were taken into custody at a US Coast Guard base.

7 January 1997

A knife-wielding Bosnian refugee facing deportation seized Austrian Airlines Flight 104, a twin-jet MD-87 with 33 persons aboard, en route to Vienna from Berlin. The aircraft returned to its point of departure, landing at Tegel Airport, where, jumped by police commandos, the hijacker was overpowered and detained after tumbling out of an open door on to the tarmac.

Index

Transportes Aereos Portugueses EP (TAP)/Air
  Portugal: 10 Nov 61, 20; 22 Oct 78, 141; 6 May
  80, 143
Transporturi Aeriene Romana Sovietica (TARS)
  (Romania): 17 Jun 48, 11; 29 Apr 49, 12; 9 Dec
  49, 12
Trans World Airlines (TWA) (US): 4 Jul 68, 119;
  11 Dec 68, 25; 17 Jun 69, 28; 31 Jul 69, 29; 29
  Aug 69, 68; 31 Oct 69, 121; 2 Dec 69, 31; 8 Jan
  70, 68; 4 Jun 70, 123; 24 Aug 70, 35; 6–12 Sept
  70, 70; 15 Sept 70, 124; 11 Jun 71, 52; 23 Jul 71,
  52; 27 Nov 71, 37; 29 Jan 72, 128; 10 Sept 76,
  136; 11 Jan 77, 136; 25 Aug 78, 140; 21 Dec 78,
  141; 5 Dec 81, 80; 27 Oct 82, 148; 14–30 Jun
  85, 85; 11 Dec 88, 47
Tunis Air (Tunisia): 12 Jan 79, 79
Turkish Airlines (THY): 16 Sept 69, 121; 3 May
  72, 129; 22 Oct 72, 131; 30 Apr 76, 135; 13 Feb
  77, 136; 19 Mar 77, 78; 13 Oct 80, 61; 24 May
  81, 145; 15 Apr 83, 149; 28 Jun 85, 153; 8–9
  Mar 96, 164
Uganda Airlines: 10 Nov 85, 153
Union des Transports Aeriens (UTA) (France): 12
  Jul 72, 130
United Airlines (US): 11 Jan 69, 26; 25 Jun 69, 29;
  26 Dec 69, 31; 11 Mar 70, 31; 1 Nov 70, 35; 4
  June 71, 126; 7 Apr 72, 101; 2 Jun 72, 102;
  17–18 Aug 72, 131; 25 Apr 75, 39; 15 May 75,
  134; 21 Dec 76, 136; 13 Mar 78, 40; 27 Aug 78,
  140; 27 Jan 79, 141; 20 Jul 79, 40; 22 Aug 79,
  142; 1 Mar 82, 43; 30 Dec 82, 149
United Arab Airlines/Egyptair: 18 Aug 69, 67; 10
  Sept 70, 72; 12 Sept 70, 72; 16 Sept 70, 72; 22
  Aug 71, 72; 23 Aug 76, 78; 27 Mar 96, 93
US Air: 5 Oct 81, 146
Venezolana (Internacional) de Aviaciun SA
  (VIASA) (Venezuela): 19 Jun 68, 23
Viacao Aerea Sao Paulo SA (VASP) (Brazil): 25
  Apr 70, 32; 14 May 70, 32; 22 Feb 75, 59; 29
  Sept 88, 63
Western Air Lines (US): 25 Feb 71, 36; 5 May 72,
  38; 2 Jun 72, 102; 20 Aug 77, 137
Wien Consolidated Airlines (US): 18 Oct 71, 37
Xiamen Airlines (China): 12 May 88, 159; 6 Nov
  93, 163
Yemen Airlines (North Yemen): 25 Aug, 73, 74; 23
  Feb 75, 77
Unknown: 28 Oct 69, 30

HIJACKINGS RESULTING IN A CRASH AND/OR A HEAVY LOSS OF LIFE

Aeroflot (USSR): 18 May 73, 57
Air Vietnam (South Vietnam): 15 Sept 74, 58
Cathay Pacific Airways (UK): 16 Jul 48, 11
China Southern Airlines: 2 Oct 90, 63
China Southwest Airlines: 2 Oct 90, 63
Compania Cubana de Aviacion SA (Cuba): 1 Nov
  58, 16
Egyptair: 23–24 Nov 85, 86

Ethiopian Airlines: 23 Nov 96, 65
Iraqi Airways: 25 Dec 86, 88
Korean Air Lines (South Korea): 23 Jan 71, 51
Malaysian Airline System: 4 Dec 77, 60
Pan American World Airways (US): 6 Sept 86, 88
Philippine Airlines: 21–23 May 76, 59
Tajikistan International Airlines: 28 Aug 93, 65
Xiamen Airlines (China): 2 Oct 90, 63

SABOTAGE/ATTEMPTED SABOTAGE BY EXPLOSIVES

Aden Airways: 22 Nov 66, 21
Aerocesar Colombia: 21 Dec 80, 145
Aerovias Condor de Colombia Ltda (Aerocondor):
  29 May 67, 119
Aerolineas Abaroa (Bolivia): 8 Dec 64, 20
Aerolineas Nicaraguenses (Aeronica) (Nicaragua):
  12 Dec 81, 147
Aerolinee Itavia SpA (Italy): 27 Jun 80, 144
Aerovias Nacionales de Colombia SA
  (AVIANCA): 27 Nov 89, 160
Air Ceylon: 7 Sept 78, 140
Air France: 19 Dec 57, 16; 10 May 61, 18; 17 Sept
  80, 144
Air-India: 11 Apr 55, 15; 23 Jun 85, 152
Air Lanka: 3 May 86, 154
Air Malta: 13 Oct 81, 80
Air Manila (Philippines): 15 Sept 72, 131
Air Vietnam (South Vietnam): 22 Dec 69, 121; 19
  Mar 73, 131
Alia Royal Jordanian Airlines: 24 Aug 71, 126
American Airlines (US): 12 Nov 67, 119; 15 Nov
  79, 143
British European Airways (BEA): 13 Apr 50, 13;
  12 Oct 67, 119
Burma Airways: 26 Aug 78, 140
Canadian Pacific Air Lines/CP Air: 8 Jul 65, 99; 23
  Jun 85, 152
Cathay Pacific Airways (Hong Kong): 15 Jun 72,
  129
China Airlines (Taiwan): 20 Nov 71, 127
Commercial Airways (Comair) (South Africa): 1
  Mar 88, 158
Compania Alas Chiricanas SA (Panama): 19 Jul 94,
  92
Compania Mexicana de Aviacion SA (Mexico): 24
  Sept 52, 14; 8 Sept 59, 17
Continental Air Lines (US): 22 May 62, 98; 19
  Nov 68, 120
El Al Israel Airlines: 16 Aug 72, 74; 17 Apr 86, 87;
  26 Jun 86, 88
Empresa Consolidada Cubana de Aviacion (Cuba):
  6 Oct 76, 136
Ethiopian Airlines: 11 Mar 69, 120
Gulf Air (Bahrain, Oman, Qatar, United Arab
  Emirates): 23 Sept 83, 82
Indian Airlines: 26 Apr 79, 142
Jugoslovenski Aerotransport (JAT) (Yugoslavia):
  26 Jan 72, 127

SABOTAGE BY FIRE

SABOTAGE BY SHOOTING

AIRCRAFT ATTACKED IN THE AIR

United Airlines (US): 31 Dec 86, 113
Zimex Aviation (Switzerland): 14 Oct 87, 114

AIRCRAFT ATTACKED ON THE GROUND

Alia Royal Jordanian Airlines: 4 Apr 85, 85
Arkia Israel Inland Airlines: 9 Apr 73, 74
British Airways: 2 Aug 90, 91
El Al Israel Airlines: 26 Dec 68, 67; 18 Feb 69, 67;
    13 Jan 75, 77
Iran Air: 15 Oct 86, 113
Jugoslavenski Aerotransport (JAT) (Yugoslavia):
    13 Jan 75, 77
Middle East Airlines (Lebanon): 27 Jun 76, 110
Pan American World Airways (US): 17 Dec 73, 75

MISCELLANEOUS ACTS OF TERROR

Aeroflot (USSR): 3 Sept 75, 135
Aerolineas TAO (Colombia): 18 Jul 72, 130
Air Djibouti: 17 Oct 77, 138
ALAS (El Salvador): 20 Jan 84, 150
Allegheny Commuter (US): 8 Jun 86, 154
British Airways: 14 Jan 90, 160
Federal Express (US): 7 Apr 94, 163
Pacific Air Lines (US): 31 Jul 61, 19
Pennsylvania Airlines (US): 28 Oct 83, 150
Philippine Air Lines: 5 Nov 68, 120
Royal Air Maroc (Morocco): 21 Aug 94, 163
Servicio de Aeronavegacion a Territorios
    Nacionales (SATENA) (Colombia): 22 Aug 79,
    142
Swiftair (Philippines): 31 Mar 77, 137
United Air Lines (US): 12 Mar 70, 122